Developing Thinking Skills Through Real-Life Activities

Lillian S. Stephens
State University of New York
College at Old Westbury

Allyn and Bacon, Inc.

Boston London Sydney Toronto

ABOUT THE AUTHOR

Lillian Stephens has an extensive background in education as a classroom teacher, reading supervisor, curriculum coordinator, and college professor. She has developed innovative approaches to teaching that address the practical needs and concerns of teachers. Dr. Stephens is the author of *The Teacher's Guide to Open Education*— a main selection of three teachers' book clubs and a milestone text on open classrooms. She has conducted numerous seminars and workshops for teachers and lectured at major conferences in the United States and Japan. Dr. Stephens is currently a professor of teacher education at the State University of New York, College at Old Westbury, and Director of the university's teacher-training program in Bristol, England.

Photo on page 117 from National Park Service, by Cecil W. Stoughton. Other photos by Allyn and Bacon staff photographers.

Library of Congress Cataloging in Publication Data

Stephens, Lillian S.
  Developing thinking skills through real-life activities.

  1. Basic education—Curricula.   2. Life skills—Study and teaching (Elementary)   3. Cognition in children.   I. Title.
LC1035.2.S73   1983   372.13   82-20728
ISBN 0-205-07977-6

Printed in the United States of America

10 9 8 7 6 5 4 3 2 1 87 86 85 84 83 82

CONTENTS

*The activities in this book are grouped into clusters of related topics. This table of contents lists only the clusters and not the specific activities.
Each section of activities has a letter designation. These letters are used throughout the book to identify the activities in a subject area. See **page 6 for a list of these letter codes.

Appendix: ACTIVITIES SKILL
CHARTS   241

A complete list of all the activities and the skills
stressed by each is included on the charts in the
Appendix. They are arranged sequentially by
chapter.

PREFACE

Children computing the cost of operating electrical appliances . . . reading advertisements critically . . . measuring and comparing the water retention of different brands of paper towels . . . writing community histories. . . . These are a few of the almost 500 challenging and motivating activities in this book, each designed to involve children with real tasks while improving their basic skills and stimulating higher-order thinking. *Developing Thinking Skills Through Real-Life Activities* was written with these dual purposes to develop children's facility in applying a wide range of skills to real-life problems and—as important—to teach them about significant issues in society, thus adding an important dimension to the traditional curriculum.

This book is for the busy teacher. Many features make it possible for teachers to incorporate real-life activities into their classrooms with a minimum of preparation. Each topic contains extensive background facts and lists of resources, eliminating the need for further research. The activities address the students directly, enabling teachers to reproduce and assign activities without rewriting.

The book is divided into six parts, each on a major theme: energy, consumerism, environment, careers, publishing, and media. Within each part, the activities are grouped in clusters comprising coherent units on a topic. Teachers can select relevant clusters to integrate with existing curricula or larger sections to substitute for particular units. The activities can be assigned to a few students as independent or group work, or to the whole class. They should prove particularly helpful to teachers seeking additional work for gifted youngsters or for students who have difficulty with the regular curriculum and require more concrete tasks.

Other practical features of the book include:

- Objectives for each unit
- Suggestions for integrating activities into specific areas of the curriculum
- Teacher notes
- List of materials required for each section
- Suggestions for implementation and extension of the activities
- Methods of introducing the topics
- Evaluation of completed work
- Activity skill charts detailing the specific skills addressed by each activity

These features are described in more detail in the Introduction (pages 5–10).

Many people have contributed to this book, particularly teachers who shared their classroom experiences. In addition to those in the United States, I gained from my association with educators in England whom I visit regularly as part of my responsibilities as project director for the New York State teacher-training program in Bristol, England. A few people bear special mention. My sister, Anne Wild, an elementary school teacher, reviewed parts of the manuscript and tested some of the activities with her pupils. Bill Schreiber, a talented artist, is responsible for the informative illustrations. The late and highly regarded consumer expert, Sidney Margolius, was of invaluable assistance with the consumerism chapters. Bob Kaplan of the Shoreham-Wading River middle school acted as consultant for the media chapter. I am also grateful to Marcia Handler, of the Merrick school district on Long Island for her support and help, and to the following people who shared material from their outstanding cultural journalism projects: Dr. Tom Arceneaux, Chamberlin Elementary School, Port Allen, Louisiana; Bernie Griff, Wade Thomas School, San Anselmo, California; James Harris, Thomas Jefferson Elementary School, Wausau, Wisconsin; Elizabeth Roberson, Bear Grass School, Williamston, North Carolina; Michael Brooks, SUVA Intermediate School, Bell Gardens, California; Jay Kaufman, Frederica Academy, St. Simons Island, Georgia; and Charles Lindsey, Chickamauga Elementary School, Chickamauga, Georgia.

This book would not have been possible without the counsel, encouragement and affection I received from members of my family: my husband, Bernard, an editor and writer who also provided professional expertise; my son, Mitchell, and his wife, Esther; and my daughter, Beth.

Lillian Stephens

INTRODUCTION

Sisyphus was a character in Greek mythology eternally condemned to push a boulder up a high hill. Just as the boulder reached the top, it tumbled down, and he was forced to start over again. Educators may have received a similar sentence. Each generation appears condemned to debate the same issues. Once again we are agonizing over questions such as social promotion, testing, grouping, minimum competency, needs of the gifted, and what constitutes the basics.

Limiting the basics to reading, writing, and arithmetic has been criticized as "simplistic" in a joint statement issued by twelve education associations. The statement further declared: "By rejecting these simplistic tendencies, educators will avoid concentration on training in a few skills at the expense of preparing students for the changing world in which they must live" and added, "Educators should resist pressures to concentrate solely upon easy-to-teach, easy-to-test bits of knowledge. . . ."[1]

Other critics of the back-to-basics movement have suggested that it leads to disproportionate emphasis on drill and memorization, neglecting higher-order cognitive skills. Even advocates of the movement have warned of "dangers," stating that "some schools may emphasize the mechanics of the basic subjects at the expense of broader knowledge and understanding," and noting that "perhaps the most obvious danger of back to basics lies in that word back."[2]

I would underscore this latter remark. I believe there is a need for a fresher approach to the teaching of the basics and a redefinition of what is basic in education. At issue is not whether reading, writing, and arithmetic should be the sole basics or whether other subjects, such as science, social studies, or art should be included. At issue is what is taught—the content of the curriculum and what constitutes literacy in our society. "Skills and abilities do not grow in isolation from content."[3]

Rabelais, a French satirist of the sixteenth century, wrote of a giant, Gargantua, who was educated so narrowly that at the age of fifteen he could do little else but recite the alphabet backwards. Are we, too, emphasizing a curriculum that has little relation to the real world? There is at least a suspicion of this in statistics that report alarming ignorance about energy, consumerism, environment, and government among teenagers and young adults. Twenty percent of all adults are declared functionally illiterate,[4] unable to decipher the questions on a driver's license; and the National Assessment of

---

[1]"The Essentials of Education." Joint statement of American Alliance for Health, Physical Education, Recreation and Dance; American Council on the Teaching of Foreign Languages; Association for Supervision and Curriculum Development; International Reading Association; Music Educators National Conference; National Art Education Association; National Association of Elementary School Principals; National Council for the Social Studies; National Council of Teachers of Mathematics; National Science Teachers Association; Speech Communication Association; National Council of Teachers of English.
[2]George Weber, "Back to Basics Has Its Pitfalls," *The New York Times*, January 8, 1978, ED 20.
[3]"The Essentials of Education," op cit.
[4]*Social Indicators*, 1976, U.S. Department of Commerce.

Educational Progress finds that only three of ten adults can figure unit prices on food and only 17 percent of those aged 26 to 30 can balance a checkbook.

The back-to-basics movement of the past few years has not succeeded in solving the problems of those youngsters in our school population who have difficulty mastering the three Rs and who frequently become disaffected. It may be that students today balk at learning the basics in the same manner as their ancestors did, at math instruction that involves students primarily with writing numbers on pages filled with algorisms. It is pertinent that even as math computation achievement scores have started to rise, the scores on problem solving have declined. Mathematicians point out that drill alone may be detrimental to sound math teaching. Unless children are taught to apply what they learn, they may be able to add fractions but have no knowledge of what a fraction is; they may know how to solve simple division examples but be stymied when they need to determine the price of one item if two sell for 49 cents.

A similar problem exists with reading material whose concepts may be unfamiliar and lack interest. This unfamiliarity with "words and ideas" in upper-grade reading material is the reason offered for the decline of reading scores after the fourth grade, particularly for inner-city youngsters. Bettelheim insists: "Children want to be taken seriously, and unless we do so they will have a hard time being serious about the things we want them to achieve, such as becoming literate. If, however, we were to give them . . . stories that respect children, by depicting their contributions to family life and to society at large as more significant than just being cute and having fun, then we would not need to worry later about their lack of interest in reading and in matters of the mind."[5]

At the turn of the century, Dewey warned of an artificial separation between school and society. Today there is even less justification for such a separation. Children are products of an electronic era in which not only their own communities, but others many thousands of miles away are also familiar to them. Yet we frequently ignore this *outside* learning and the different ways in which children acquire information. The isolation of school from society has been held to be a contributing factor to school *dropouts*. Students are said to drop out because they do not perceive of a relation between their learning in school and the issues they encounter in real life. There is the world of school, the world of home and community, and the world of television. Each is separate. This separation spawns what has been described as the *disconnected* child, unable to make connections among separate worlds. To this child, school does not make sense. If the point of learning is only to pass a future test, the need to remain in school becomes obscured.

It is these factors that lead me to suggest that the basics be redefined to add a fourth R—*the real world;* that a basic education must include a contemporary component; that literacy must imply functional literacy, awareness of *real* issues, and facility with *real* problems. It is not acceptable for adults to be unable to complete drivers' licenses, compute unit prices, or balance checkbooks or for the schools to graduate students who are able to write but not to prepare a résumé, able to compute symbols but not interest rates, able to read but not items on a food label and who are ignorant of other basic information such as what constitutes a *synthetic fuel*. Such ignorance prevents them from becoming contributing citizens, from participating in decision making, and from effectively influencing the quality of their lives. When we draw an artificial demarcation between what is addressed in school and what exists outside, we may instill in our students a sense that they are incapable of understanding

---

[5]Bruno Bettelheim, "Learning to Read," *Harper's Magazine* (April 1978), p. 58.

real questions, powerless to affect *real* issues. Unfortunately, such attitudes remain to haunt their adulthoods as many remain nonparticipants.

It is the contention of this book that the real world can be part of the curriculum at all grades. Children have a *right, responsibility*, and the *competency* to be informed of and participate in significant matters to a degree consonant with their ages, abilities, and maturity. The fact is that even young children can make valid contributions to their communities and need to recognize their responsibility to do so. Children have to acquire basic skills, but this need not preclude a meaningful curriculum. Each of the chapters in this book faces outward—toward the real world. Each suggests participatory activities. In the process each also reinforces reading, writing, and arithmetic. Each chapter also promotes higher-order cognitive skills. Children are encouraged to go further than memorization and recitation—to also research, observe, classify, predict, experiment, infer, compare, analyze, synthesize and apply.

What is being proposed here is not an enlarged curriculum: one is not unmindful of the many demands on teachers. What is proposed instead is a revised curriculum—substituting some of the suggested topics for those now taught or integrating them into current units. The chapters that follow describe methods of doing this. Many teachers have successfully utilized *real-world* activities along with more traditional approaches. Reports of such experiences in schools throughout the country are included here.

It is hoped that introduction of real-life activities in a more comprehensive manner may have an additional advantage. It could be a decisive factor in solving one of the more serious problems in education today—the inability to reach a large segment of minority youngsters who fare badly under current teaching methods. If we relate school to life and substitute concrete activities for abstract ones, it may be possible to tap their unrealized potential and aid them to acquire language and mathematics literacy as well. But the book's approach is not limited to a segment of the school population. Gifted children need an opportunity to expand their interests and can pursue the activities independently; newly mainstreamed youngsters need an individualized curriculum that can be provided by the activities; all children need to learn to function in the real world.

This book is addressed primarily to elementary and middle-school teachers, although all teachers may find they can adapt sections for their students. The earlier years were chosen because they are crucial, formative years, the curriculum is more flexible on these levels, and the responsibilities of youth are first defined then.

This is an activity book. The format was deliberately selected because it is consonant with the premise that children should be involved in their learning and that they learn by engaging in meaningful tasks. Theoretically, the book draws on the works of Dewey, Piaget, Bruner, and Kohlberg. Dewey's influence lies in his concepts of the relation between school and society and of children as productive participants in both, as well as in his formulations of the nature of experience, of problem solving, and of *education as life*. Piaget and Bruner contributed to the notions of structure of intelligence describing how children reason, and how children learn. Kohlberg's insights into stages of moral development added a concern that school experiences be provided that prevent children from being *stalled* at a low level of moral reasoning.

OVERVIEW

THE MANY WAYS TO USE THIS BOOK

It was March 23, and the Easter holiday was due to start in three days. The teacher had just completed a social studies unit and did not consider it advisable to begin a new topic so close to the break. Instead she selected a few activities on *product testing* (see Chapter 5: CS 27–30), providing students with a significant and motivating experience during those few days. This is one way of utilizing this book, choosing a few special activities as fillers for short periods of time. There are many others that will be described.

But first it should be noted that this is a resource book. No teacher would be expected to include all the topics; teachers will select those that have the most interest and relevance for their students. In the writing of this book, consideration was given to the oft-expressed complaint of teachers: "I realize that energy, consumerism, and other contemporary topics are important, but how can I fit them into my already crowded curriculum?" Although each of the parts of this book comprises a whole and coherent curriculum unit, the activities are so arranged that individual sections can be isolated. Each is a complete topic for students. Furthermore, the *Teacher Notes* that precede each section, together with the detailed student activities, eliminate the need for extensive teacher preparation before starting a topic.

The activities may be incorporated into the regular classroom program in a variety of ways:

■ Substitute one of the units for a curriculum unit in science or social studies, such as *energy* for *space* or a section of *environment* for *communities*. Suggestions for this approach are noted in *Curriculum Integration* at the beginning of each part.

■ If you cannot complete an entire unit, select a chapter, topic, or activity cluster for the whole class, and then permit groups to work on additional aspects, later sharing their findings.

■ Select some activities to supplement the regular curriculum. For example, include those related to air pollution with a study of air or fossil fuels with a study of the Middle East.

■ Reinforce basic skills by pinpointing students' needs and assigning specific activities. The Activities Skill Charts, which can be found in the Appendix, note specific skills addressed by each activity. Thus if a student needs practice in applied math computations, single out activities that offer this.

■ Assign some activities for homework. A number lend themselves to independent work outside of school and to parent involvement.

■ Use activities for enrichment—as extra, motivating work for students who finish their other tasks. In this respect, the activities can be especially valid to meet the needs of gifted youngsters.

■ Try a thematic approach. Select one of the topics as a class theme. For a period of time, much of the work of the class will revolve around the theme. It can serve to teach, reinforce, and integrate many subjects in the curriculum. (Basic instruction in reading and mathematics will continue apart from the theme during this period.) Incidentally, the titles of the six parts of the book reflect a thematic approach. For a description of how the titles can be related to classroom organization, see the introduction to "Part Five: The Classroom as a Publishing House."

■ Consider an individual topic approach. Have each child select a topic from one of the chapters: a source of energy, advertising, air pollution, and so on. Children can then work either independently or in small groups to research their topics. Work on such topics can proceed during free time, during a set period each week, or even at home. Records of work are kept as directed in each activity, and findings eventually are presented to the class. In pursuing topic work, children learn how to investigate a problem in a logical sequence and how to organize, summarize, and present their data.

■ Finally use the activities to teach, supplement, enrich, reinforce; as fillers, or complete units; and for children who need a more concrete and less verbal approach to learning or for gifted children who are ready to explore contemporary topics independently.

ORGANIZATION OF THE BOOK

The book is divided into six parts. Each includes a complete unit on one of the following:

Energy
Consumerism
Environment
Careers
Publishing
Media

Within each part, chapters cover one or more topics related to the unit. Each topic can be completed separately. Background material has been included throughout the book as follows:

1. Each part starts with:
   An introduction
   Objectives of the unit
   Suggestions for curriculum integration
   Suggestions for unit extensions

2. Each of the individual topics leads off with Teacher Notes which include:
   Background
      Facts about the topic for the teacher
   Activities requiring special materials
      Details any special materials or preparations, although most of the activities can be completed with materials readily available in classes.
   Implementation
      Suggests methods of organizing the activities and further possibilities for integrating specific topics with other subjects.
   Modification and extension
      Included where applicable
   Evaluation
      Specific suggestions for evaluation of activities are stated. Other factors will influence the teacher's evaluation as well:

   a. Evaluation will be largely of expressive activities rather than pen and pencil tests. Teachers will check filmstrips, posters, tapes, oral reports, bulletin boards, and so on.
   b. Teachers will also evaluate whether students are achieving in some of the following:

Are they growing in ability to conduct research, use reference material, work independently, or work in groups on common tasks?

Are they able to take notes, organize data, draw conclusions—generally gaining in higher-order process skills?

Are they acquiring an awareness of real problems as they are affected by them and attitudes of responsibility?

Are they beginning to recognize areas where they can make a valid contribution to the community in which they live?

   c. The Activities Skills Charts (described below), by specifying skills to be developed in each activity, can be employed as additional guides to evaluation.

Activity or chapter starters

Most chapters include suggestions for introducing the individual topics to students.

3. Resources

At the conclusion of each part, there is a listing of selected resources including available free material.

4. Activity Skill Charts are included in the Appendix.

There is a separate chart for every topic. The charts enumerate all the activities on the topic and the skills stressed by each. They are arranged sequentially by chapter and can be utilized by teachers as follows:

■ As an index to the activities in the book.

■ To select activities that emphasize particular skills required by their classes or individual children. For example, if teachers wish to reinforce research or specific math skills, they can easily locate related activities by just glancing at the charts.

■ To identify those activities more appropriate for upper grade levels. In view of the wide range of ability in most classes, these distinctions have been kept to a minimum. The teacher is best qualified to determine the match of a particular activity to a class. Where grade level has been noted, the following key is used:

I = Intermediate level (approximately 3–4)
U = Upper levels (approximately 5–8)

ORGANIZATION OF THE ACTIVITIES

The activities are clustered in related groups with the objectives of each cluster stated.

They are lettered and numbered by topic.

Key to Activity Lettering
  Energy (all activities start with E)

Energy Awareness	EA
Fossil Fuels	EFF
Solar Energy	ESE
Wind Power	EWIP
Water Power	EWAP
Nuclear Power	ENP
Sources of Energy (an overview)	ESEN
Energy Conservation	EC

  Consumerism (all activities start with C)

Shopping	CS

Advertising	CAD
Economic Concepts	CEC
Rights and Responsibilities	CRR
Money Management	CMM
Culminating Activities	CC

Environment (all activities start with N)

Air Pollution	NAP
Water Pollution	NWP
Waste Disposal	NWD
Environmental Mathematics	NME

Careers (all activities start with R)

Self-Awareness	RSA
Career Awareness	RCA
Future Studies	RFS

Publishing (all activities start with P)

Writing Books	PWB
Cultural Journalism	PCJ
Greeting Cards	PGC

Media

| All Activities | M |

STRUCTURING THE ENVIRONMENT

The activities have been designed to permit independent work by students. Methods of facilitating this and for organizing activity work are presented below. Teachers will select those that best fit their classroom.

Prepare task cards   About 500 activities are included in this book, written so they may be copied onto activity cards, reproduced as worksheets, or duplicated, cut apart, and stapled or pasted onto index cards or oaktag. The cards may be covered with clear contact or, if possible, laminated.

The cards can be classified by topic: career awareness, solar energy, advertising, and so on, or by subject: math, language, and so forth, or by skill: topics for research, surveys, and so on. For ready reference, place the cards in activity boxes labeled to indicate classification.

Students may be assigned specific activity cards or given a choice of some. For example, every child may be expected to choose one *topic for research* or three *math problems* or to complete a survey and graph results. The activities may be considered part of a child's regular work or homework or, be part of a personal topic for exploration. (In the use of activities, it is frequently advisable to assign some and permit a choice among others. In this manner, teachers can insure that students complete activities that reinforce specific skills.)

Organize Learning Centers   Learning centers may correspond to particular units, such as a consumer center, career center, and so on. The centers would include activity cards related to the topic, any special materials needed for the activities (ascertained by the notes at the beginning of each section), books, articles or other related information, baskets or display areas to place finished work, and a method of recording participation in the centers.

A permanent publishing or media center may be made part of the class. Here children can bind their finished reports or original pieces or make slides or filmstrips to illustrate their findings.

Working on Activities Some teachers schedule one or more activity periods each week when students work on assigned or self-selected activities. In these periods, the class frequently works in groups, each group focusing on a different aspect of a unit.

It has been noted that students will also work on activities independently. Frequently, a teacher will assign an activity cluster as a concentration for a period of time (one or two weeks). During that period, students are expected to schedule their work so as to include activities from that cluster.

Time spent on a particular topic will vary. A class that has become energy-conscious may wish to engage in energy activities all of the school year. A permanent learning center on that topic can facilitate this.

Records It is important that teachers keep records of students' work on activities. In many instances the finished work will act as a record, but where children are permitted choices and freedom to work independently, more details may be necessary. Teachers may prepare a class list with the activities available to the class. When a student selects or is assigned an activity, a slash (/) is placed next to the student's name; when he or she completes it, an X is made. In the accompanying illustration, the first student is working on Activity CS 7 and has completed CS 6, and the second student has completed CS 6, 7, and 8 and is working on CS 9.

	Activity Card Numbers			
Students	**CS 6**	**CS 7**	**CS 8**	**CS 9**
John Allen	X	/		
Jane Brown	X	X	X	/

Such a list may also be placed in a learning center, and students can indicate when they start and complete an activity.

Summarizing and Presenting Data Work on activities should culminate with opportunities for students to report their findings. Most activities include suggestions for doing this, but teachers may adjust requirements to meet the needs and abilities of individual students. Some students may be expected to write reports or booklets; others, to report orally. For still others, an expressive art activity may be most appropriate. The following are additional suggestions:

■ Request that students keep all their completed work on a topic in one notebook or folder that can be reviewed regularly.
■ A number of experiments are included in the activities. Students can be required to keep a *science lab book* in which work on all experiments is recorded. This is excellent training in the scientific method of organizing and recording data. The lab book should have the following information for each experiment completed:

Title: Name of experiment (from activity).
Objective: What students were trying to find out.
Materials: What they used.
Procedures: Specifically what they did.
Hypothesis (optional): They may include in advance a hypothesis of the results.
Findings: What they observed and concluded.

■ Each of the topics involves a specialized vocabulary. Students can be asked to start a *vocabulary book* in conjunction with each part. In the book they would list and define key words.

■ A *book of facts*—a large book made of construction paper and held together with three rings—can be maintained for each part. In this, interesting facts are noted: how much sugar in certain cereals, the cost of heating the school, and so on. This "Book of Facts" can later be donated to the school library.

■ Maintain a bookbinding and media center where children can bind their booklets (see Chapter 11, PWB 15) and also produce their own filmstrips (see Chapter 12, Activities M6–10). One method requires only ordinary white paper to make a film strip.

Some of the activities suggest roller movies, displays, or strip movies as a means of summarizing information. Directions for these follow.

■ *Roller Movies* Roller movies are sometimes called *television sets* and can be made from any container or box. Empty lunch milk containers are serviceable. To make a roller movie:

Cut a rectangular opening in the front of the box.
Cut holes above and below the opening and insert sticks or dowels.
Draw scenes onto a continuous sheet of paper. Each scene should be the size of the opening. Staple or tape the top end to the top stick.
Roll up the paper like a scroll, and then attach the bottom to the lower stick.

Roller movie depicting "people who work at school." See Chapter 10, Activity RCA 2.

■ *Displays Boards* Make large boards attached accordion-style on which students place pertinent information.

Large displays can also be placed on easels. Students write and illustrate their findings on long sheets of paper customarily used for painting.

■ *Strip Movies* Students illustrate their report in frames on a long strip of paper. Two slits are made in a piece of cardboard or oaktag the size of one frame. The strip is then pulled through the slits one frame at a time. The student may give an oral report to accompany the *movie*, or older students may write an accompanying script so that members of the class may view the movie and read the script at their seats.

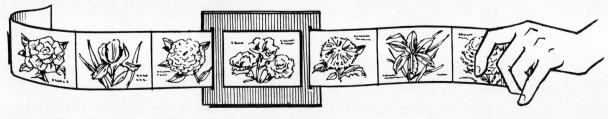

PARENT AND COMMUNITY INVOLVEMENT

Many of the activities help foster closer relations between school and community. Parents can be involved in a number of ways: They frequently serve as resource people, their cooperation is essential for transportation and supervision of out-of-school tasks, and they help plan community activities. Others in the community are also invited to participate. Many of the culminating activities open the schools to residents, inviting them to view consumer or energy fairs or visit classes in conjunction with oral history projects. Students go into the community as responsible, concerned participants. They share their findings through posters or displays in local stores or libraries. A relation between schools and retirees in the community can be a further outgrowth of students' work. The final result should be a partnership between school and community—with benefits accruing to both.

THE CLASSROOM AS A DEPARTMENT OF ENERGY

An energy fair was in progress in the classroom. It was the culmination of a month-long study of energy that had started as a science unit and then had been integrated into the entire curriculum. The children had researched energy sources, written reports and energy stories, and calculated costs of kilowatts.

The fair had been organized in two sections: sources of energy and conservation. Children had built models of windmills, solar heaters, oil wells, volcanoes, and woodburning stoves. They displayed samples of coal and pictures of geysers. On large maps they had indicated where the oil-producing countries of the world were located.

The conservation section had a list of electric appliances and the kilowatts used by each. Posters had been designed to encourage energy conservation. Many of them had been placed in community stores. An energy saver's club had been organized, and the name *SWAT* selected. *SWAT* was the name of a local television show, but the children had given the acronym a new connotation. It now stood for "SAVE WATTS ALL the TIME." Round lapel disks made of felt were distributed with the inscription "Join the SWATS."

In a corner of the room, children were demonstrating how to read an electric meter, which had been loaned to them by the local utility company. Other children were computing the yearly cost of gasoline for different models of cars, assuming that each drove 15,000 miles per year.

As a result of the efforts of this class, the whole school had become more energy-conscious. Lights were no longer automatically switched on in the classrooms, nor did they remain on when a class left the room. Children understood why the school thermostats had been lowered and used energy more discriminatingly at home.

There was no doubt of the value of these experiences for the children, no question of the importance of an energy curriculum. Yet the fact is that the study of energy is still not widely mandated. Many believe it should be. A national survey of adults aged 26 to 35 revealed that 95 percent "believed that topics like basic energy knowledge, energy problems, the future of energy, etc., should definitely be an important part of every school's curriculum."[1] The survey also found widespread ignorance of energy facts among the population studied.

There are compelling reasons for studying energy. Few topics can be considered more *basic* today. The current supply of fossil fuels may well be depleted in the lifetimes of our school children. Alternative sources need to be carefully evaluated. Decisions made today will affect the quality of life in the future. Without adequate information, young people experience a sense of powerlessness to deal with the future and even exhibit a recklessness in their use of energy that may seriously affect them at a later time. Teenagers in this country are among the largest users of electricity for personal use in the home. Yet children can become conscious of the need for conservation; they are capable of understanding basic energy concepts. Energy can be studied at any grade level.

In Part 1 the study of energy is divided into three components:

Energy Awareness
Energy Sources
Energy Conservation

All of the components need not be included in the curriculum. A teacher may elect to emphasize one aspect, such as conservation, or select a few activities from each component.

[1]National Assessment of Educational Progress, "Energy Knowledge and Attitudes," A National Assessment of Energy Awareness Among Young Adults, Aged 26 to 35 (December 1978), p. 30.

OBJECTIVES OF AN ENERGY CURRICULUM

Students will:

■ Be able to define energy and be familiar with key concepts related to it, to a degree consistent with their ages and abilities.
■ Become informed of various sources of energy—those frequently used as well as alternative sources.
■ Be aware of some of the problems associated with each source.
■ Be mindful of the energy shortage—its causes and implications.
■ Assess the potential effects of the energy shortage on personal and impersonal levels.
■ Be convinced of the need for energy conservation and become *energy savers*.
■ Publicize energy conservation methods.
■ Gain a greater degree of understanding of their own environment.
■ Acquire habits of scientific investigation of problems.
■ Improve reading, writing, speaking, and mathematical skills.
■ Enhance self-concepts by opportunities to contribute to solution of *real-life* problems.

CURRICULUM INTEGRATION

Science

An energy unit may be substituted for another science unit at any grade level. It is particularly appropriate for classes studying the earth, the solar system, and/or matter and energy.

Social Studies

The following chart indicates the recommended focus at different grade levels and how energy topics relate.

Grade	Focus	Related Topics
K, I	Local environment	Energy awareness Energy is all around us: sun, wind, water Energy from food Family dependence on energy
II	Community	Community helpers related to energy Energy used in community
	Transportation	Need for energy in transportation The automobile as major user Ways in which energy is collected, transported
III	Communities around the world	View from perspective of energy-rich and energy-poor communities. Effect on lives of people.
IV	U.S. history and people	U.S. resources of fossil fuels, alternative resources (water, wind, geothermal, oil shale) Alaska oil, pipeline Nuclear energy—issues Environmental considerations Energy legislation
V & VI	Regions of the world	Energy resources of Canada, Mexico, Middle East, OPEC Political, social, economic implications of location of resources

In addition to the topics in the preceding chart, conservation can be included at all grade levels as *responsible citizenship*, and the following also viewed from an energy perspective.

Geography: World location of energy resources
Natural resources for potential alternatives
Effect of climate on use and development of alternatives: sun, wind, water
Economics: Cost of energy
Effect on economy of countries

Mathematics

Computations can be based on usage, reading meters, energy units, costs of gasoline to operate automobiles, cost of operating various appliances, and potential savings as a result of conservation.

Language Arts

Debates   Vocabulary extension
Interviews   Research
Reports   Stories
Letter writing   Poetry

Art

Posters   Murals
Mobiles   Puppets
Collages   Models

UNIT EXTENSIONS

1. Culminate the unit with an "energy fair." It enables children to display the work they have completed, involves parents and community, and is educational for participants and viewers alike.
2. Schedule a class or schoolwide energy "teach-in." Invite speakers: parents and other people from the community working in the energy field.
3. Start a "10 Percent Club." Students in Milwaukee participated in a successful program to reduce the use of energy in metropolitan Milwaukee by 10 percent. Encourage similar conservation methods.
4. Set up an energy learning center. Materials can include:

    Activity cards from this chapter.
    Kits for experiments (see activities).
    Books related to energy.
    Magazine and newspaper clipping file (children can add to this).
    Meters: utility companies may lend some. Children can also construct them.
    Charts compiled as result of activities.

ENERGY AWARENESS

All life on earth depends on energy. But what is energy? The word itself is relatively easy to define; it is *the ability to do work*. The concept of energy, however, is difficult for children to grasp. Energy is invisible. It is stored all about us—in the foods we eat, in fuels, and in atoms. It must be extracted from these sources and converted into forms that can be utilized—heat, light, motion, and sound (the latter is a form of motion). In the process of conversion the amount of energy remains the same, but some of it becomes useless to us.

In this chapter, activities introduce basic facts about energy and also highlight its role in our daily existence.

TEACHER NOTES

BACKGROUND

The universe is composed of matter and energy. Matter is anything that occupies space and has mass. No two pieces of matter can occupy the same place at the same time. Examples of matter are air, water, and minerals.

Energy does not take up space or have a mass. It is invisible, but we can see examples of it all about us—in the light from a bulb, the heat from a stove, the movement of a car. Although described separately, matter and energy are interrelated—both are parts of the basic building blocks of nature.

Energy has been defined above as *the ability to do work*. Another term frequently associated with a discussion of energy is *power*. Power is the rate at which work is done. The power of machinery is frequently measured in units of *horsepower*—the rate at which a mythical strong horse can work. Engines of automobiles, for example, used to be described in this manner and were said to have anywhere from about 50 to 350 horsepower. To move an automobile at the same rate as an engine, a team of 50 to 350 horses would need to be hitched to the car. Other measurements: electrical energy is measured in watts. A kilowatt is equivalent to 1,000 watts. The energy content of food is expressed in calories.

The law of *conservation of energy* is basic to an understanding of energy. It states: *Under ordinary circumstances energy can be neither created nor destroyed but can be transformed from one form to another.* This may appear confusing, implying as it may that because energy cannot be destroyed, we can never exhaust it. But as has been noted, as we convert energy for use some of it changes to a form that is lost to us.

Energy may be described as *potential* or *kinetic*. Potential energy is stored energy. It is the energy a body has because of its *condition*, such as the tense, wound spring of an alarm clock; its *position*, such as the weight on top of the table or water stored at the top of a dam; or its *chemical state*, such as gasoline, coal, or gas.

Kinetic energy is the energy a body has because of its motion. It is energy in action. When potential energy is used to create heat, light, motion, or sound it becomes kinetic energy. Heat, for example, results from molecules in motion. Energy is constantly changing from one state into another, from potential to kinetic and back, in a process called *transformation of energy*.

Energy has different forms including mechanical energy, chemical energy, electrical energy, atomic energy, and solar energy. Each of these can be converted to light, heat, sound, and motion energy.

ACTIVITIES REQUIRING SPECIAL MATERIALS

EA 2, 3, and 4: Access to plants.
EA 3: See experiment for details.
EA 6: Objects brought from home.
EA 8: Old magazines or newspapers.

IMPLEMENTATION

Establish the definition of energy *(the ability to do work)*. See Activity Starter.

Depending on the level of children, introduce some of the concepts from the Background notes.

MODIFICATION

Activities EA 8–11 may be included with the chapter entitled "Energy Conservation."

EVALUATION

Check drawn or written responses in EA 1, 4, 5, 7, 9, and 11.
Information in EA 1, 2, 4, 5, and 7 may be tested by pen and pencil.

ACTIVITY STARTERS

The teacher slumped into her chair. "Sorry," she informed her first-grade class, "I don't know if I can find the *energy* to take you out to the playground during our recess. Would you just as soon stay indoors?"

The children objected, and the teacher relented. After the recess, she reminded them of her statement that she lacked "energy." "Have you ever felt that you didn't have any energy—that you couldn't move, just wanted to sit or lie down?" she asked. After they responded affirmatively, she continued, "What is energy?"

A number of definitions were offered. "Energy moves things." "It lets us work." From this discussion, the teacher developed a definition of energy: *Energy is the ability to do work.*

"Where do our bodies get energy?" was the next question. Two other concepts were generated: We receive energy from the foods we eat. People use energy to work, move, keep warm and grow.

A teacher placed a heavy weight at the edge of a table. Below were some pieces of egg shell. He called the attention of the students to the weight and then nudged it off the table onto the egg shells, which broke into numerous pieces.

"At what point did the weight possess energy?" he asked. In the course of the discussion, he was able to develop the concept of two states of energy: *potential* and *kinetic*. The weight possessed energy at both points. On the table it possessed *potential* energy; as it was released and fell, it possessed *kinetic* energy.

ACTIVITIES ON ENERGY AWARENESS

Become informed about energy and recognize how much we take it for granted.

ACTIVITIES EA 1–4: Learn some basic facts about energy:

a. Energy is invisible but we know it is there.
b. It does work for us; it produces light, heat, motion, and sound.
c. The sun is the source of most energy on earth.

EA 1   What is energy?

We cannot see energy, but we can see forms of it—light, motion.
We cannot feel energy, but we can feel a form of it—heat.
We cannot hear energy, but we can hear a form of it—sound.
Light, motion, heat, sound—these are all forms of energy.

Let's explore this further. On a large sheet of paper write the heading "Forms of Energy." Now fold the paper into four columns, labeling each either *light, heat, motion,* or *sound.* What form of energy does each of the following illustrate? (Some may be more than one.)

The thrust of a rocket
The roar of a lion
The steam from a radiator
The clang of a bell
The song of a bird
The race of a long-distance runner
The glare of the sun
The hiss of a boiling teapot

Add other examples to each column.

EA 2   Energy from the sun.

Do you know where we obtain energy? From the food we eat, which in turn received its energy from the sun. Plants get energy directly from the sun through a process called *photosynthesis,* animals obtain theirs by eating plants, and people get theirs by eating plants and animals.

The sun is the source of most of the energy on earth. It causes winds to blow and water to flow, and the energy stored in plants and animals millions of years ago is used today when we burn wood, oil, coal, or natural gas. (See Chapter 2: "Energy Sources.")

Find out more about *photosynthesis.* What is it? Analyze the two parts of the word: *photo* and *synthesis.* Relate these to the process.

Think about plants. What would happen if they were deprived of light? Prove it.

EA 3   More about photosynthesis.

In photosynthesis, the chlorophyll in the leaves of plants using the energy from the sun, combines water and carbon dioxide to produce sugar, then starch and fats. The following experiment demonstrates the presence of starch in a plant exposed to the sun.

You will need:

Geranium plant
Tincture of iodine
Pan with boiling water
Tap water
Wood alcohol
Black paper and paper clips
Small dish and aluminum pie plate
Slice of potato

To proceed:

1. Place the geranium plant in a dark closet until the leaves turn white.
2. Cover portions of a few leaves with strips of black paper, and expose the plant to sunlight until the leaves turn green again.
3. Meanwhile, prepare an iodine solution (10 parts water to one part iodine). To demonstrate that iodine indicates the presence of starch, put a few drops of the solution on a slice of potato. It should turn blue-black.
4. Pick the partly-covered leaves from the plant and discard the strips of paper.
5. Place the leaves in boiling water for a few moments.
6. Remove the chlorophyll from the leaves by next immersing them in warm wood alcohol. To warm the alcohol, place the dish with alcohol in the pot with boiling water. (Just surround the dish with the water, do not heat it again or boil the alcohol.) The alcohol will remove the chlorophyll and the leaves will turn white.
7. Now carefully remove the leaves, rinse, place on an aluminum pie plate, and cover with a few drops of the iodine solution. The part that was exposed to the sun should turn blue-black indicating the presence of starch. The covered part will remain brown, the color of the solution.

EA 4 Plants are phototropic.

Phototropic is defined as being stimulated by light to grow toward it.

Design an experiment to prove that plants are phototropic. Keep careful records of your findings.

ACTIVITIES EA 5–6: Distinguish between potential and kinetic energy.

EA 5 Two states of energy.

Potential energy is in an object but is not being used. It is referred to as *stored* energy.

Kinetic energy is actually being used to do work—to create heat, light, motion. It is energy in action.

Think of potential energy as in objects at rest, kinetic energy as in objects in motion, as in examples below.

Prepare two charts: one illustrating objects with potential energy and the other the same objects with kinetic energy.

(Examples: Potential Energy: A bow in an arrow before it is shot. An automobile waiting at a red light. A piece of coal. Kinetic Energy: The bow discharged. The automobile moving. The coal burning.)

How many can you depict?

EA 6 Demonstrate examples of potential and kinetic energy.

In class show how potential energy can be changed to kinetic and vice versa, by doing the following:

Create a pendulum.
Wind an alarm clock; then let it ring.
Wind up a toy and let it move.
Find other examples.

Make a display of objects with potential energy. Place a card next to each indicating the conditions under which the potential energy in the object will change to kinetic. (For example: Next to a candle, the card would state "light it.")

ACTIVITY EA 7: Identify other kinds of energy.

EA 7 More ways to think about energy.

There are many different ways that energy is produced.

Chemical energy: By burning fuel.
Mechanical energy: By running machines.
Solar energy: From the rays of the sun.
Atomic energy: Splitting or combining atoms.
Electrical energy: Movement of electrons in atoms.

Illustrate these facts by making a filmstrip (see Chapter 12, Activities M 6–10) showing each kind of energy with examples.

ACTIVITIES EA 8–9: Energy in our everyday lives. Note how dependent we have become on it.

EA 8   Design an energy collage.

Find as many pictures as you can of things that use energy, such as cars, trains, appliances, machines.

Have each student make an individual collage of pictures collected. Then combine all the collages into a tremendous one. The finished product should depict how very much energy is a part of our lives.

EA 9   Can you do without energy?

Do you recall a power blackout when there was no gas or electricity? Imagine such a day with a shortage of gasoline, as well.

Construct a booklet or roller movie titled "Life Without Energy." Describe a day in which there is no gas, electricity, or automobile fuel available. Start with the time you awaken, then note how the lack of energy would affect your day in school. Compare your notes with classmates.

ACTIVITIES EA 10–11: Compare the use of energy in the past and present, and then project into the future.

EA 10   Create a past and present energy mural.

Compare the use of energy by a family in the seventeenth century with one in the present. You may have to do research to be accurate.

Working with a group, prepare a large mural with scenes depicting the energy used in the past and present for activities such as the following:

Awakening
Securing and preparing food
Washing dishes; cleaning homes
Lighting homes
Transportation
Entertainment

What will your mural illustrate about changing patterns in the use of energy?

EA 11   Life in the future.

Imagine how a family in the year 2050 will accomplish the activities described above. Will it require more or less energy?

You may write about it or create a future energy mural to accompany the one in EA 10.

2
ENERGY SOURCES

People have lived on the earth for over one million years, but it is only in the past 200 years that the demand for energy has become acute. The development of the steam engine, electric power, automobiles, airplanes, and ever more sophisticated machines has created insatiable clamors for fuel, to the point that in only 200 years we have come close to exhausting the earth's known supply of fossil fuels.

The history of human beings on earth may be viewed from the perspective of their use of energy. Early people utilized only their own muscle power to gather food and provide shelter and clothing. Later as they discovered fire to fashion tools, they were able to combine these with human energy to build complicated structures. The pyramids in Egypt, for example, were built by the energy of thousands of slaves. People also discovered other sources of energy—the wind to sail vessels, the sun to heat and cook, and animals that they could domesticate and train to do work.

In the United States, wood was the primary source of energy until about 100 years ago when improved methods of mining coal led to its widespread use. Since the middle of the twentieth century, oil and natural gas have replaced coal as our major source of energy. They were considered cleaner, less polluting, and easier to extract. The problems that have now arisen with oil and gas—their cost, associated dependence on foreign powers, and the possible depletion of resources—have led to the current feverish concern about energy. It has been postulated that the survival of the human race depends on its ability to safely harness new sources of energy.

In this chapter and the one that follows, students are introduced to the primary and alternative sources of energy, as well as to problems associated with the use of each. It is important that children understand that all conversion of matter to energy may have undesirable environmental impacts. This sets the foundation for a later discussion of conservation.

Chapter 3 concludes with activities related to sources of energy in general. Teachers should review these activities before starting this topic. Some may in fact be used as an introduction to the topic or simultaneously with activities on specific sources. For example, consider the following methods of organizing work on sources of energy:

1. Use the general activities on pages 53–55 with the entire class and have individuals or small groups work independently on different specific sources.
2. Select a specific source, such as solar energy or fossil fuels for the entire class, either as a separate unit or as part of a related science or social studies topic, and supplement with general activities.

ACTIVITY STARTERS

Two comic books offer an excellent introduction to energy sources and some problems associated with each. They are "Mickey Mouse and Goofy Explore Energy"[1] and "The Best Present of All."[2] If possible, read them to class.

Review the definition of energy (*energy is the ability to do work*) and the concept that energy produces heat, light, and motion.

Establish the notion that there must be a source for energy. Utility plants, for example, need fuel to produce electricity. They are like "giant monsters gobbling up ever more scarce fuel." Ask what else demands fuel?

Lead children to recognize that there are many sources of energy by questioning the source of energy for each of the following:

A child running
An automobile
A train
A sailboat
A hydroelectric plant
A beating heart
An atom bomb

Relate the Greek myth of Prometheus who stole fire from the gods and gave it to primitive people. Inquire if there is any source of energy today that someone might wish to steal. This can lead to a discussion of nuclear energy, its advantages and disadvantages. The class may then be asked whether there are any problems associated with other sources of energy. An investigation of sources of energy then follows.

THE FOSSIL FUELS

Our primary sources of energy today are the three fossil fuels—petroleum, natural gas, and coal.

TEACHER NOTES

BACKGROUND

Petroleum, natural gas, and coal are called fossil fuels because they were formed from the remains of plants and animals that lived millions of years ago. At that time the surface of the earth was moist, much of it covered by water. Tiny plants and animals lived in mud, in shallow water, and along the coastlines. As they died, their remains settled in the mud. The process continued for thousands and thousands of years, the remains accumulating in succeeding layers. Oceans formed and receded; more sand, mud, and water pressed down on the layers. This pressure, together with the action of bacteria and heat beneath the surface of the earth, is believed to have formed the fuels.

[1]Walt Disney Educational Media Co., 500 South Buena Vista St., California, 91521. Copies may also be secured from the Public Affairs Department, Exxon, U.S.A. P.O. Box 2180, Houston, Texas 77001.

[2]*Ranger Rick's Nature Magazine,* April and May/June 1974 issue, National Wildlife Federation, 1412 Sixteenth St., N.W., Washington, D.C. 20036.

Petroleum became trapped in sedimentary rocks. Natural gas is generally found with petroleum.

Coal was formed in a similar process from plants that had no flowers—ferns and mosses. As these plants decayed, they fell into muddy swamps in a process that was repeated over the eons with new plants growing over the old. At first the decayed matter became peat, but with more pressure, over the years it became coal. It is estimated that it takes a thickness of five to eight feet of rotted plants to produce one foot of coal. The plants from which coal was formed originally contained carbon, oxygen, and hydrogen. With the intense pressure on them, much of the oxygen and hydrogen were squeezed out, leaving the carbon. The more carbon and the less moisture in the coal, the more valuable it is.

Coal was the most utilized fuel in this country from the end of the nineteenth century until about 1950, but because burning coal pollutes the environment and some types of mining deface sections of the earth, there was a shift to other sources of energy—petroleum and natural gas. Most of the energy used today comes from oil, much of it imported.

Petroleum or oil is pumped out of the ground through oil wells in the form of crude oil. It is refined to produce gasoline, home heating, diesel and lubricating oil, kerosene, and a broad spectrum of products. Chemicals made from petroleum are used to make paints, detergents, nylon, synthetic rubber, plastics, cosmetics, drugs, and so on. Petroleum and the gasoline that is made from it also pollute the environment. In addition, occasional oil spills from wells or tankers may destroy sea life and pollute oceans and beaches. Still other problems result from the high consumption of petroleum. Dependence on foreign oil has left much of the world at the mercy of a small group of oil-producing countries. Whenever they decide to raise prices, inflation results for people around the globe. Serious, too, is the prospect that in the foreseeable future current stocks of petroleum may be exhausted.

ACTIVITIES REQUIRING SPECIAL MATERIALS

    EFF 1: Clay or Plasticine.
            Leaves or bones (fish or chicken).
    EFF 3: Samples of rocks.
    EFF 7 and 18: Materials brought from home.
    EFF 9: World maps.
    EFF 12: See activity.
    EFF 13: Out-of-school research.
    EFF 14: See details of experiment.
    EFF 17: Maps of United States.

IMPLEMENTATION

These activities lend themselves to integration with geography, United States history, and regions of the world. Encyclopedias or other books describing fossil fuels should be accessible.

Contact local utility companies. Many have material available for classes.

EVALUATION

Check:

Written responses: EFF 5, 10, 15, 16, 20
Research data: EFF 2, 3, 4, 5, 6, 7, 9, 10, 15, 16, 17, 18, 20, 21, 22, 23

Graphs, visuals: EFF 2, 4, 7, 8, 9, 14, 17, 18, 24
Mathematics: EFF: 12, 13, 24

Key questions:

What are the three fossil fuels?
How are they formed?
Where are the most abundant supplies of each?
What problems are associated with the use of each?

ACTIVITIES ON FOSSIL FUELS

Find out about the three fossil fuels and study each individually.

ACTIVITIES EFF 1–2: Explore fossils and fossil fuels.

EFF 1   What is a fossil?

Research this question. Find out too how they were formed, where they are found, and what value they have to us.
Create fossils.
Impress leaves or bones of fish or chicken in clay or Plasticine. Remove. Let the clay harden.

EFF 2   What are the fossil fuels?

Petroleum, coal, and natural gas are called fossil fuels. They are our main sources of energy.
Research how they were formed and why they are called *fossil fuels*. How long does it take for them to form? Why do you believe it necessary to conserve them?
Depict the above information in a display or filmstrip.

ACTIVITIES EFF 3–10: Focus on petroleum (or crude oil).

EFF 3   In what kind of rock is petroleum found?

Secure samples of three different kinds of rock: igneous, metamorphic, and sedimentary. Place a drop of oil on each.
Which rock is porous? Which tends to absorb the drop of oil? In which would petroleum be found?

EFF 4   Draw a model of an oil well.

Find out:
How do the drillers know when they have struck oil?
How is the oil brought to the surface?

EFF 5   Drilling for offshore oil.

Rich deposits of oil are believed to lie beneath the waters. Some of these have already been tapped in the North Sea near England and the Gulf of Mexico, for example.

Find out other locations of offshore oil and some of the problems of drilling for it.

In your report, include a short piece stating whether you think you would like to be part of a crew digging for offshore oil.

EFF 6   Danger of oil spills.

Some oil is spilled when tankers that carry it are involved in accidents; or it suddenly gushes uncontrollably from wells.

Can you find examples of each and why this is a particular concern of environmentalists.[3]

See also Chapter 8, Water Pollution; Activity NWP 4.

EFF 7   Products from petroleum.

Note the many products made from petroleum, Figure 2.1.
Bring in samples of as many of these as you can and create a display.

EFF 8   Refining crude oil.

Draw a diagram showing how crude oil is refined. (See illustration.)
Indicate how the refined oil is transported—pipeline, truck, and/or tanker.

EFF 9   Locate oil reserves.

On a map of the world, show the location of the major known reserves of oil. (See Figure 2.2)
Are there any countries without any oil?
What are the implications of the distribution of oil reserves? Discuss these.

EFF 10   Study the oil-rich countries.

In what part of the world are they?
Do a report on one.
What is meant by OPEC?

ACTIVITIES EFF 11–13: Concentrate on gasoline: A key product of petroleum.

EFF 11   A shortage of gasoline.

Discuss the following in class:

What is the cause of a shortage of gasoline?
What is the effect?
Does a gasoline shortage affect you personally?
How?

[3]Write for "Oil Spills and Spills of Hazardous Substances," pamphlet, Environmental Protection Agency, Washington, D.C., 20460.

What Can You Make From 'Energy'?

Every one of the following products and thousands more are made from chemicals that are made from petroleum.

Credit cards	Upholstery	Sports car bodies	Vinyl tops	Plastic wood	Eye shadow
American flags	Uniforms	Stoppers	Digital clocks	Stuffed animals	"Tiffany" lamps
Eyelashes	Phonographs	Straps	Draperies	Car mats	Typewriter keys
Aspirin	Hearing aids	Smocks	Ice chests	Soft contact lenses	Wire insulation
No-wax floors	Welcome mats	Tennis balls	Life jackets	Dog leashes	Desk organizers
Permanent-press clothes	Car sound insulation	Tires	Audio tape	Dice	Fake furs
Oxygen masks	Racks	Tablecloths	TV cabinets	Trash bags	T-shirts
Golf balls	Pacifiers	Measuring cups	Model planes	Thermal blankets	Electric scissors
Ink	Dresses	Rulers	Car battery cases	Drinking straws	Golf bags
Lighter fluid	Cassettes	Ring binders	Measuring tape	Afghans	Skin conditioners
Heart valves	Garment bags	Reclining chairs	Insect repellent	Pole vaulter poles	Photographs
Hair spray	Track shoes	Boat covers	Hockey pucks	Foam insulation	Outdoor carpeting
Attache cases	Dominoes	Tote bags	Ice buckets	Hand lotion	Tool boxes
Crayons	Fences	Dishwashing liquids	Fishing nets	Shampoo	Salt shakers
Steering wheels	Car polishers	Unbreakable dishes	Fertilizers	Shaving cream	Screen door screens
Wet suits	Luggage	Toothbrushes	Hiking boots	Aquariums	Sculptures
Disposable diapers	Kitchen counter tops	Extension cords	Hair coloring	Sails	Caulking
Food wraps	Protractors	First-aid kits	Knitting yarn	Soft bumpers	Fan belts
Laxatives	Antifreeze	Notebooks	Toilet seats	Safety glass	Tape recorders
Parachutes	Earphones	Combs	Towel bars	Erasers	Distributor housings
Stretch pants	Flashlights	Watchbands	Denture adhesive	Radio cases	Window shades
Trash cans	Windbreakers	Darts	Frisbees	Awnings	Dog food dishes
Telephones	Whistles	Flight bags	Hair rollers	Knitting needles	Curtains
Rubber duckies	Motorcycle helmets	Toothpaste	Light fixtures	Fan blades	Dog toys
Brassieres	Pillows	Flea collars	Loudspeakers	Wigs	Lids
Enamel	Clothesline	Drip-dry dresses	Movie film	Window shutters	Pan handles
Seed tape	Dune buggy bodies	Tents	Panties	Salad bowls	Slippers
Wall coverings	Carpet sweepers	Stadium cushions	Electronic calculators	Epoxy glue	Tennis shirts
Transparent tape	Antibiotics	Plastic varnish	Fishing boots	Punching bags	Tent pegs
Card tables	Checkers	Finger paints	Candles	Model ships	Tennis shorts
Acrylic paints	Chess boards	Foul weather gear	Diving masks	Shavers	Vitamin capsules
Antiseptics	Shower doors	Foot pads	Hairbrushes	Plywood adhesive	Dashboards
Golf cart bodies	Soap dishes	Refrigerants	Body suits	Parkas	Ribbons
Vacuum bottles	Yardsticks	Rugs	Water pipes	Football suits	Putty
Vinyl siding	Shorts	Nightgowns	Pails	Cameras	Percolators
Slips	Syringes	Sandals	Car enamel	Shoelaces	Swings
Shoe trees	Slip covers	Hair curlers	Guitar picks	Swizzle sticks	Skis
Safety flares	Sugar bowls	Lamps	Vinyl shingles	Piano keys	Tool racks
Warm-up suits	Shoes	Lipstick	Switch plates	Bikinis	Folding chairs
Bearing grease	Paddles	Laminates	Shower curtains	Bracelets	Charcoal lighter
Overcoats	Decoys	Ice cube trays	Sponges	Football helmets	Gas siphons
Ping-pong paddles	Volley balls	Typewriter cases	Detergents	Anesthetics	Robes
Rafts	Tobacco pouches	Visors	Beach balls	Plungers	Picture frames
Bubble bath	Sleeping bags	Swimming pool liners	Ties	Artificial turf	Air mattresses
Purses	Refrigerator linings	Laundry softeners	Sunglasses	Patio furniture	Petticoats
Sockets	Pencils	Electric blankets	Bird houses	Ashtrays	Seat covers
Bookends	Electrician's tape	Ear plugs	Panty hose	Lawn sprinklers	Slacks
Weed killers	Model cars	Tennis rackets	Backpacks	Artificial limbs	Hampers
Flippers	Midi-skirts	Shirts	Bathinettes	Rain hats	Lighting panels
Planters	Kites	Drinking cups	Records	Bandages	Yarn
Football pads	Folding doors	Canisters	Typewriter ribbons	Dentures	Jars
Tiles	Mini-skirts	House paint	Footballs	Belts	Stools
Deodorant	Floor wax	Lamp shades	Disposable lighters	Tongs	Rollerskate wheels
Puzzles	Garden hoses	Computer tape	Doorknobs	Paneling	Movie film
Air conditioners	Mascara	Cough syrup			

Figure 2.1 Products from Petroleum. (Courtesy of Union Carbide Corporation.)

Sources and resources

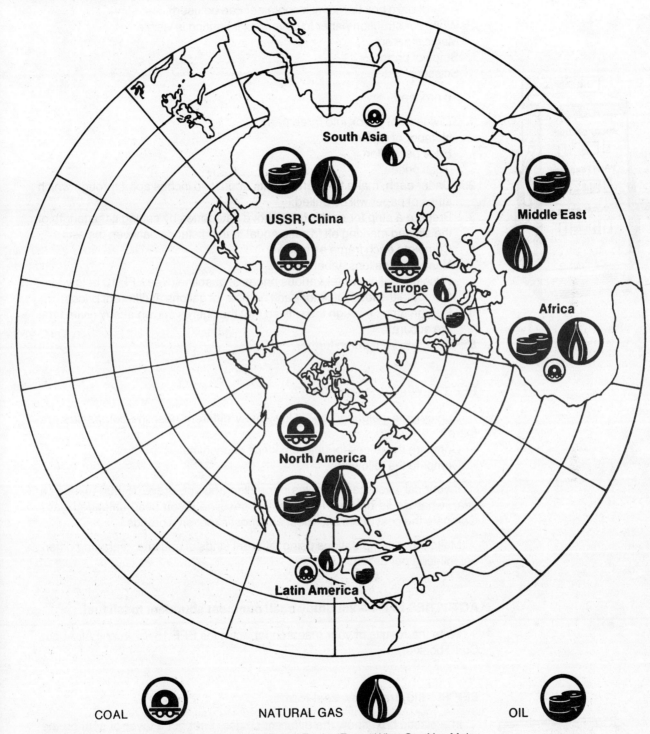

Figure 2.2 Location of World Resources of Fossil Fuels. (From "What Can You Make from Energy?", teaching kit, Union Carbide Corporation, 1978. For information on how to obtain full kit, write ENERGY, Union Carbide Corporate Communications Department, 270 Park Avenue, New York City, 10017.)

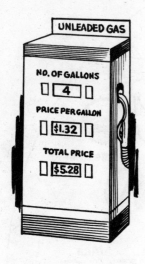

EFF 12 Construct a gasoline pump.

You will need:

A cardboard box (large milk container can be used)
White construction paper to cover box if printing is visible
Magic markers
Strips of paper
Scissors

To proceed:

1. Divide front of box into three parts:
   Number of gallons
   Price per gallon
   Total price
2. Under each, make two vertical slits about two inches apart through which strips of paper will be pulled.
3. Prepare a strip for each of the above categories by cutting it the length of the slit and marking off frames equal to the distance between the slits.
4. Complete each frame as follows:
   Number of gallons: label *1* to *15*
   Price per gallon: Enter various prices of gasoline (See EFF 13 below.)
   Compute the total price for each number of gallons at different prices.
5. Pull the strips through the slits so that the figures shown at any given time are accurate.
6. Decorate your pump further.

EFF 13 What price gasoline?

Survey your neighborhood. How many different gasoline companies are there?
Compare the prices for different kinds of gasoline.
Compute the following:

If your car averaged 20 miles per gallon and you drove 15,000 miles in a year, what would be the yearly cost of gasoline if you used unleaded gas? Compare the cost of the cheapest and most expensive brands.

Make other computations using different kinds of gas and averaging different mileage per gallon.

ACTIVITIES EFF 14–20: Study coal: our most abundant fossil fuel.

Write the results of your research for activities EFF 15–17 in an "All About Coal" booklet.

EFF 14 Illustrate how coal forms.

In a plastic box, show the different stages. First put a layer of coal on the bottom. This represents the final stage. Over it put peat moss (peat will eventually become coal). Then add decayed plants mixed with mud. On top of these, add soil and rock.
As you look through the side of the box, you can observe the various layers of earth under which coal is finally formed.

EFF 15   Extracting the coal.

Read about coal mining.
Why is mining considered a hazardous occupation?
Find out about the life of a coal miner.

EFF 16   Research the different kinds of coal.

Define: bituminous, anthracite, lignite.
Which has the highest sulphur content?
Why is this important?

EFF 17   Locate coal reserves in the United States.

Where are coal reserves found? Indicate these on a map of the United States. (See Figure 2.3.)

EFF 18   Products from coal.

What are some products made of coal? List them on a chart. Bring some in and display .

EFF 19   Debate the use of coal as a source of energy.

Construct two puppets or stick figures.
Label one "A Friend of Coal," the other "An Enemy of Coal."
Stage a debate between the two.

ACTIVITIES EFF 20–24: Investigate natural gas: the third fossil fuel.

EFF 20   Research natural gas.

Gas was formed over a period of billions of years, just as the other fossil fuels were formed from the remains of animals and plants that lived on earth. It is usually found with deposits of petroleum.
Natural gas consists of *hydrocarbons,* mainly methane and ethane, but frequently others as well, such as propane and butane.
The United States has one of the largest reserves of natural gas in the world.
Research the following:

Which states have the largest deposits?
How is the gas brought to the surface of the earth?
How is it transported from these states to your home?

Write a report on your findings and illustrate it with diagrams.

EFF 21   The discovery of natural gas.

It is said that natural gas was first discovered accidentally in Greece. A shepherd noticed that his sheep were behaving peculiarly whenever they came to a certain place.
The religious leaders of the time investigated and decided that the strange vapors were the breath of the Greek god Apollo. A temple was built on the

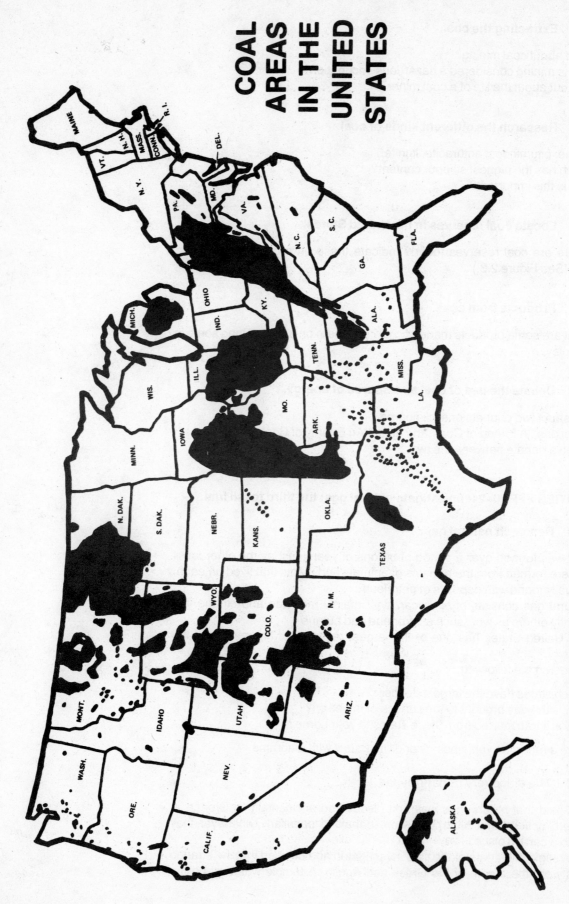

Figure 2.3 Coal areas in the United States. (Courtesy of National Coal Association, Washington, D.C. 20585.)

spot: The Temple of Delphi. (The vapors were, in fact, natural gas escaping from a fissure in the earth.)

Read more about Delphi. Who was the oracle at Delphi?

Find other tales associated with the history of natural gas. Make a book about some of these. Illustrate and bind it. (See Chapter 11, Activity PWB 15.)

EFF 22   The uses of natural gas.

Gaslight is important in the history of our country. Can you find out when it was used?

Much of the natural gas was at first wasted—burned at oil wells. What is the relation between natural gas and oil? How is natural gas brought to the surface? Research its many uses.

EFF 23   Manufactured gas.

Much of the gas used in this country is not, in fact, natural gas. Some of the kinds of manufactured gas include coke oven, carbureted water, and oil. Investigate how these and others are made.

EFF 24   Learn to read a gas meter.

Gas is measured in cubic feet. Gas meters are similar to electric meters. Here's how to read a gas meter.

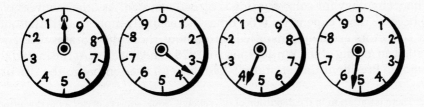

Read the dials from left to right, as you would a numeral. If an indicator falls between two numbers, always record the smallest of the two.

Your utility bill does not record the actual thousands of cubic feet. In the example shown, the meter reading would be 345.

Practice making cardboard meters and reading them. If you can, read your meter at home at the beginning and end of a month, and check to see how much cubic feet of gas was used during that month.

(See also Chapter 4, Activity EC 4: You can read an electric meter.)

SOLAR ENERGY

As other forms of energy become increasingly expensive or less desirable, we are fast becoming "sun worshippers," looking to the sun to solve our energy crisis.

TEACHER NOTES

BACKGROUND

People have always relied on the sun for energy—directly for heat and light and indirectly as the source of most other energy on earth. It is the solar energy stored in fossil fuels that we burn, the waters evaporated by the sun's heat that return to earth and fill dams for hydroelectric power. It is the action of the sun on the surface of the earth that creates winds and the energy from the sun that enables green plants to create our foods. Moreover, it is to the energy still lodged in plants that we look for one promising alternative source (see Biomass).[4]

Direct use of the sun for energy is an attractive concept. Solar energy is plentiful, free and nonpolluting. In the course of a year, more than 500 times as much solar energy is "delivered" to the surface of the United States as is consumed in all other forms. Yet there are obvious problems with utilizing solar energy. The sun does not shine constantly. There are long hours of darkness during the night and in many parts of the country, particularly during winter, there are limited hours of sunshine.

Direct use of solar energy generally embraces solar heating and solar electricity. Solar heating is not a new concept. It was used by prehistoric people. Efforts to heat homes with solar energy are described as *passive* or *active*. A passive system relies on the placement of a house so that it maximizes the heat gained from the sun in the winter and provides landscaping and an overhang to shade the house in the summer. Active systems provide collectors to capture the sun's heat, which is then distributed throughout the house to heat water or, in some cases, heat and cool the entire house. The solar collectors can be supplements to conventional systems, which are still required for cloudy days.

The technology for solar heating is already known. As other sources of energy become more expensive, it becomes increasingly more practical. Rooftop solar collectors are being installed throughout the United States. They were installed on a wing of the White House in 1979 to heat water. At the installation ceremony, President Carter stated: "No one can ever embargo the sun or in-

---

[4]Note: There is variation in the definition of *solar energy*. Some sources prefer a narrow interpretation, concentrating on direct sunshine; others take a broader view encompassing all renewable sources of energy, which in addition to direct sunshine, include biomass, wind and water power, ocean thermal and tidal waves. Predictions that solar energy will supply as much as 20 percent of our energy needs by the year 2000 are based on this broader definition of solar energy.

For easier analysis of different sources, this chapter relies on the narrow interpretation of solar energy. Students, however, should be made aware that the other forms of energy mentioned originate from the sun.

terrupt its delivery to us." Although this is true in the larger sense, problems could easily develop with widespread installation of solar collectors. Regulations will have to be passed by communities to prohibit new trees or buildings from shading existing collectors. The legality of this has not been established.

Sunlight can be converted to electricity by the use of solar cells that contain strips of *silicon*. As the light strikes the silicon, an electric current is produced by a "photovoltaic effect." Today solar cells are routinely used in camera light meters, to provide electricity for space vehicles, and for communication and signaling equipment in remote areas. They are prohibitively expensive for widespread use. Research is focusing on producing cheaper solar cells utilizing material less expensive than silicon. But for solar cells to become a significant source of electrical energy for routine use, much more technological development is required.

Large-scale solar collectors for commercial use are also being tested. Plants have been constructed for this purpose in the United States and abroad. France operates one in the Pyrenees mountains. Experiments have attempted to use large mirrors or lenses to concentrate the heat of the sun onto a boiler, which creates steam that, in turn, powers a turbine and generator to produce electricity. Suggestions have also been made for orbiting satellites with solar collectors. At the moment these are not considered feasible. There will undoubtedly be increased research in the use of solar energy. Projections vary, but a target of 20 percent of energy needs supplied by all forms of solar power is mentioned for the turn of the century.

ACTIVITIES REQUIRING SPECIAL MATERIALS

ESE 1, 2: Thermometer.
ESE 3: Magnifying glass.
ESE 4, 5, 6, 8, 9, 11, 12, 13, 14: See details of experiments.

IMPLEMENTATION

This section lends itself to ready integration with a study of the solar system.

Teachers may also use the activities to reinforce methods of conducting science experiments.

Activities can be completed over a long period of time if the curriculum does not permit concentrated study. A folder or book should be maintained by students summarizing experiments and information gained.

Some of the activities may be assigned as homework. (Such as ESE 1 and 2).

Consider including Activities EA 2, 3, 4 in Chapter 1 with this section.

EXTENSION

Celebrate Sun Day.

Have a sun fair. Display your finished activities. You might suggest visitors estimate the temperature on the sun (see Activity ESE 7). Have children compute the closest answer and offer a prize to the winner. This offers excellent math practice. (*Surface temperature on the sun, approximately 11,500 degrees Fahrenheit, 6,371 degrees Centigrade.*)

EVALUATION

Check:

Ability to experiment and record data: ESE 1 to 6, 10, 12, 13
Research: ESE 7, 13, 15
Construction of models: ESE 8, 9, 11, 14
Written work: ESE 16, 17, 18

Key concepts:

Sun provides heat and light energy that can be used for many different purposes. To fully utilize solar energy, we must be able to collect, store, and concentrate the heat of the sun and identify materials that retain heat best.

Students should also be able to distinguish between passive and active solar heaters, describe how solar heaters work, and be prepared to offer examples of other applications of solar energy.

ACTIVITIES ON SOLAR ENERGY

The sun drenches the earth with energy. If we could find efficient ways of capturing solar energy, there would be no energy shortage. These activities investigate the sun as a source of energy and inspiration.

ACTIVITIES ESE 1–7: Survey aspects of the sun's heat.

ESE 1   Heat from the sun.

Take the temperature of the air in different spots outside the school: a shady area, a sunny area.
Keep a chart of your findings as follows:

TEMPERATURE READINGS

	9:00 a.m	11:00 a.m	1:00 p.m.	3:00 p.m.	(Later if possible)
Sunny area					
Shady area					
Temperature difference					

What does this chart tell you about the heat produced by the sun?

ESE 2   Can the sun heat water?

Pour equal amounts of cold water into two similar containers.
Put one container in the sun and the other in the shade. Check the temperature of each at regular intervals. Record the results.
(*Note:* As a variation of this, experiment to see if the sun can brew tea. Place tea bags in a jar of water and leave in the hot sun.)

ESE 3 More heat from the sun.

Using a magnifying glass, focus the sun's rays on a piece of paper. What happens?

ESE 4 Which materials store the sun's heat best?

A problem with the widespread use of solar energy is to collect and store the sun's heat for times when the sun is not shining. Different materials have been suggested for storing it. The following experiment permits you to test some.

Which of the following retains heat best: sand, pebbles, salt, water?

To find out you will need:

Plastic food wrap
Cardboard box large enough to hold four jars
Black paint
Four small jars of equal size (such as baby food jars)
Four thermometers
Sand, salt, water, pebbles

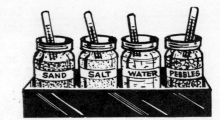

To proceed:

1. Paint the outside of the cardboard box black.
2. Fill each of the jars with one of the materials—sand, salt, water, or pebbles.
3. Place a thermometer in each jar.
4. Put the jars into the box, cover box with plastic wrap, and place in the sun. Record the temperature every half hour for two hours. Now remove the box from the sun and record temperature every half hour for one hour. Construct a chart as follows:

TEMPERATURE READINGS AT TIMES SHOWN

Substances Tested	In Sun				Out of Sun	
	9:00 a.m.	9:30 a.m.	10:00 a.m.	10:30 a.m.	11:00 a.m.	11:30 a.m.
Sand						
Pebbles						
Salt						
Water						

Which substance retains heat best? Which the least? What conclusions can you draw for storing solar heat?

Repeat this experiment with different materials such as sugar, strips of paper. Add the results to the above chart.

ESE 5 Which colors retain heat best?

Some colors absorb more light from the sun than others. Those colors, therefore, retain heat best. The light becomes heat energy. You can demonstrate this by completing the following two experiments.

You will need:

Black and other colors of paint
Thermometers
Cans of equal size

To proceed:

1. Paint the outside of one can black and the others in different colors, and leave one can unpainted.
2. Fill each of the cans with the same amount of cold water.
3. Place a thermometer in each can and leave the cans in the sun.
   Check the temperatures at regular intervals.
   In which colored can is the water the warmest?
   Record the results.

   Repeat the experiment, but use hot water instead of cold.
   Compare your findings for both experiments.
   List the colors tested in order of those that retain heat best to least.

ESE 6   How can you concentrate solar energy?

Set up a mirror outdoors so that it reflects the sun's rays onto a pan of cold water. Take the temperature of the water after two hours.
Now repeat the experiment with the same amount of water but without the mirror.
Did the mirror help heat the water?
(Note: Large parabolic mirrors are used in solar collecting systems to concentrate heat. A parabolic mirror is shaped like a parabola. This experiment illustrates the reason for the use of mirrors.)

ESE 7   How hot is the sun?

Here's a research project:

Find out how hot the sun is.
Where does it get its heat?

ACTIVITIES ESE 8–14: Investigate uses of solar energy: for heating, telling time, purifying water, and cooking.

ESE 8   Solar energy for heating.

There are basically two ways to use the sun to heat houses: passive and active. In a *passive* system, a house is built so that it receives the maximum amount of sun in the winter while trees and overhangs shield it from the sun in summer. As a means of achieving this, houses should generally be built with windows facing south. Passive systems have long been known. Native Americans utilized this knowledge in building their homes.
In an active heating system, solar energy is collected and stored to provide heat on cloudy days and during the night.
Construct a solar collector.
Using the information you obtained by completing Activity ESE 5, decide what color to paint the bottom of your collector.

ESE 9   Build a rooftop solar collector.

Solar collectors are placed on rooftops to enable the sun to heat water, or air in the collector. The hot water or air is then distributed through pipes into the house. Additional hot water is stored in tanks or, in the case of air, in beds of crushed rocks or pebbles.

As an advanced project, make a model of a house with a rooftop solar collector.

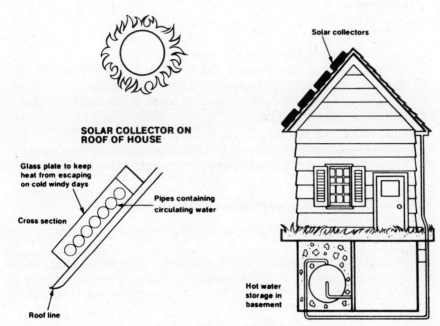

Uses of solar energy in the home. (Book 1, Energy Reader, *What Is Energy* (Washington, D.C.: U.S. Department of Energy, May 1980).)

ESE 10   Demonstrate a problem with solar collectors.

This experiment shows a difficulty encountered in building solar collectors because of the movement of the earth and the relative shift of the position of the sun.

Starting with the morning, circle a spot on the classroom floor where the sun strikes. Indicate the time. Now follow the shift of the sun's reflection throughout the day, circling new spots each hour.

Discuss how this phenomenon may create a problem in placing solar collectors.

ESE 11   Build a sun dial.

The movement of the earth in relation to the sun has enabled people to use the sun to tell time.

The easiest sundial to construct relies on noting the shadow of a stick in the ground or a large nail on a board. Mark the time as the shadow moves about.

(For greater accuracy, the angle of the nail to the board should be equivalent to the latitude at which the dial is located. The shadow will then rotate at a uniform 15 degrees per hour.)

You may wish to research more complicated sun clocks and experiment with constructing them.

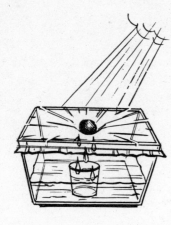

ESE 12   Can solar energy purify water?

Build a solar still to determine this.

You will need:

A pan
A glass (about 2½ inches shorter than the top of the pan)
Plastic wrap
A small rock
Muddy water

To proceed:

1. Place the glass in the center of the pan.
2. Fill the pan with muddy water to about ¾ of the height of the glass.
3. Tape the plastic wrap securely around the top of the pan.
4. Put a small rock on the plastic over the glass, but do not permit the rock actually to touch the glass.
5. Place the pan in the sun. Check it at regular intervals. Note that, as the water evaporates from the pan, tiny drops condense on the plastic.
6. Carefully observe the drops of water in the glass. What do you conclude?

ESE 13   Can solar energy produce salt from seawater?

To find out, place seawater into a large flat pan and put it in the sun. What happens?
(If seawater is not available, use one teaspoon of salt to one cup of water.)
Additional research: (a) Find out where salt is being produced by the *solar* method. (b) Locate the Dead Sea and the Great Salt Lake. How were they formed?

ESE 14   Solar energy for cooking.

Have you ever heard the expression "It's so hot outdoors, you could fry an egg on the sidewalk!"
This could, in fact, be true. Solar energy has been used for cooking. You can start by constructing a small cooker to roast a marshmallow:

1. Line a large, pointed paper cup (you can make one) with aluminum foil. Insert the marshmallow on a pointed stick through the cup, face it toward the sun, and turn until roasted.
2. You can make a larger cooker. The key factor is a curved reflector that will focus the sun's rays on the food.

ACTIVITIES ESE 15–18: Consider more facts about the sun and be inspired by it.

ESE 15   Can the sun's rays be harmful?

Ask the school nurse why you should not stay in the sun for long periods of time. Report on this.

ESE 16   How would the sun's absence affect us?

Write a story of a week, a month, a year without the sun. What would happen? What changes would there be in your life?

ESE 17   The sun in literature and myth.

Ancient people worshiped the sun and frequently devised stories about it.

Find out the names of the sun gods in Egyptian, Greek, and Roman history. What were some of the legends associated with each?

Research also the story of Archimedes, the Greek scientist, who is said to have used the sun to defeat the Romans.

Pretend that you are a member of a primitive people with no scientific knowledge about the sun. Write a story about one of the following:

Where the sun goes at night.
Why it shifts position in the sky.
What happens during an eclipse.

ESE 18   Be inspired by the sun.

Sit outdoors on a bright, sunny day. Paint a picture reflecting the colors about you. (You may wish to read how Van Gogh, an artist, was influenced by the sun.)

Write a poem about the sun.
Create photograms with the sun. (See Chapter 12, Activities M14–M16.)

3
OTHER
ENERGY
SOURCES

Faced with the uncertainty of a continued foreign supply of oil and natural gas, and the fact that our own resources of these fossil fuels may be depleted by the turn of the century, the United States is embarked on a massive search for alternative sources. One of the most promising, solar energy, was explored in the last chapter. In this chapter other alternatives will be examined. All, with the exception of nuclear power, are in fact indirect forms of solar energy. Some are relatively recent sources—nuclear power and biomass; others, such as wind and water power, are among the earliest known. Thirteen activities presenting an overview of sources of energy complete the topic.

WIND POWER

Wind power is a proven source of energy. It has been employed extensively to sail ships, pump water, turn mills to grind flour from grain, and activate generators to produce electricity. In the Netherlands, windmills were used to regain lands from the sea. Here in the United States, it was a significant source of power until the end of the nineteenth century, when the steam engine replaced it.

TEACHER NOTES

BACKGROUND

Once again there is interest in wind power as a source of energy. Just as the sun, the wind is free and nonpolluting. However, obstacles exist to its development. Generating electricity by wind is expensive, strength and frequency of winds vary, and for widespread use, large land areas would be required to install the mills. Despite these problems, experimental wind turbines are being built in areas throughout the country to assess means of capturing and marketing wind power. Small turbines are already in use in many localities, and there is indication that larger projects are planned. A proposal to build twenty windmills in a valley in California was made in the spring of 1979. At that time it was projected that the twenty mills would supply power for 1,000 people and save 175,000 barrels of oil a year. The announcement of the plan stated:

Five years ago, it would not have been competitive to make power with windmills; it's only because the cost of oil has gone up so much that it is now. It'll take into the

1990s before enough windmills are up to make an impact on our use of oil, but the sooner we get started the sooner we get there.[1]

The California project will be constructed in Pacheco Pass, a valley where winds whip through at 16 to 20 miles an hour. It is not always possible to find such areas, but extensive research is being conducted to identify sites and improve the design of the mills. The California State Legislature has set a goal of "10 percent of electrical energy from wind power by the year 2000."

Meanwhile, there are other examples of interest in wind power. The Long Island Lighting Company has proposed a plan to build windmills in Montauk on the tip of Long Island. Federally funded power-generating windmills have been built in New Mexico, in Puerto Rico, in North Carolina, and on Block Island. Small communities throughout the states have experimented with them. Two windmills made it possible for Navaho children in a remote reservation in Arizona to attend their own school. The children had been commuting to schools out of the community. In order to build a school on the reservation, they needed electric power. But it would have cost about $100,000 to bring in electricity. Instead they built the windmills, at a cost of $20,000 (labor was donated by the Navahos). The windmills charge batteries that provide electricity.

Although wind power is not viewed as a major source of energy, it will undoubtedly supply some of our needs in the future as the technology becomes more refined. It may be particularly apt for agricultural areas and rural homes.

ACTIVITIES REQUIRING SPECIAL MATERIALS

EWIP 2: Outdoors.
EWIP 3, 5, 6: See details of constructions.

IMPLEMENTATION

Organize as individual or small-group activities.

EXTENSIONS

Young children can make kites, gliders, and parachutes in conjunction with a study of wind. Note how wind holds these up.

Older children may wish to explore causes of hurricanes, typhoons, and windstorms. Those interested in speed of wind (see Activity EWIP 6) may be introduced to the Beaufort Wind Scale that follows:

Beaufort Scale Numbers	Wind Designations	Velocity in Miles per Hour
0	Calm	0–1
1	Light air	1–3
2	Slight breeze	4–7
3	Gentle breeze	8–12
4	Moderate breeze	13–18
5	Fresh breeze	19–24
6	Strong breeze	25–31
7	Moderate gale	32–38 (continued)

[1]Norman Moore, *The New York Times*, April 22, 1979, p. 52.

Beaufort Numbers	Wind Designations	Velocity in Miles per Hour
8	Fresh gale	39–46
9	Strong gale	47–54
10	Whole gale	55–63
11	Storm	64–75
12	Hurricane	Above 75

EVALUATION

Review research: EWIP 5.

Check constructions—children should understand function of different wind instruments.

Further evaluation will depend on emphasis placed on this section. Do children understand what causes wind? Why can sun be said to cause wind? How can windmills produce electricity?

ACTIVITIES ON WIND POWER

Have you ever been blown so hard by the wind that you have had difficulty standing? If so, you know the power of the wind. These activities explore the nature of wind, its force, and its use as an alternative source of energy.

ACTIVITIES EWIP 1–6: Think about the wind.

EWIP 1   Wind power.

a.   What is wind?
Wind is moving air. The air in our atmosphere is constantly circulating as warm air rises and expands, and cool air becomes heavier and sinks back to the surface of the earth. It is this unequal temperature and weight of the air in different parts of the earth that causes winds.

Note the movement of air over a stove or furnace as the air is heated. Design experiments to prove that the air is hotter toward the ceiling.

b.   What does wind do?
List as many effects of the wind as you can. Your list should include the following:

It moves things.
It lifts things.
It cools things.
It dries things.
It creates music.
It helps produce electricity.

On a long strip of paper paint a series of pictures illustrating each of the above.

EWIP 2   Observe the power of the wind.

Take a walk on a windy day. List all signs of the wind.

EWIP 3   Construct a weather vane

Weather vanes indicate the wind's direction. They have an interesting history. It is said that a Roman builder, Vitruvius, first observed an object like a weather vane in 50 B.C. on a tower in Athens, Greece. He copied the idea for Roman buildings. Much later, in the year 900 A.D., churches in Rome were ordered to place weather vanes in the shape of crowing cocks on their roofs. For many years only churches and royal palaces could have weather vanes on their buildings.

Although some weather vanes are quite decorative, any pointer that is mounted freely so that it can turn in the wind can be used as a weathervane. Here's one suggestion:

You will need:

A flat stick
Plastic drinking straw
Scissors and straight pin
Index cards
Clay or Plasticine

To proceed:

1.   Cut a slit at each end of the straw.
2.   Draw an arrow tip and pointer on separate cards and insert each at a different end of the straw. You may need glue to keep them secure.
3.   Attach the straw to the top of the stick by inserting the pin through the straw—slightly off center so that it is closer to the tip. Make the hole in the straw large enough so that the straw can spin around.
4.   Anchor the stick firmly in a large ball of clay.
5.   To indicate directions, write or paint the four points: N, E, S, W on the sides of the clay.

EWIP 4   Make pinwheels.

Blow on them gently, then faster.
Note that the more wind the faster they turn.
Take them outdoors on a windy day. Note the action of the blades.

EWIP 5   All about windmills.

Windmills are used to produce energy. The wind turns the blades of the mills activating gears inside. These move shafts and rods that make machinery run or drive electric generators.

Find out about their use in the past and their projected use in the future.

What are the advantages and disadvantages of wind power as an alternative source of energy?

As an added activity, build a windmill.

EWIP 6   Build an anemometer.

An anemometer is an instrument used to measure the speed of the wind. You can build one as follows:

You will need:

2 sticks about 1″ wide by 2′ long
1 stronger stick about 3 feet long (such as a 2′ x 4′ board).

Plaster of Paris or a square piece of board for a pedestal.
4 paper cups or 2 rubber balls cut in half
Washer or wooden bead
Nails, thumb tacks

To proceed:

1. Attach paper cups or rubber balls to the ends of the sticks so that each faces in an opposite direction. Color one cup or ball so that it stands out.
2. Now nail the two sticks together through the center and into the three-foot-long stick. Place a washer (or wooden bead) between the smaller sticks and the long stick so that the sticks are free to rotate.
3. Anchor in plaster of paris or on a wooden pedestal (see illustration)
4. Observe your anemometer revolving in the wind. The faster it turns, the greater the speed of the wind. You can compute the approximate speed by counting the numbers of complete revolutions of the colored cup in six seconds.
5. Check to see where the wind is strongest near your school.

WATER POWER

About fifty years ago, water power was responsible for generating almost 30 percent of the electricity used in this country. Gradually, as more reliance was placed on fossil fuels and fewer hydroelectric plants were built, its relative contribution has decreased. Water, however, remains a significant source of energy.

TEACHER NOTES

BACKGROUND

Water has long been employed as a source of power. At first simple water wheels were built by the sides of rivers, and as the water flowed on the blades, the wheels turned and powered machinery or ground grain. Later people noted that, unlike the power of the wind or the sun, water power could easily be stored and released as needed.

Dams were built to collect the water and raise its level to produce more power when it was released. The flow of water could be directed through turbines, which, in turn, activated generators that produced electricity. This is the premise of hydroelectric plants.

Water power or hydroelectric power is an existing source of energy in the United States and in many countries throughout the world. It produces about 15 percent of the electricity used in this country, with plants located in almost every state. States leading in the utilization of hydroelectric power are Washington, California, Oregon, and Tennessee. New York State has a hydroelectric plant at Niagara Falls.

Expanding the use of water power is deceptively appealing. Water is cheap, safe, nonpolluting, and naturally recycled. But other factors need to be considered. There are limited additional sites available for large hydroelectric plants. Environmentalists oppose flooding sites to create new dams because of the potential danger to wildlife in the areas, and because it could result in the elimination of recreation areas. An alternative has been suggested that entails minimal environmental damage; that is, to build small plants to be powered by the flow of ordinary streams. These could be used for local energy needs. Many feel that a partial solution to the fuel shortage lies in a combination of small-scale projects utilizing water or wind where appropriate.

ACTIVITIES REQUIRING SPECIAL MATERIALS

EWAP 3.   Round top of can, nail, two corks, scissors
EWAP 5.   Maps of the United States

IMPLEMENTATION

Integrate with science unit on water or complete as short unit.

EVALUATION

Children should be able to define *hydroelectric* power and understand how it can be used.
Review research: EWAP 2, 4, and 5.

ACTIVITIES ON WATER POWER

At a very early age, children experience the effect of water power as they bathe, shower, or splash in water. These activities are directed to expanding their experiences and relating water power to the production of energy.

ACTIVITIES EWAP 1–5: Focus on water power

EWAP 1   Can water move things?

Using a water hose or other source of water, design an experiment to demonstrate that water can move things.

EWAP 2   Can water cut rock?

Read about the Grand Canyon in Arizona. How did water help form this canyon? What does this illustrate about the power of water?
Research the history of the canyon in your encyclopedia and write a report.

EWAP 3   Construct a water wheel.

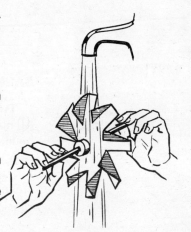

Secure a round top of a can, a long nail, and two corks.
Punch a hole in the center of the top with a nail. Make the hole large enough so that the top can turn freely around the nail.
With a scissor that will cut tin, make six equal cuts in the top.
Bend each of the cuts back with pliers.
Place the can top on a long nail, and hold it in place by putting corks through the nail on both sides of the top.
Put the wheel under a faucet. Note how you can control the speed of the wheel with the force of the water.
(*Note:* Younger children can construct a wheel from cardboard.)

EWAP 4   What are hydroelectric plants?

Why are these plants called "hydroelectric"? Check the origin of the word. Create a filmstrip illustrating how they work.

(*Note:* In hydroelectric plants, water turns turbines fast enough to activate generators, which, in turn, produce electricity by moving wires through a magnetic field.)

EWAP 5   Where are hydroelectric plants located?

On a map of the United States, identify areas where large hydroelectric plants are located. Why are they there?

Do you see any other potential sites?

What are some environmental problems that could be created by building new plants? Share your ideas in a group discussion.

NUCLEAR POWER

Nuclear power, particularly since the accident at the Three Mile Island plant in Harrisburg, has become the most controversial of all alternative sources.

TEACHER NOTES

BACKGROUND

Two methods exist for securing energy from the atom—fission and fusion. All nuclear reactors today rely on *fission*. Nuclear power results when an atom, usually the uranium atom, is split. (Plutonium, which is not a natural element, may also be used.) Tremendous heat results from the splitting or fission. This heat is then used like any other fuel to heat water to form steam. The steam spins the blades of turbines, which then turn generators producing electricity.

Although the technology for producing energy from nuclear fission is well established, problems dealing with its safety remain unresolved. They include questions of the effect of low-level radiation released into the atmosphere, dangers of a nuclear accident, concern over further spread of the know-how, and failure to devise an acceptable plan for disposing of nuclear waste products that may remain radioactive for over 25,000 years. The Harrisburg accident in the spring of 1979 highlighted some of the concerns about the safety of nuclear plants.

The volume of wastes produced by reactors is considerable. The waste must be stored in a manner that will isolate it from people for tens of thousands of years. Various disposal sites have been suggested: deep in the earth, under the sea, in glaciers, or even in outer space. No resolution of the storage problem has been made.

Nuclear fusion, as a means of producing energy for commercial use, is still in early stages. In fission, the atom is split; in fusion, two nuclei fuse or combine to form a larger one. The larger one has less mass than the two original ones. The difference in mass is converted into considerable amounts of energy. Fusion has been accomplished only once, unhappily in the production of the hydrogen bomb. If a method were perfected for nuclear fusion, the projection is that it would be safer than fission. Fuels that are very common and cheap, such as deuterium contained in sea water, could be used. However, energy from nuclear fusion is considered distant.

ACTIVITIES REQUIRING SPECIAL MATERIALS

None require special materials.

IMPLEMENTATION

Integrate into science units on matter and energy.

More advanced children can report on the actual problems that developed at Three Mile Island by studying newspaper articles of April 1979 as well as the report by the President's Commission on the Accident at Three Mile Island.

They can debate whether plants already built should be licensed to operate.

Some may wish to research the history of the development of nuclear energy.

EVALUATION

Check:

Accuracy of diagrams: ENP 1 and 3
Research: ENP 4
Ability to take survey: ENP 6
Ability to marshall facts in debate: ENP 5. Do arguments demonstrate comprehension of problems (such as waste disposal)? Has consideration been given to both sides in debate? Is there evidence of deeper understanding of issues?

ACTIVITIES ON NUCLEAR POWER

How safe are nuclear plants? Is nuclear energy a desirable alternative source? These remain unresolved questions.

ACTIVITIES ENP 1–6: Become informed about nuclear power and some of the problems associated with its use.

ENP 1   What is an atom?

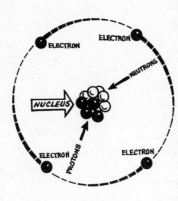

Draw a diagram of an atom.
Show the nucleus and its parts.
(You may also wish to make a model of an atom.)

ENP 2   Nuclear energy through fission or fusion.

Nuclear energy is currently created by *fission*—splitting of atoms. This is accomplished as follows. The atom has a nucleus and electrons. The nucleus contains protons and neutrons. In fission, a neutron is released, which strikes the center of the atom, causing it to split into many fragments and also causing a chain reaction splitting the nuclei of other atoms. Nuclear reactors control this chain reaction. The process of fission generates tremendous heat.

Fusion is as yet unperfected. In fusion, atoms would generate heat by combining into a smaller mass.

You can demonstrate the difference between fission and fusion.

Fission: Use a paper towel to represent an atom. Tear it apart. The atom is split.

Fusion: Use two separate pieces of paper toweling. Wet them so they will stick together, and fuse them, overlapping a bit to create a smaller mass.

ENP 3   Nuclear energy produces electricity.

Draw a diagram showing how nuclear energy is used to create steam to generate electricity.

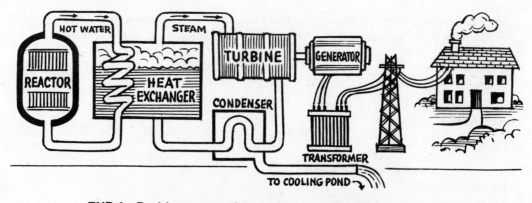

ENP 4   Problems associated with nuclear power.

What are the problems associated with the use of nuclear power? Find out about nuclear wastes. How are they disposed of? How long do they remain radioactive? Why are there these hazards?

Report on your findings.

ENP 5   Should nuclear plants be built?

Organize a debate on this topic.
Then have the class vote.

ENP 6   Take a survey.

Ask as many people as you can whether they believe nuclear plants should
be operated.
Classify the answers by groups (age groups, for example).
Graph and publicize the results.

ADDITIONAL ALTERNATIVES

A number of alternative sources have been discussed in this and the preceding
chapter: solar energy, wind, water, and nuclear power. Less-known alternative sources are also receiving serious consideration. Most are relatively expensive, but with the rising cost of imported fuels and the infusion of government funds into research and development, they may well become a part of
our energy future. This will be particularly true if a solution to the energy
crisis, as some have suggested, lies in small, varied projects catering to local
communities rather than to large areas. These sources utilize local resources.

Background notes are presented here on biomass, synthetic fuels, waste,
and geothermal and ocean thermal energy. Mention is also made of tidal
waves and volcanoes. Specific activities have not been included on any of
these. Each can be assigned as a topic for investigation by a small group.[2]

BIOMASS

Plants are a natural storehouse of energy. During the process of photosynthesis, they capture energy from the sun. Some of this is utilized by the plants
for their own growth; some, by animals and people who eat the plants as food;
but much of the solar energy remains in the plants. It can be released as heat
energy when the plants are burned. The term *biomass* refers to the plant material available as a potential source of energy.

Plants have long been recognized as a source of energy. Fossil fuels were
formed over millions of years as a result of the decay of plants. But there is
interest now in growing plants specifically for fuel. Many can be grown
quickly; they are a renewable source and burn easily. Experiments are currently underway to determine the practicability of this alternative approach.
A number of crops have been suggested: grains, beet and cane sugar, fast-
growing trees, rubber plants, cattails, desert shrubs, and even water plants.
Some fast-growing algae and water hyacinth could conceivably be grown in
bodies of water—from ponds to oceans—and harvested for fuel.

Alcohol can be derived from plants with high sugar content. This is cur-

[2]Teachers may wish to make volcanoes in the classroom to demonstrate this potential source.
Instructions follow:
Shape a volcano on a board with plaster of Paris. Make a crater on top and insert a small can.
The volcano may be painted.
Place a few tablespoons of ammonium dichromate in the can, and light it with a match. The
volcano will give off hot sparks and a substance like lava.
An eruption can also be caused by first placing four tablespoons of baking soda in the can, and
then adding a mixture of ½ cup water, ¼ cup liquid detergent, and ¼ cup vinegar. You may need
to stir the mixture for it to erupt.

rently being done and the alcohol later combined with gasoline to produce *gasohol*, sold as a substitute for gasoline alone. It burns with greater efficiency than gasoline and produces fewer pollutants. If car engines can be adjusted to run on higher percentages of alcohol to gasoline, *gasohol* would save large amounts of oil. Actually, alcohol can be produced from any starch or sugar, even from fermented garbage. Wood is another form of biomass. Renewed attention is being given to woodburning stoves with efforts focusing on making them more energy-efficient.

Arguments against cultivating biomass for fuel note the worldwide shortage of food and question the morality of using land for energy crops rather than food crops. Additionally, "energy farms" could require large amounts of water, which, particularly in some areas, could pose a major problem. To meet these arguments, consideration is being given to cultivating areas not now useful for food and using even arid or semiarid lands. Desert shrubs and some species of plants that grow wild have been identified as potential sources of energy.

SYNTHETIC FUELS

The term *synthetic fuels* refers to the oil and natural gas produced primarily from coal, oil shale, and tar sands, although fuel from biomass is sometimes included in the definition. Methods of extracting the synthetic fuels from each of the three major sources are, for the most part, clearly established. They are the following:

■ *Coal:* Crude oil and natural gas are created by crushing the coal, burning it under high pressure, and exposing it to catalysts. Hydrogen is used in the process.
■ *Oil shale:* Large deposits of oil lie in rock formations called *shale.* In the United States, they are primarily in Colorado, Wyoming, and Utah. The shale can be mined and oil extracted by heating it at extremely high temperatures, 900 degrees Fahrenheit. A material called kerogen is formed that becomes oil. In another process, not yet perfected, the shale would be heated underground until a liquid is formed and then pumped to the surface.
■ *Tar sands:* Most commercial deposits of tar sands are located in the Alberta province of Canada, although some fields do exist in Utah. The sands are combined with hot water and steam and then refined into coke, crude oil, and natural gas.

Synthetic fuels have previously been produced. At the beginning of the century, a gas was produced from coal; and during World War II, Germany used gasoline derived from coal to alleviate a fuel shortage. But the widespread effort envisioned at this time has never been attempted. Concern has been expressed at the high cost of synthetic fuels and the environmental impact of their manufacture. It is feared that coal liquids carry cancer-causing agents and that burning coal will release pollutants not completely removed by the planned processes. Problems exist, too, with shale. The process for extracting oil results in large amounts of spent shale that need to be disposed. It also requires large amounts of water. Some opponents of synthetic fuels have pointed to the huge amount of energy required in their production, questioning whether the net energy gain is worth the high cost. The United States government has allocated substantial funds for development of synthetic fuels. Efforts to combat the negative environmental implications have been promised.

FUEL FROM WASTES

There is an incredible amount of waste discarded daily by the American public, an estimated one billion pounds, much of it a potentially valuable source of energy, metals, and other materials. About 75 percent of the waste is combustible and could be burned to produce energy. Converting waste into fuel is a tantalizing idea. It could solve both an energy problem and another serious problem—waste disposal. The fact is that we are running out of places to dump garbage, and in the areas in which we have already buried it, the garbage remains to haunt us. It pollutes the water, land, and air.

To make it economically feasible to convert garbage to fuel, we would also need to recycle other waste products, a process that would save still more energy. For example, recycled aluminum requires only 5 percent of the energy needed to produce it from raw ore. It takes eight times more energy to mine and produce new copper than to recycle it.

What is required is a shift from a "throwaway" economy to one of conservation. Garbage would have to be sorted and viewed as a potential resource. Some beginnings have been made. Plants have been established to convert waste into fuel in a number of states. (See also Background Facts, Chapter 9.)

GEOTHERMAL ENERGY

Geothermal energy results when the natural heat of the earth in hot underground rocks comes in contact with water. Steam is produced that is forced through cracks in the earth's surface in the form of geysers or hot springs. Other deposits remain below the earth's surface. The steam can be captured and used to power electric generators or provide heat. In Iceland, geothermal heat provides almost all the heat for the capital, Reykjavik. There is a geothermal plant currently operating in Italy. In the United States, there is one in California. Most of the geothermal resources in this country are found in the West.

As with other alternative sources, problems have been pinpointed. A method of releasing geothermal energy is to inject water into the earth to bounce off the hot rocks below. Some warn that this process has not been adequately studied and could trigger earthquakes. Another concern is with the odor released during the procedure. It comes from hydrogen sulfide, which smells like rotten eggs. Those familiar with hot springs may recall that this odor is often associated with them.

OCEAN THERMAL ENERGY

Mechanical energy can be captured from the flow of heat energy between a hot and cool region. Many ocean areas have large differences in temperature between the surface waters warmed by the sun and the cold waters toward the bottom. This has been viewed as a potential source of energy.

An ocean thermal energy system is currently being tested in Hawaii. The hot surface water is used to heat a liquid with a low boiling point (such as ammonia), which then turns to vapor that drives turbines just as steam does when heated. Cold water from the bottom of the ocean then cools the vapor, condensing it back to a liquid, and the process is repeated. Underwater cables transmit the energy to shore.

TIDAL WAVES AND VOLCANOES

Both of these have been mentioned but mainly on a theoretical level, although France and the Soviet Union have had some experience with tidal energy. Canada is interested because of the huge tides in the Bay of Fundy between New Brunswick and Nova Scotia. Tides are said to average 37 feet twice a day in this area.

Other sources will undoubtedly emerge in the next decades, but in reality one of the most practical sources of energy is one readily available to all—conservation. It is to this we shall shortly turn.

SOURCES OF ENERGY: AN OVERVIEW

This overview presents some general activities that can be studied independently or included with any of the preceding sources.

TEACHER NOTES

ACTIVITIES REQUIRING SPECIAL MATERIALS

ESEN 3: World maps.

IMPLEMENTATION

To enable integration of these activities with the preceding ones relating to specific sources, they have been grouped as follows:

Introductory activities: ESEN 1–3
Those relating to specific sources: ESEN 4–7
Culminating activities: ESEN 8–13

Books and other research material should be available to students during this unit.

EVALUATION

Assess ability to work in groups.
Check:

Research data ESEN: 2, 3, 4
Speaking, debating skills: ESEN 5, 6
Writing: ESEN 11
Graph: ESEN 8
Creative thinking: ESEN 10

Key concept: There are many potential sources of energy but also problems associated with the use of each.

ACTIVITIES ON GENERAL SOURCES OF ENERGY

Survey the many sources of energy that heat and cool our homes, run our machines, and affect our daily lives.

ACTIVITY ESEN 1: Note how energy sources have changed through the years.

ESEN 1   Prepare an energy time line.

Construct a mural depicting the sources of energy from earliest times to the future.

Start with primitive man using body energy, then using crude tools such as rocks, and finally discovering fire, leading to more sophisticated tools.

Include the use of wind to sail boats, water to power mills, and the sun to provide light and heat.

Depict the domestication of animals to do work.

Add invention of steam for engines, electricity, automobile engines, and airplanes.

Finally, note the discovery of nuclear power. Can you predict a future source?

As a more extensive activity, your time line may include dates of important inventions (such as the steam engine) and key people involved.

ACTIVITIES ESEN 2–3: Research some of the sources of energy, and where they are found.

ESEN 2   Devise a "Sources of Energy" chart.

Draw or bring in pictures of different sources of energy—oil wells, windmills, coal mines, and so on. Be imaginative; include little-known sources, such as volcanoes.

ESEN 3   Locate the sources of energy.

On a map of the world indicate where there are deposits of petroleum, natural gas, coal, uranium, hot springs, and other sources of energy described earlier. (See Chapter 2, Figure 2.2 for information on fossil fuels).

For a more complicated version: Indicate the sizes of the deposits by different colors: red for a large deposit, blue for a medium one, and green for a small one.

ACTIVITIES ESEN 4–7: Focus on specific sources.

ESEN 4   Research a specific source of energy.

Find out all you can about that source. You may prefer to work in groups. (Information about specific sources can be found earlier in this and the preceding chapter.)

Determine where the source is found, its availability, potential uses, practicability, and problems associated with its use.

Report to the class. Prepare visuals—models, pictures, dioramas, graphs, diagrams, filmstrips to accompany your report.

Consider also a bound book for presentation to the library that will summarize your investigations. (See Chapter 11, Activity PWB 15.)

ESEN 5   "Sell" a particular source of energy.

Plan an advertising campaign to "sell" your source.

Describe its advantages.

Write a slogan for your campaign. Design posters. Prepare television commercials.

ESEN 6   Prosecute a polluter.

Conduct a mock trial of a source of energy for polluting the environment. Choose a defense attorney, a prosecuting attorney, and a judge. The class may act as jury.

The decision will be as to whether the source should be permitted to be used as it is at present, be required to follow new guidelines, or be "banished for life."

ESEN 7   Pantomime a source of energy and an application.

Can you show the sun drying clothes? The wind moving boats? Coal being dug from the ground, transported, and used to heat a building? Find other examples.

Have the class identify the source of energy pantomimed.

ACTIVITIES ESEN 8–13: Culminating activities. Apply and display your knowledge about energy.

ESEN 8   Energy in your home.

Survey the members of your class to find out the sources of energy used in their homes for heating and cooking food.

Make a graph illustrating your findings.

As an added activity: Investigate which is the cheapest and which the most expensive way of heating homes: gas, electricity, or oil. Report this to the class.

ESEN 9   Energy in the school.

Interview the school custodian.

What are the sources of energy used in the school?

Are any alternative sources being considered?

What would be the problems in changing to other sources?
Discuss the information garnered in class.

ESEN 10   Daydream about energy in the future.

a.   Invent a new source of energy.
     Can you think of a source of energy not currently being used? Look about
     you for ideas.
     Draw a diagram of your invention.
     Or create a comic strip character to introduce it.
b.   Design a car of the future.
     How will it be powered?
     Summarize the ideas of class members in a chart.
c.   Design a city of the future.
     Indicate energy-saving aspects: garbage for fuel, moving sidewalks in-
     stead of cars, people able to fly with the use of giant kites.
     Prepare a display illustrating these.
d.   Design a house of the future.
     What will be the energy sources?
     Write a statement with your forecasts.

ESEN 11   Write a poem.

   Immortalize an energy source in poetry. Try a cinquain, quatrain, limerick.
(See Chapter 11, Greeting Card Activity PGC 8.)

ESEN 12   Consider a special bulletin board.

   Plan an energy bulletin board outside your classroom.
   Highlight alternative sources of energy. Give facts about each. Include diagrams, pictures.

ESEN 13   Plan an open house or energy fair.

   Invite people to visit your classroom to see displays on sources of energy.

4
ENERGY CONSERVATION

The Arab oil embargo in 1973 marked the close of the era of cheap energy in the United States, and also brought a realization that the supply of fossil fuels was finite and that new sources of energy would have to be developed. Most alternative sources are still economically unfeasible or pose serious environmental hazards. There is, however, a major alternative source of energy that poses no threat to the environment, no pollution, and could save billions of dollars. That source is *conservation*. Many believe that this is potentially the largest untapped source of energy.

TEACHER NOTES

BACKGROUND

The United States with six percent of the world's population uses about 30 percent of the world's energy resources. Each American consumes about seven times as much energy as a person in another country. The nation wastes millions of barrels of oil each day through inefficient use of energy in homes, buildings, industry, and transportation. It has been estimated that "the United States can use 30 or 40 percent less energy than it does, with virtually no penalty for the way Americans live."[1]

An investigation of the energy problem in the United States identified three categories of conservation:[2]

1. Curtailment: forced through limitation of supplies.
2. Overhaul: rearranging patterns of work and life.
3. Adjustment: more efficient use of energy. Also called *productive conservation*.

The authors of the study noted that the first two categories were frequently identified with conservation but that they somehow appeared "repressive," "Un-American," and were, therefore, less desirable. It was the third alternative, *adjustment*, that they felt should be actively pursued. As an example of how adjustment can be made without changes in life-style, the authors offer the process of making toast. It can be prepared in three different ways: on a barbecue, in a broiler, or in a toaster. Each requires different amounts of energy, but the end product is the same.[3]

Impressive statistics support the claim for productive conservation:

[1]Robert Stobaugh and Daniel Yergin, eds., *Report of the Energy Project at the Harvard Business School* (New York: Random House, 1979), p. 182.
[2]Ibid., pp. 138–139.
[3]Ibid., p. 137.

If simple insulation packages . . . were installed in 20 million poorly insulated homes, it has been estimated that energy use in the residential sector could be cut by a quarter.[4]

Reducing the thermostat from a twenty-four hour setting of 74 degrees to 68 degrees during the day and 60 degrees at night can reduce heating loads by as much as 20 percent.[5]

Similarly, significant savings are possible in industry, commercial buildings, increased mileage per gallon of gasoline used by automobiles, and more energy-efficient appliances. In homes, even some minor changes could have an effect—drawing drapes on cold nights and showering instead of bathing to save hot water.

It has been noted that young people are among the largest consumers of energy for personal use in the home. They do not perceive a relationship between their behavior and an energy shortage. They do not view leaving a television set on when they leave a room, requesting to be transported when they can easily walk or bicycle, turning on an air conditioner, or using to excess appliances such as hair dryers as contributing to the shortage. Yet wasteful patterns of children can more easily be corrected than those of adults. Children can be taught to be energy-conscious, to conserve energy, and in the process they can influence adults to do the same.

The goals of this section are to make children aware of the need for conservation, of areas where they can conserve, and to help them recognize that their efforts can be significant. Students can view themselves as in the vanguard of the battle against energy waste and for conservation.

ACTIVITIES REQUIRING SPECIAL MATERIALS

EC 5: Paper pie plates and metal fasteners.
EC 16: Necessitates children's leaving classroom—may be during or after school hours.
EC 17, 18, 20: See experiments for details.
EC 22: Small piece of plastic food wrap.

IMPLEMENTATION

Though not essential, children's understanding of this section will be enhanced by reference to facts about energy (Chapter 1) and information from background notes pertaining to alternative sources.

Some utility companies will lend the class an electric meter or provide simulated meter faces. See Activities EC 4, 5.

Activities include checking usage of electricity at home. Teachers should be aware that this may be a sensitive question for some families.

MODIFICATIONS

Methods of reporting results of surveys have not been specified for some activities (see EC 8–10). This enables teachers to adapt them for different grade levels. Teachers may suggest that younger children discuss findings; older ones may discuss and/or write conclusions.

[4]Ibid., p. 172.
[5]Ibid., p. 176.

Other adaptations can be made for younger children. Many activities require calculations. Smaller numbers can be used as in EC 4. Similarly, EC 16 can eliminate requirement for computation of savings.

EVALUATION

Check:

Math computations: EC 3 to 8, 10, 11, 12, 13, 15, 16, 19, 20
Written responses: EC 1, 2, 12
Research data and reports: EC 2, 6, 7, 8, 9, 10, 12, 14, 15, 16, 20 to 23
Records of experiments: EC 17, 18, 20, 21, 22, 23
Visuals: posters, filmstrips, and graphs EC 12, 14, 25–28, 31

(In reviewing the preceding items as well as oral reports, evaluate whether there are evidences of serious consideration of problems, awareness of *energy crisis*, and practical suggestions.)

(*Note:* The objectives of this section are largely attitudinal. Evaluation should focus on changes in children's energy behavior at school and their reports of their actions at home.

Emphasis on conservation should continue after the completion of the unit.)

ACTIVITY STARTERS

Young children may not understand the word *conservation*. In addition to defining it, it may be demonstrated. One teacher explained that there were only 100 sheets of construction paper left for the next ten days. The children had previously been using it at the rate of 20 per day. He asked how they could manage to leave some for each day.

Another teacher referred to children's allowances to define *conservation*. What would happen, she asked, if children expended their entire weekly allowance in one day.

In one class the teacher asked, "Do you think that one person could solve our energy crisis?" When she received a negative reply, she continued, "What if one person decided to become an energy saver and enlisted one other person to do the same; and on the following day, each of them enlisted one other person for a total of four; and on the following day each of the four enlisted one other person for a total of eight, each of whom on the following day enlisted one other person. . . . How many people would be energy savers at the end of a month?" she inquired. The children soon realized that technically they could reach every person in the city in a short period of time. While it was not conceivable that they could actually do this, realistic possibilities did exist. What if all 25 people in the class pledged to become energy savers? From how many additional people could pledges be secured? The children added up friends, members of their families, and neighbors and realized that they could in fact contact a large number of people.

Another teacher dramatized the concept that energy sources can be depleted by the following demonstration. She distributed materials for the children to complete an electric circuit to light a small bulb by using a dry cell battery. When they accomplished this, she suggested they add additional bulbs to the circuit. Eventually, each bulb became dimmer and dimmer and finally was extinguished. By discussing this, the children realized that the energy stored in the dry cell had been *depleted*. The teacher related this to the depletion of other sources of energy.

ACTIVITIES ON CONSERVATION

Review the many demands for energy and how you can become an energy-saver.

ACTIVITIES EC 1 and 2: Study the word *conservation*.

EC 1   What does conservation mean?

Define the word. Play with it: How many three- or more-letter words can you find in conservation?

Can you make it into a new word by just transposing two letters? (Hint: The new word means a discussion among people.)

Make an acrostic from the word *conserve*.

One class made the following into a poster:

C   ar pool
O   pen windows instead of using air conditioning
N   o energy waste
S   olar energy
E   conomize fuel
R   ecycle garbage
V   olcanoes for energy
E   xtra efforts save energy

EC 2   Why do we need to conserve energy?

People in the United States use about seven times as much energy as people in other countries. Why do you think this is true? Discuss this fact in class.

Why do we call fossil fuels *finite* resources? Look up the meaning of the word *finite* to explain this.

Can you do without energy? (See Chapter 1, Activity EA 9.)

Write an essay entitled "It is important to conserve energy because . . . "

ACTIVITIES EC 3–10: Learn about kilowatts, meters, and the cost of electricity.

EC 3   What is a kilowatt?

A kilowatt is the equivalent of 1,000 watts. Electricity use is recorded in kilowatt hours (kwh).

An electric light bulb has a number stamped on it—100, 75, 60, and so on. This means that the bulb will use that many watts of electricity in one hour. For example, a 100-watt bulb will use 100 watts of electricity in one hour, 1 kilowatt in ten hours.

How many watts would a 60-watt bulb use in 2 hours, 8 hours, 10 hours?

EC 4 You can read an electric meter.

Electric meters are maintained by utility companies to indicate how many kwh of electricity have been used. They then charge the customer for this amount.

Here's how to read a meter.

Read the dials from left to right as you would read a numeral. The farthest right dial represents the unit column; the next, the tens; and so on, as in our decimal system.

When an indicator lies between two numbers, always record the smallest number. Note that some of the dials read clockwise and some counterclockwise.

The number in the illustration would be 12594.

To determine how many kwh have been used, you would have to know the previous reading and subtract this from the current one. For example, if the previous reading on these meters had been 11232, then 1,362 kwh of electricity would have been used (12,594 − 11,232 = 1,362).

(See also Chapter 2, EFF 24; Learn to read a gas meter.)

EC 5 Construct meters.

Using paper pie plates or cardboard, make meters. Attach moveable hands with metal fasteners.

Practice reading meters by setting them for different readings, such as 20659, 18345. Have one student set the meter and another read it.

Practice, too, *before* and *after* readings. Complete a chart such as the following. (Add other figures to it.)

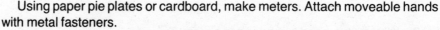

Meter as of May 1	Meter as of June 1	Electricity Used in Month of May
21345	22456	?

EC 6 How much does a kilowatt hour cost?

To find out, call your local electric company.

Based on this information, compute the cost of the electricity used in the month of May in the preceding activity.

EC 7 Check your electric meter at home.

How many kilowatt hours of electricity do you use daily? Weekly? Monthly? To find out, read the meter at the same time each day, week, and month.

EC 8   How much does your family pay for electricity?

Based on the information from Activities EC 6 and EC 7, compute the approximate daily, weekly, and monthly cost of electricity. Compare your results with the actual electric bill.

How much could be saved if your family used 10 percent less electricity? Can you devise a plan in cooperation with other family members to save money and energy?

EC 9   What is the cost of electricity to the school?

Find out how many kwh of electricity the school uses and the cost of the electric bill each month.

Could students help reduce this cost? How?

EC 10   Electricity uses fuel.

Electricity is generated by burning fuel; about 75 percent of our gas, coal, and oil is used to manufacture electricity.

It takes about one gallon of oil to produce 12.7 kilowatts of electricity.

How many gallons of oil were needed to produce the electricity used in your home and school last month?

ACTIVITIES EC 11–14: Analyze the use of energy by appliances.

EC 11   How much energy does that appliance use?

Below is a list of the average amount of energy used by different appliances.[6] The actual wattage of an appliance will vary depending on the brand used.

Appliance	Average Wattage
Blender	300
Broiler	1140
Coffee Maker	1200
Dishwasher	1201
Range with Oven	12200
Toaster	1146
Clothes Dryer	4856
Iron	1100
Washing Machine	512
Room Air Conditioner	860
Hair Dryer	1000
Radio/Record Player	109
TV—Tube type	
Black and White	100
Color	240

Note the one that uses the most and the least. What is the difference between these?

Here's an interesting calculation: Find the average amount of energy used by all the appliances listed.

[6]Based on Long Island Lighting Company's figures, July 1979.

EC 12 Which appliances are most commonly used?

Make a list of all the appliances used in your home.

Compare your list with those of other classmates. Graph the results.

Now on a chart note the five most common appliances found in the homes. What is the average wattage used by these?

As an added activity, find out which of these were available when your grandparents were children.

EC 13 Cost of operating an appliance.

To compute the cost of operating an appliance for a year:

1. Write down the wattage. You may use the chart in EC 11 or check for the exact figure. This is usually found on an attached plate on the appliance.
2. Multiply this by the number of hours operated in a week and the number of weeks operated in a year.
3. Divide the total by 1,000 to find kilowatt hours.
4. Multiply by cost of kwh. (Wattage × Annual Use) ÷ 1,000 × cost of kwh = Annual Cost.

APPLIANCES	HOW MANY WATTS?	HOURS OF USE PER WEEK	HOURS OF USE PER YEAR	COST OF KILOWATT HOURS PER YEAR	IN USE BY GRANDPARENTS
TOASTER					
WASHING MACHINE					
VACUUM CLEANER					
COFFEE MAKER					
ELECT. REFRIG.					

EC 14 Are all appliances necessary?

If you could only have three appliances, which would they be?

Compare these choices with other members of your family. Are they the same?

Now collect all the students' choices and illustrate the results in a bar graph. Include the name of the appliance and the number of people who selected it.

ACTIVITIES EC 15–16: Consider car pooling to save gasoline.

EC 15 Collect information on car pooling.

Do you know any adults who drive to work? Ask them to complete the following questionnaire.

Do you drive to work?
How many ride in the car with you?
How many miles do you drive (round trip)?
How many miles can you drive on each gallon of gasoline?
What is the average price you pay for a gallon of gasoline?

Tabulate the results of the questionnaires and compute the following: How much gasoline could be saved if each car contained at least three passengers? How much money could be saved?

EC 16   Complete a transportation survey.

Stand on a corner during commuting hours in teams of three. Have one person record all the cars with one passenger, another with two, and the third with three passengers or more.

Compute the savings in gasoline if each car contained at least three passengers. Estimate that the cars will drive about 50 miles round trip and receive about 15 miles per gallon of gas.

ACTIVITIES EC 17–18: Investigate insulation.

EC 17   What is insulation? Which materials insulate best?

Some materials are said to be low-heat conductors; that is, they prevent heat from escaping quickly through them. Such materials are called *insulators*. Installing them in areas of the house (such as around hot-water heaters, walls, floors, and attics) is one of the most important ways to save fuel. Special materials have been designed to insulate homes and buildings.

You can experiment to see which common materials insulate best.

You will need:

Various materials: cotton, wool, aluminum foil, paper, plastic wrap, nylon, and so on
Styrofoam cups
Thermometer
Boiling water

COTTON   WOOL   ALUMINUM   PAPER   PLASTIC WRAP

To proceed:

1. Place an equal amount of boiling water in Styrofoam cups. Wrap each in a different material. (You can compare a few at a time.)
2. At the end of an hour, test and record the temperature of the water in each of the cups. Which materials were the best *insulators?* If you wished to keep a baby's bottle warm, in which would you wrap it?
3. Try additional experiments with these materials. For example, what happens if you wrap a few thicknesses of the material around the cups?
4. Keep careful records of your results.

EC 18   Test for cold retention.

Repeat the preceding experiment using uniform-sized ice cubes instead of hot water. Wrap each cube in a different material.

After stated periods of time—half-hour, hour, more if necessary—check the cubes. In which does the ice melt quickest? Slowest? Record your results.

Which material insulates best? Compare your findings with those in the preceding activity. Are the same materials effective heat and cold insulators?

ACTIVITIES EC 19–23: Examine more energy-saving tips.

EC 19   Lower thermostats and save money and heating fuel.

The following chart indicates the percentage of savings on the price of heating fuel if thermostats are lowered from 70 degrees Fahrenheit to the temperatures shown for the period of time indicated.

If your heating bill last year was $1,000, compute the savings if the thermostat were lowered from 70 to 55 degrees for eight hours each night.

(For additional math practice, compute the savings for *each* of the periods of time shown, again assuming a heating bill of $1,000 and a thermostat previously set at 70 degrees.)

Temperature	Four hours	Eight hours
65°F	2½%	5 %
60°F	5 %	9½%
55°F	7½%	14½%
50°F	9½%	19½%

EC 20   Save energy when cooking.

Which boils quicker: water in a covered or an uncovered pot? How much difference is there?

Design an experiment to determine this.

What conclusions do you draw?

And for scientists: Collect more exact data.

Construct a chart as follows:

HOW LONG DOES IT TAKE WATER TO BOIL

	Boiling Time in Seconds		
Quantity of Water	Covered Pot	Uncovered Pot	Difference
1 quart			
2 quarts			
4 quarts			
6 quarts			

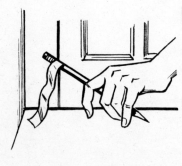

EC 21   Shower or bath?

Which uses more water: a shower or a bath?

Design an experiment to find out.

Which would enable you to save energy for heating hot water?

EC 22   Avoid waste of energy through drafts.

Heat is wasted on cold days because of drafty areas in the home.

To check for such areas, make a "draft detector." Scotch-tape a strip of plastic food wrap, about 5 inches by 10 inches to a stick or pencil. Use it to test for drafts near windows, doors.

If you discover drafts, find out how these can be sealed.

EC 23   Does this door need weather stripping?

Try slipping a quarter under the door. If it goes through easily, the door needs weather stripping. Call this to the attention of a parent.

ACTIVITIES EC 24–33: Help the school and community become energy savers, too. Here are ten ways you can organize to save energy.

EC 24   Organize the class as a team of "energy savers."
Select a name for your team.
Agree on a symbol (a light turned off, the sun, a windmill).
Urge others to enroll on your team.

EC 25   Conduct a contest for an energy conservation slogan.

One class used "Kill-A-Watt"; another, "Don't Be Fuelish, Save Energy."
Make buttons with the winning slogan. They can be made of felt or actual ones can be purchased and sold.
Design stickers to be pasted on book covers with your slogan.
How else can you popularize it?

EC 26   Plan a poster campaign.

Prepare posters for display in school and neighborhood stores.
Use energy slogans and specific suggestions: "Turn off a 100-watt bulb for a total of ten hours and save a kilowatt." "Use your body energy—walk or bike instead of driving."

Poster displayed at energy fair, Morris School District, Morristown, N. J.

EC 27 Make energy filmstrips.

Inexpensive filmstrips can be made (see Chapter 12, Activities M 6–10) and distributed to other classes.
Include ideas for saving energy. (See more specifics later in this chapter.)

EC 28 Create a comic character or puppet.

Give it a name. One class called their puppet "Prometheus" based on the Greek mythological character; another the "Energy Elf."
Write comic strips featuring your character indicating how it saves energy, and also have it call attention to wasteful practices.

EC 29 Be an energy "private eye."

Check for signs of energy waste at home. Are lights left on in empty rooms? Does the radio or television operate after you leave a room? Do you keep opening the refrigerator door?
Make a list of other possible energy wasters.
Look for examples of energy waste in school. Discuss these in class.
What suggestions can you make to save energy?

EC 30 Schedule an energy-saver day.

Have each of the students ask their parents if they could stage an energy-saver day. Eliminate as much use of energy on that day as possible. Try to wash with cold water, eat cold foods, use minimum lighting, and use no appliances.
Discuss in class the actions you took and how you felt.

EC 31 Issue an energy-savers fact sheet.

Research ways to save energy. Include the headings: turn off, turn down, use less, and save. Examples of each are the following:

Turn off: lights, radio, television, electric blanket, air conditioner, faucets.

Turn down: furnace (thermostats), air conditioner (if you need it on).

Use less: make fewer car trips, use a car pool, shower instead of bathing, pull curtains at night, use only bulb wattage necessary, and don't let water run when brushing teeth or washing hair. Wash with cold water when possible (particularly clothes).

Save: stuff cracks, close doors and windows when air conditioner is on, close refrigerator door quickly, do fewer washes in machines, hang clothes to dry instead of using dryer, set thermostats lower at night, use fluorescent lights instead of incandescent where possible. Use mass transportation.

Research also facts such as the following:

If every house in the United States lowered its thermostat by an average of six degrees for 24 hours, there would be a savings of more than 570,000 barrels of oil each day.

Assuming that a person bathes in half-hot and half-cold water, substituting one five-minute shower for one bath each day would result in a saving of 2,000 gallons of hot water in a year.

Two lightweight sweaters add more warmth than one heavy one.

Publicize these facts to the community.

EC 32 Prepare an energy news program.

Broadcast energy-saving tips (such as those in EC 31), and also ask the children to report what they have done to save energy.

Read the names of super energy savers and list their methods on a large chart in the hall.

EC 33 Complete an energy report card.

Each week have members of the class rate themselves on the report card (Figure 4.1).

Award a scroll to those who have *perfect marks*.

MY ENERGY REPORT CARD

	Need No Improve-ment	Need a Little Improve-ment	Need Lots of Improve-ment
Name_____ Week_____			
Ways I Saved Energy This Week:			
Turned off lights when not needed			
Turned off radio and TV when not in use			
Kept doors and windows closed in cold weather			
Requested fewer car trips			
Opened refrigerator door less			
Used fewer electric appliances			
Used cold water instead of hot where possible			
Wore warmer clothes on cold days so thermostat could be lowered			
Conserved supplies			
Other			

(Adapted from "Project Save," Merrick Public Schools, Merrick, New York.)

Figure 4.1 Sample Form of Report Card.

RESOURCES FOR PART 1

Write to the following requesting free energy materials for the classroom, and for a list of other available publications and films.

American Gas Association
Educational Services
1515 Wilson Boulevard
Arlington, Virginia 22209

Edison Electric Institute
90 Park Avenue
New York, N.Y. 10016

Exxon USA
Public Affairs Department
P.O. Box 2180
Houston, Texas 77001
    Request single copies of comic books: "Mickey Mouse and Goofy Explore Energy" and "Mickey Mouse and Goofy Explore Conservation."

League of Women Voters
1730 M Street N.W.
Washington, D.C. 20585

National Coal Association
Coal Building
1130 Seventeenth Street N.W.
Washington, D.C. 20036

National Science Teachers Association
1742 Connecticut Avenue N.W.
Washington, D.C. 20009

National Wildlife Federation
1412 Sixteenth Street N.W.
Washington, D.C. 20036
    Request reprints from *Ranger Ricks Nature Magazine*, April and May/June 1974 "The Best Present of All," and "Special Report on Energy."

Standard Oil Co.
Mail Code 3705
200 East Randolph Drive
Chicago, Illinois 60601

Superintendent of Documents
United States Government Printing Office
Washington, D.C. 20402

Union Carbide Co.
270 Park Avenue
New York, N.Y. 10017

United States Consumer Information
Pueblo, Colorado 81009
    Request "Tips for Energy Savers" DOE/CS 0020

United States Department of Energy
Office of Public Affairs
Washington, D.C. 20585

United States Department of Energy
Technical Information Center
Post Office Box 62
Oak Ridge, Tennessee 37830
    Excellent source of materials. Single copies of many publications are issued to teachers. Request the following:
        Energy Fact Sheets
        Award Winning Energy Education Activities DOE/IR 0015

Energy from the Winds DOE/OPA 0013
Winter Survival DOE/OPA 0019
Interdisciplinary Student/Teacher Materials in Energy, the Environment and the
Economy. Specify grade levels.

In addition to the above, state education departments and local utility companies may
have material available.

THE CLASSROOM AS A CONSUMER BUREAU

The room appeared more like a math lab than an ordinary classroom. Students were working in small groups on a variety of mathematical calculations. Some were computing unit costs from empty packages: cans, boxes, bottles. Others were computing costs per serving from information on the packages. One group was comparing the percentage of sugar in different brands of cereal. Another was graphing the results of a survey on the effects of advertising on purchasing habits.

Every Tuesday morning this particular classroom was a "consumer bureau." The three Rs were emphasized through consumer education activities. Children read consumer pamphlets, labels, instructions. They read analytically, critically. They wrote letters to manufacturers and consumer agencies and published fact sheets. But more than the three Rs was involved: the activities incorporated science, social studies, and art.

Consumer education is in itself becoming recognized as a basic facet of a child's education. Arguments supporting its introduction into the curriculum from early childhood on are impressive. In a 1973 poll[1] it was found that children aged eight to twelve years spent $2 billion to $5 billion annually. Today that figure would be much higher. American teenagers spend about $15 billion on bicycles, soft drinks, jewelry, cosmetics, T-shirts, and records. In addition to independent purchases, children influence parents' expenditures especially for products like toys, breakfast cereals, and clothing. Manufacturers are well aware of children's purchasing power. Substantial amounts are spent on advertising geared to young children.

Successful consumer education projects have been reported in schools throughout the country. Children have studied basic economics, analyzed advertisements, tested products, published consumer information, and actually handled community consumer problems by contacting manufacturers. In one school, they conducted an "operation price watch" inspired by a parent who belonged to a labor organization that had a similar campaign. They monitored the prices of ten specific items over a period of time and reported when they exceeded federal guidelines.

Many of the activity clusters in this part can be introduced as separate topics. For example, teachers can select those related to shopping for toys, reading labels, or product testing in the next chapter; or television commercials in the chapter on advertising. Furthermore, teachers can readily create an awareness of consumer issues by substituting some of the activities stressing mathematics for the story problems in math texts. This unit also affords an excellent means of teaching critical thinking, distinguishing fact from fiction, and imparting other higher-order cognitive skills.

OBJECTIVES OF CONSUMER EDUCATION

Students will:

- Acquire knowledge of basic concepts of consumerism.
- Gain insight into how their buying patterns are formed.
- Recognize themselves as consumers.
- Be able to evaluate purchases and become wiser shoppers.
- Learn to analyze advertisements critically.
- Be better managers of money.
- Gain an understanding of some basic economic facts.

[1]Rand Youth Poll. Reported by Sally Williams. Address, "Television and the Young Consumer." International Festival of Children's Television, Washington, D.C., 1974.

- Become more aware of their rights and responsibilities as consumers.
- Clarify their own values, needs, and wants.
- Enhance their self-concepts by performing useful tasks.
- Be more capable of making objective decisions based on information, critical evaluation.
- Practice skills of problem solving, inquiry, analyzing, comparing.
- Gain experience in speaking.
- Read for information.
- Practice writing business letters.
- Practice mathematics skills.

CURRICULUM INTEGRATION

Mathematics

Part Two lends itself particularly well to integration with mathematics, offering practice in both computations, measurements, and problem solving. Each of the four operations are included as follows:

Addition: totaling costs of shopping lists, menus, food coupons
Subtraction: comparing prices of items and weights
Multiplication: computing costs of a number of items
                    practicing percentages
Division: computing unit prices
            determining the price of one item if a price is based on larger quantity (three for 95 cents)
            price per serving

Language

Reading: labels, instructions, consumer reports, advertisements (particularly critical reading)
Writing: booklets, consumer reports, letters, commercials, skits, advertisements
Research
Listening: critically to commercials
Speaking
Vocabulary extension

Social Studies

Consider substituting consumerism for a social studies unit such as a unit on a community or the United States. It can also be introduced as an economics unit.

Science

Integrate with health or study of the human body.
Activities on food shopping and labels are particularly appropriate as part of a unit on nutrition.
Relate activities to scientific method of investigating problems.

Art

Children create posters, puppets, filmstrips, collages.

UNIT EXTENSIONS

1. Organize a consumer fair. Have children demonstrate their findings through displays, charts, filmstrips, posters.
2. Maintain a consumer learning center where children can check containers and continue to test products.
3. Older children may be interested in making some basic cosmetics. Information on ingredients can be obtained from Food and Drug Administration.
4. Investigate hazardous products. Research additives: nitrites, food coloring, controversy about saccharin.
5. Research use of common, everyday products for cleaning (lemon, milk for stains) as substitutes for commercial products. Interview older people for suggestions.
6. A unit on consumerism leads naturally to a study of nutrition. Discuss latest guidelines on nutrition by Federal Department of Agriculture and warnings about too much sugar and salt. Check food containers for evidence of this.

UNIT STARTERS

"Who is a consumer?" "Are children consumers?" Start the unit with a definition of consumer *(someone who buys or uses something)*. Establish that children are consumers. They eat food, wear clothes, play with toys, all previously bought. Many also have money to spend. In addition, they influence their parents' purchases. Seek examples of this. "Have you ever asked an adult to buy something for you?"

Give each child a fixed amount of paper money (such as $50 or $100). Ask the children to list what they would like to buy and the approximate cost of each item.

Note the prices they estimated. How realistic were they? Consider, too, the choices made. What was included? How did they know of the item? It may be interesting to compare their choices with those of younger and older children. For a more involved project, students can survey other classes in the school and tabulate their preferences and knowledge of prices by age levels.

CHAPTER

5
SHOPPING

Children need to "become aware that there is only a limited amount of money available to most people for most of their lives and that choice has to be made . . . ; that they cannot always take things at their face value."[1] They are subjected to constant exhortation to buy—in television commercials, comic books, even on cereal boxes. Few counterforces exist urging them to evaluate, shop critically. Williams warns: "Unless a counterbalance is provided by the teacher . . . children will grow to believe that the name which is shouted the loudest and publicized the most heavily is that belonging to the best and highest quality product."[2]

The activities in this chapter include shopping for food, clothes, and toys and reading labels. They are designed to make the student an aware, discriminating consumer. They span all age levels. Even young children can participate in consumer education as noted by the many activities for all grades.

TEACHER NOTES

BACKGROUND

The need for practical information about shopping is clear. Children are uneducated consumers, swayed by advertising, emotion, surface appeal—with little notion of price or value. They may not even be aware that different stores charge different prices for the same product. Particularly in this period of inflation, children need to be helped to evaluate their purchases, to shop wisely. It needs to be borne in mind, however, that buying practices reflect values—personal needs, goals, and life-styles. What is appropriate for one consumer may not be so for another. A woman who works all day and then is responsible for preparing an evening meal cannot appreciate that savings result from preparing food from scratch. Nor can a person without a car chase food specials.

ACTIVITIES REQUIRING SPECIAL MATERIALS

CS 4:   Three containers of different size and sand or salt.
CS 19: Children are asked to bring toy premiums.
CS 24: Fruit juice.
CS 26: Children are asked to survey different stores.
        Permission to telephone from school may be considered.
CS 27–30: Products to be tested. Check also for details of experiments.
CS 31: Suggests children accompany parent to supermarket.
CS 33: Containers with labels.
CS 35: Cereal boxes.
CS 39–50: Toys will need to be examined both in school and home.

[1]Alma Williams, *Educating the Consumer* (London: Longmans, 1975), p. 45.
[2]Ibid., p. 32.

CS 46: Toy catalog.
CS 52: Catalogs, newspapers, magazines.
CS 54–56: Fabric swatches.
CS 55: See details of experiment.

IMPLEMENTATION

It will be necessary to accumulate empty containers of all kinds: food packages, particularly dry cereal, and toy boxes, cans, wrappings of paper goods and frozen foods, plastic wrappings—as many containers as possible. Each will need to have the price and labels left intact.

Magazines, newspapers with advertisements, and catalogs should also be available.

If possible, schedule a class visit to the supermarket. Permission can generally be secured if it is scheduled for a quiet period during the day. The store manager may permit the children to go into the back of the store to see where food is delivered and stored. As preparation for the visit, suggest children first accompany their parents (see activity CS 31).

You will find that some activities, such as those on toys and clothes (CS 39–57), lend themselves better to holiday seasons.

EXTENSIONS

A clothing exchange for outgrown boots, mittens, and jackets can be established in cooperation with parents.

Children may make their own toys, such as games, puppets, or puppet theater instead of buying toys.

See also culminating activities at end of chapter.

EVALUATIONS

Check:

Math computations: CS 6, 8, 9, 10, 12–18, 20, 21, 23, 27, 35, 46, 52
Graphs: CS 53, 55
Written work and research reports: CS 3, 4, 7, 8, 11, 13, 22, 33, 34, 37, 38, 41, 42, 44, 45, 47, 49, 51

In addition, assess children's ability to collect data, organize experiments, draw conclusions, evaluate findings.

Determine by objective measures whether children have become wiser shoppers. For example, given three items, can they more accurately assess the price of each; can they interpret food labels, critically survey packages, compare prices?

ACTIVITY STARTERS

The teacher held up two boxes of cereal—one larger than the other. "Which has more cereal?" he asked. When the children indicated the larger box, he called their attention to the quantities listed. Actually, the smaller one had more.

He displayed two cans of food—one a supermarket brand and the other a nationally advertised one, which was much more expensive. "Which would you choose?" was the next question. "Let's check the ingredients," he suggested. They were identical. Both brands were, in fact, made by the same company. "Let's learn to be smart shoppers!" he proposed.

ACTIVITIES ON SHOPPING

Investigate how to be a *smart shopper* by examining packages, analyzing prices, evaluating purchases, testing products, visiting your supermarket, and scrutinizing labels, toys, clothing, and fabrics.

ACTIVITIES CS 1–5: Examine packages and assess their effect on consumers' purchases and prices.

CS 1 Units of measurement.

How do we measure the following?

The amount of dry cereal in a box
Vegetables in a can
Fresh vegetables
Milk and juices
Napkins in a box

Make a chart entitled "How Are Products Measured?" On it list as many products as you can and the units used for measurement. Draw or find pictures illustrating your chart.

CS 2 Classify packages.

Select all the empty cereal boxes from your class collection.
In how many different ways can you classify them? (Include size of box, weight of contents, price, product.) Sort them according to each of these classifications in turn.

CS 3 Compare packages.

As you sort the boxes, observe the following: Size of box: Do the larger boxes always have the most cereal? Compare the size to the weight.
Price: Compare price to weight. Does the largest amount of cereal always cost the most?
Product: Is there a difference in price for the same product depending on brand?
Were you surprised by any of the results? Keep a record of your findings.

CS 4 How does packaging influence purchasing?

a. You will need:

Three containers of different sizes and shapes.
Tall narrow jar (such as a shampoo jar).
Plastic bag.
Wide, squat jar.
A dry ingredient (such as sand or salt) that you can pretend is valuable for molding models.

TALL JAR
PLASTIC BAG

SQUAT JAR

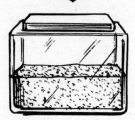

To proceed:

Fill each of the containers with the same amount of the ingredient.
1. Now line up the three containers and study them. Do they all look as if they have the same amount? Which would you be more apt to purchase?
2. Try this experiment: Ask others who are not aware that each package contains the same amount which they think has the most ingredients and which the least. Record your results. What conclusions can you draw about packaging from this experiment?

b. Here's still another way to analyze packaging:
Note the pictures on the outside of cereal boxes.
Is there a picture of a sports hero? What message does this imply?
Is the cereal shown with fruit? If so, is the fruit included?

CS 5   Does packaging add to price?

Examine boxes of toys that you have received. How much room is actually taken by the contents? How much is to display the contents?

Remove the contents of a box that contains a coloring set or different parts of a toy. Place the contents in a plastic bag. Compare the bag to the box.

Which seems more valuable to you? Would you pay as much for the toy if it were packed in the bag?

Look for other examples of packaging that just increase the price of the product, not the actual worth of the contents.

ACTIVITIES CS 6–15: Learn about prices.

CS 6   What is unit price?

The unit price is the price of an item divided by the actual quantity. For example, two packages of lollipops may each cost 50 cents and contain the same size and kind of lollipop. However, one may contain five lollipops and the other eight. The unit price of the pops in the first package would be 10 cents each and in the second 6¼ cents each. Which would be the wiser purchase?

In the evaluation of purchases, it is important that we check unit price. Practice this by determining:

The price of each napkin in a package
The price of each ounce of a cereal
The price of each ounce of juice

Supermarkets now show unit price on the shelves where products are stored. You can use this information to compare prices of different-sized containers or different brands.

CS 7   Record unit prices.

Make a card for each of the empty containers collected by the class. The following information should be included:

Product	Manufacturer	Quantity and Unit	Total Price	Unit Price

Sort the cards by products.

CS 8   Unit prices as a guide to shopping.

If unit price were the only consideration, determine the best buy for each product from the cards completed in the preceding activity. What is the difference between the lowest and highest unit prices for each product?

Is one brand consistently more expensive than another?

Now consider another factor: What other than price might be a consideration in shopping *(taste, family preference, nutrition,* and so on)?

Complete the following: When shopping for a product, these are some of the considerations . . . .

CS 9   Price per serving: another way of comparing prices.

Cereal boxes and many others indicate the number of servings in a package and also the size of a serving.

The price per serving will be determined by the price of the item divided by the number of servings.

Find the price per serving for different brands of cereal. How will this information affect your decision as to which is the best buy?

CS 10   Which size is cheaper?

Is it usually cheaper to buy larger or smaller quantities of a product? Using the information you have accumulated about unit prices and price per serving, examine a number of products and find out. Hypothesize in advance what the answer will be.

When might it be unwise to buy a larger size even if it were cheaper? Give examples.

CS 11   Does advertising affect prices?

You will need to research the prices of store or generic brands of products as well as advertised brands. *For the purpose of this experiment you are assuming that the brands are equal in quality. This is not necessarily true.*

Find examples of food products or cosmetics that are regularly advertised, and then investigate the prices of other brands of these items. Construct a chart illustrating your findings:

| | | Advertised | |
Product	Unit Price	Yes	No

Do you see any relation between the price of a product and whether it is advertised? Why might this be true?

CS 12   Play "The Price is Right."

Get to know the price of different items.

Each day select a panel of experts.

Choose five items. Ask each to write down the price. Who came closest? How much did the prices vary?

Use different kinds of items—food (a dozen eggs, a box of cereal, a bottle of juice), clothing (a pair of jeans, a sweater), and toys.

For a variation, for each of the items to be priced also indicate what could be purchased for the same amount.

CS 13   What is the cost of a lunch for four?

Plan a menu for a lunch for four. Estimate the cost.
Now list all the items and figure the actual cost.
How close was your estimate? Compute the difference.

CS 14   What can you buy for $5.00?

How much tuna fish? How much peanut butter? How much milk? How much soda?
Estimate; then find out.

CS 15   Practice consumer math.

If one of a product costs a certain amount, what would three cost? Make up problems like this, using specific products and actual costs, such as the following:
If two cans of beets cost 45 cents, what does one cost?
If a pound of chicken costs 69 cents, what does a three-pound chicken cost?

ACTIVITIES CS 16–26: Be a comparison shopper: More tips to help you critically evaluate your purchases.

CS 16   Buy what you need.

Find an item that is sold in large quantities, such as onions—3 pounds for 99 cents. If you need only one pound, can you buy it, or must you take the packaged amount? Ask the store manager. What would the price of one pound be?

CS 17   What price beans?

Compare the price of fresh, frozen, and canned string beans. Which is more expensive? How might the season influence the results?

CS 18   How expensive are frozen products?

Stores have to pay for energy to store frozen products so that they would usually tend to be more expensive. But this may not always be true.
Prepare an analysis as follows:

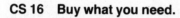

Product	Quantity	Price Fresh	Price Frozen

To be accurate, you would have to gather your data at different times of the year.
What can you conclude from your analysis? Could there be an advantage to using frozen products even if they were slightly more expensive?
How does the price of freshly squeezed orange juice compare with frozen juice? Which do you prefer?

CS 19 Was that *premium* worth its price?

Bring in items you have "won" from gum machines. Tell how much you actually paid for them. Was it worth it?

How about the premium you sent for from a package or comic book ad? Was it as it looked on the ad? Was it worth it?

CS 20 Learn to read food advertisements.

Look for advertised specials in food ads. Compare these with prices in stores where the item is not on special. Compute how much you would save by buying the special. Why might the special not prove cheaper? *(Store too far, quantity too large.)*

CS 21 How much are food coupons worth?

Clip all the food coupons in a newspaper in one week. Total them. How much would you save if you used them all?

And a more extensive activity: A practical service to residents.

Establish a coupon service.

Clip food and other coupons from the newspapers.

Request that parents contribute coupons or box tops that they do not need.

File these by category—cereal, coffee, salad dressing, and so on.

Make them available to other parents, residents, and local retiree groups. You may need to post a regular list of coupons on hand.

CS 22 How can you determine quality?

Is there any difference in quality between brown and white eggs?

Is there any difference in nutritional value between cans marked "Grade A," "Grade B," "Grade C"?

How do the various grades of meat differ?

Write to your local consumer agency to find out.

CS 23 Comparing prices of different-sized eggs.

Which are better buys: large, medium, or small eggs?

Generally, the larger size is worth about 7 to 8 cents more per dozen.

The United States Department of Agriculture offers more precise figures:

Comparing sizes and costs of eggs	Buy the larger size if the price per dozen is less than
Extra large and large	$1/9$ of the price of extra large
Large and medium	$1/8$ of the price of large
Medium and small	$1/7$ of the price of medium
Large and small	$1/4$ of the price of large

Find out the prices of different-sized eggs in your communities and determine which is the best buy.

CS 24   Juices vs. juice drinks.

Know the difference:

A juice must be 100 percent fruit juice.
A nectar may contain some water as well.
A punch contains water and sugar as well.
A drink may contain 10 percent to 33 percent fruit juice; the rest is water and sugar.

Mix your own drink. Start with the juice and dilute it. Compare the price of 8 ounces of a commercial drink and your own mixture. What do you conclude?

CS 25   Juices vs. cola drinks.

Did you know that cola drinks contain caffeine and sugar? Check with your school nurse or health teacher to find out why this could be a problem.
Did you know that orange juice contains Vitamin A, Vitamin C, and potassium, all needed by our bodies? Cola drinks contain none of these.
Which should you drink when you are thirsty?
Publicize these facts. Make posters explaining them.

CS 26   Do all stores charge the same?

List the different kinds of stores in your community and the kinds of products each sells.
Have students check with these stores for the price of similar items—tennis balls, games, for example. Post the prices. Do all stores sell a similar product at the same price? If you find a "great buy," publicize it.

ACTIVITIES CS 27–30: Organize a product-testing laboratory.

CS 27   Test paper products.

You will need:

A graduated millimeter cylinder or narrow tube on which you can indicate quantities
Aluminum foil or pie plates
Watch with second hand
Water
Paper products

To proceed:

1. Have students bring in samples of paper products used in their homes: napkins, towels, toilet tissues, tissues. Each one should be accompanied by a card stating:

Brand Name	Price per Package	No. in Package	Unit Price

Sort cards by product. Determine which are most widely used. Assign "popularity" rating to each product: *Popularity rating* = the number of students who brought that product.

2. Work in groups. Devise tests for each product to determine which is most absorbent.

The following are two possible tests:

(a) Place a piece of paper in a pie plate. Pour two teaspoons of water on the paper. After five seconds remove the paper and pour the remaining water back into the cylinder. Record how much water the paper absorbed and how much was left. Repeat this with each brand. (You may also test by waiting a longer period—10 seconds. See if the results change.)

(b) Place five sheets of towels or napkins in a pie plate with one cup of water. After 30 seconds remove the sheets; hold them over the plate so that all the surplus water drips back. Measure the amount of water left in the plate to see how much the papers have absorbed. Repeat with each brand.

From these and other tests you can devise, you will determine which brand absorbs water best. Rate the products with a letter *A* for best in test, *B* for next, and so forth.

Now make a chart as follows:

Brand Name	Unit Price	Popularity Rating	Test Rating

It will be interesting to compare the price and popularity of an item with its test rating.

(You may also wish to test paper products to see which is the strongest. After soaking in water for equal periods of time, gently pull at them.)

CS 28   Try taste tests.

Bring in samples of different brands of the same products: peanut butter, apple juice, cornflakes, cola drinks.

Set up a tasting panel of five students for each product.
Test one product at a time.
Put an equal quantity of each brand into unmarked paper cups, and have the students sample, then rate which taste best.

Compare the ratings with price. Are the most expensive brands the best? Consider making a chart for each product as in the preceding activity.

A tasting panel compares different brands of a product. (Photograph courtesy Public School 221, District 26, Little Neck, N. Y. Early Childhood Gifted Program, Bea Chertoff, teacher.)

CS 29 Test cleaning powders.

a. First test scouring powders by trying the following: You will need tea bags and an enamel pan or dish. Wet three tea bags and leave on the bottom of an enamel pan for about an hour. The tea will stain the enamel.

Now use equal quantities of three different cleansing powders. Which removes the stain quickest? (You might also try an old-fashioned home cleanser. Rub a cut lemon on the stain. See if it will work.)

b. Test the cleaning power of detergents or soap powders.

Stain a piece of cotton fabric with ink. Cut the fabric into equal pieces corresponding to the number of products to be tested. Dilute the powders with equal amounts of water. Pour on the stain. Time to see which acts most quickly and most effectively.

CS 30 Test other products.

Design experiments to test other cleansers, plastic wraps, and so on. One class investigated which pencils withstood sharpening best.

Look about you to see which products that you use could be subjected to your *product testing.*

ACTIVITY CS 31: Survey the supermarket.

CS 31 A trip to the supermarket.

Consumer education starts in your supermarket. Accompany your parents when they shop. If they have made a shopping list, ask to see it and estimate in advance what you think it will cost. (Check this with the actual cost later.)

Take a pencil and paper and take notes at the store.

1. What are the specials?
2. What is displayed in the front of the store?

3. How many different brands of the same products are there: soap, cleaning materials, cereals, canned fruits, canned fish? How would you decide which to buy?
4. Can you find the unit prices? What is the difference between the most and the least expensive?
5. Can you find the dates on the products?
6. Check the weights; there is usually a scale provided for customers' use. Do all packages of carrots weigh the same? Bags of potatoes?
7. Where are items such as gum, candy, and magazines placed?
8. Look about the store for other interesting observations.
9. Report to the class on your visit and compare notes with others who visited stores.

ACTIVITIES CS 32–37: Labels: Discover why they are important and how to read them.

CS 32 How reading labels can save money.

The following is a true story:

A woman had purchased a cream in a saddle shop to prevent "dried-out brittle hooves" on her pet horse. Quite coincidentally on the same day she had purchased a "nail-strengthener cream" in a cosmetic shop for her own nails. She glanced at the labels on both products and was surprised to discover that the ingredients were practically the same—the only difference was that some caramel coloring had been added to the horse cream. She also observed that the cosmetic was packaged in a fancy jar.

The difference in price between the two products: the horse cream sold for $5.95 per pound; the cosmetic cream for $10 per ounce or $160 per pound.

Although this large a difference is unusual, you will find that some brands of a product are more expensive than others, but their ingredients may be exactly the same.

Read labels of similar products to find examples of this. Start with cosmetics, cleaning products, food, drugs, and pet food.

Even young children can become aware of information on labels. (Photograph courtesy Public School 221, District 26, Little Neck, N. Y. Early Childhood Gifted Program, Bea Chertoff, teacher.)

CS 33   Rules about labels.

The federal government insists that certain information appear on labels and that it be listed in a prescribed order. This includes:

1. Nutrition information by serving: The package must show the size of a serving and the number of servings per package.
2. Also there must be listed in the following order: calories, protein, carbohydrate, fat, vitamins, and minerals together with the percentage of U.S. Recommended Daily Allowances (U.S. RDA). Cereals must also include carbohydrate content.
3. Ingredients: Most products must list ingredients and in *descending* order. The largest ingredient must be shown first.
4. Brand name and common name (if the latter is different from the brand name).
5. Name and address of the manufacturer.
6. Quantity of item.
7. Date beyond which it cannot be sold (where this is appropriate, such as in a perishable item).
8. Drugs must contain directions for use and warnings about restrictions and any side effects.
9. Appliances must carry information on the amount of energy consumption.
10. Clothing labels must indicate the type of fabric and cleaning instructions.

Here's an exercise to help you learn to read labels:

Select a few containers and copy the label information onto a form as follows:

Product

Nutrition Information
Serving size
Servings per package
Calories
Protein
Carbohydrates
Fat

Manufacturer

Percentage of U.S. Recommended Daily Allowances (U.S. RDA)
Protein
Vitamin A
Vitamin C
Thiamine
others

Total Quantity

Ingredients
(List only the first three since these are the most important.)

_____
_____
_____

CS 34   Understanding label vocabulary.

Other key words on labels and their meanings:

Enriched: additional vitamins, proteins, minerals added.

Fortified: vitamins, proteins, minerals added that are not naturally present in product.

Additives: *may* include preservatives, coloring agents, flavors, and additional nutrients.

Find examples of these on labels. Write the name of the product and the key word included.

Pay special attention to additives. Some may be of questionable safety. List all the additives and write to doctors, chemists, and the Food and Drug Administration inquiring as to what each product is and whether it is considered completely safe.

CS 35 How much sugar?

Sugar can cause tooth decay. The sugar causes a fermentation process in the mouth that creates an acid that attacks tooth enamel.

Extra sugar also leads to overweight.

To find out how much sugar there is in cereals, examine cereal boxes:

1. Look at the list of ingredients. Is sugar listed among the first three? (It may even be listed first; some cereals contain as much as 60 percent sugar.)
2. Read the carbohydrate information. This must show the amount of sugar (but don't be fooled; it may be called sucrose, dextrose, or even corn syrup). Computing this can get tricky because some manufacturers list the quantities in ounces but the carbohydrates in grams. There are approximately 28 grams to the ounce. Divide the number of grams of sugar per ounce by 28 to find the percentage of sugar in the cereal. (For example, one cereal lists 9 grams of "sucrose and other sugars" in an ounce. Nine divided by 28 would indicate that it contains about 32 percent sugar.
3. Compute the sugar content of a number of cereals.
4. Make a chart publicizing the results.

CS 36 Read ingredients.

Federal law requires that ingredients be listed in order of amount—greater amounts must be listed first.

Here are the actual ingredients as written on the labels of three different cans of beef stew:

Can No. 1: beef, tomatoes, water
Can No. 2: tomatoes, beef, water
Can No. 3: water, tomatoes, beef

Of the three cans, which would you expect to be most expensive? Which the cheapest?

Compare the ingredients of other products, such as peanut butter and peanut spread, cheese and cheese spreads. A chart such as the following will clearly illustrate your findings.

Products	Ingredient No. 1	Ingredient No. 2	Ingredient No. 3

CS 37 Look for dates.

Products that may spoil must be dated.

Before buying a food, always check the date to be certain it is still fresh. This is particularly important with dairy products.

Find the dates on food containers. Investigate further: by writing to manufacturers or interviewing your local supermarket manager, determine how far in advance the expiration dates are for these products: milk, cheese (different varieties), cream, eggs. Add others.

ACTIVITY CS 38: Help others to be smart food shoppers.

CS 38　Issue a consumer report.

Write a booklet for the community with tips on smart food shopping. Here are some suggested by the President's Consumer Affairs Office:

1. Read, read, read. Check sale items.
2. Clip coupons but use them wisely. Don't use a coupon unless it is for something you really need.
3. Make a shopping list before you go to the store.
4. Use unit pricing to determine the most economical brand and size.
5. Consider private brands or generic labels.
6. Make your own drinks instead of soda.
7. When buying eggs, look at price differential—if it's more than 8 cents between one size, buy the smaller.

Add some other suggestions to the list based on the preceding activities. *And be a smart shopper.*

ACTIVITIES CS 39–43: Be a wise toy buyer. In these activities you will be concerned with toy safety.

CS 39　How safe is that toy?

A child was electrocuted when his kite made of polyester film coated with aluminum came into contact with a power line. Another was hurt when he accidentally discharged a pellet from a toy gun.

Learn to check toys for possible hazards.

Select three toys. Examine them carefully.

List all possible hazards if the toys broke accidentally or were mishandled. (Remember some children mishandle toys).

CS 40　Can broken toys be hazardous?

Bring some broken toys to the classroom.

Inspect them carefully.

Are there any spots where a child could get hurt? (Look for sharp edges, exposed prongs, or wires.)

CS 41　Read labels on toys and games.

Look for terms like "nontoxic," "flame-retardant," and "washable materials" on stuffed animals.

What does each of these mean? Why are they important? Write a short paragraph explaining what could occur if toys were not any of these.

Look for warnings. See if there are any special instructions or warnings about misuse.

Check labels and toy boxes for examples of these.

Discuss their significance in class.

CS 42 Promote toy safety.

Issue a safety *fact sheet.*

You can help make people aware of the importance of checking toys for safety. Design a booklet or fact sheet to be distributed to the community just before a holiday period, such as Christmas or Hanukkah, in which you include guidelines for buying safe toys. The following were suggested by the Virginia Citizens Consumer Council (Toy Safety Committee):

1. Buy toys that are built to withstand investigation.
2. Look for wheels attached to pull toys, trucks and so on, with screws, not nails.
3. Look for pull cords attached with staples, not thumb tacks.
4. Be sure dolls and stuffed animals with moveable parts (such as head, arms, legs) do not use elastic, metal rods, or metal wires.
5. Examine wooden toys for smoothly sanded finishes and metal toys for rolled or turned in edges.
6. Choose toys of flexible plastic; toys made with rigid plastic or glass produce a very sharp edge when broken.
7. Check facial features on stuffed animals—cloth or painted ones are better than buttons fastened with a pin or hook.
8. For infants—buy washable, nonbreakable toys and squeeze toys with nonremovable squeakers.
9. Be sure any toy designed to be placed in the mouth (such as a whistle, a horn, or a bubble blower) is not so small or fragile that it, or any part, can be swallowed.
10. Check labels for nontoxic paint and nonflammable materials.
11. Make sure riding toys have widespread wheels and a low center of gravity to prevent tipping over.
12. Electrical toys for children, if bought at all, should be used only with adult supervision.

Are there other guidelines you would add?

CS 43. Stage a toy safety exhibit.

At the exhibit demonstrate toys that may be hazardous and ways that children can get hurt. Distribute your safety guidelines.

ACTIVITIES CS 44–51: Select toys carefully: Additional criteria for purchasing toys.

CS 44 Do you still play with that toy?

Have each member of the class make a list of the toys received last Christmas.

Combine these into a large class list.

Toy	Still in Good Condition		Poor Condition		Would You Buy It Again?
	Still Play with It	No Longer Interested in It	Parts Broken	Parts Lost	

Draw some conclusions from this list.

Can you classify kinds of toys that appear to be wise buys?

Which toys would you like to receive next Christmas?

CS 45   Which toys break easily?

From the above chart note which toys appear to break easily.
Bring in some broken toys. (See Activity CS 40.)
Examine them. Why did they break?
Were they mishandled or made shoddily?
Can parts easily be lost?
Can they be repaired?
Make a list of toys that are poor buys because they break easily.

CS 46   What do toys cost?

Using a toy catalog or asking your parent, find out what toys cost.
Make a chart by price range: Under $5.00, $5.00 to $10.00, $10.00 to $20.00. . . . Under each heading include as many toys as you can in that price range.
Which would you prefer in each price range? Compare your choices. Publicize results.

CS 47   How well-packaged are toys?

Compose a check list for toy packages:

Are directions clear?
Are age levels accurate?
Are parts, such as batteries, included?
Does toy come assembled? If not, is it easy to assemble?

Use your check list to analyze as many toys and games as you can, both those in school and at home.
Compare your conclusions with those of others in the class.

CS 48   Criteria for a good toy.

From the above activities, decide what to consider when buying toys. Some of those suggested include:

Suitable for age suggested
Develops new interests
Maintains interest
Durable, will not break easily
Safe
Fun
Challenging
Can be used creatively
Directions clear, packaging good
Price fair

Can you think of others? Make a poster listing criteria for good toys.

CS 49   Can you write directions?

Some people's jobs are to write toy directions. How well would you do at this?
Practice by writing directions for games, such as Tic Tac Toe or Concentration.
Collect directions that have been received with different toys or games. Have the class read them and, if they are not easy to understand, rewrite them.

CS 50   Organize a toy repair and exchange shop.

Now that you have learned how expensive toys are, you can appreciate the importance of keeping them in use.

Bring in toys that can be repaired. During free periods, patch boxes, find missing parts—try to fix them.

Also bring in toys that you no longer want. Have a class committee put an approximate value on them, and issue a *check* to you for that amount. The *checks* can be used to buy other toys in your class exchange.

(See also Chapter 7, Money Management Activities CMM 15 and 21.)

CS 51   Issue a toy bulletin.

Publicize information you have gained about toys from activities CS 39–CS 48. Include, too, any toys that the class believes deserve a place on an "Honor Roll" of good toy buys.

A toy bulletin issued before a holiday (such as Christmas) can be a service to the community.

ACTIVITIES CS 52–57: Choose clothes carefully. Become informed of prices, criteria, and fabrics.

CS 52   If you had $100. . . .

You will need: mail-order catalogs, newspaper and magazine clothing advertisements. You may also need to ask your parents in advance for the price of items of clothing.

Pretend that each member of the class receives the same amount, $100 or more. With this amount each is to buy all the clothes needed for one season (excluding underwear, socks, pajamas, and one pair of serviceable shoes).

List all the clothes you would buy and the prices of each. They may not total more than the set amount.

Compare your choices with those of others in the class. Be prepared to explain the reasons for your choices.

CS 53   Selecting clothes.

Some of the following considerations have been suggested for buying clothes:

Style
Comfort
Usefulness
Easy care
Price
Quality
Durability
Widely advertised

Rank these in order of importance to you.
Make a graph showing the first three choices of the students in the class.
Were other considerations suggested?

CS 54   Learn about fabrics.

Some fabrics used to make clothes are nylon, cotton, polyester, acrylic, dacron.

Ask a neighborhood fabric store for samples of these. Your parents may also have some.

Some fabrics are grown naturally; others are made in a laboratory. Research to find out how a particular fabric is made.

Create a fabric chart:

Mount a piece of fabric with information about it (how it is made, other uses besides clothing, features).

CS 55 Which fabrics absorb water more easily?

You will need:

A jar with a wide mouth
Swatches of different fabrics
Watch with second hand
Cup and water

To proceed:

1. Wrap each piece of fabric, one at a time, securely around mouth of jar (see diagram).
2. Pour an equal quantity of water onto each fabric.
3. Record the time it takes for the water to pass through the fabric into the jar below.

What are your conclusions? Which fabric would be best for rain clothes? Make a graph illustrating the results.

CS 56 Will that fabric shrink?

Select equal size pieces of different fabrics.

You are now to design an experiment that will provide the following information:

Will the fabric shrink? If so:
Will shrinkage vary with water temperature?
Can you determine the percentage of shrinkage?

CS 57 Read clothing labels.

Find the labels on your clothes.

What information do they contain? Classify by fabric, laundry instructions, and so on. Read the labels on class members' clothes to see which fabrics are most commonly used for pants, shirts.

Compare the laundry instructions on the labels. Which are the most desirable?

6
ADVERTISING

Advertising aimed at children is a big business. Sophisticated techniques are employed to induce children to buy a product. On television the commercials are fast, noisy, and colorful and promise immediate rewards to children who choose a particular doll, toy, or breakfast food. Fantasy is combined with reality so cleverly that the line of demarcation is often blurred—particularly for young children who may not even realize that the intent of the commercials is to induce them to BUY.

TEACHER NOTES

BACKGROUND

The figures are staggering. A child in the United States who watches 16½ hours of television per week, a typical amount, may be exposed to close to 8,000 commercials in one year. Over 20,000 commercials appeared on children's television programs in 1979. Many were interspersed so frequently that children had difficulty distinguishing between commercials and other cartoons.

Food manufacturers constitute the largest block of television advertisers. This fact raises another issue. It has been charged that much of the money spent promoting food products is "spent promoting food of questionable value." It was further stated:

> A recent survey of television advertisements found that almost 70% of all weekday food advertising, and 80% of the food ads on weekends, promoted foods that were high in fat, cholesterol, refined sugar, salt or alcohol. . . . Only two to three percent of the advertising promoted the consumption of fresh fruits or vegetables. . . . A by-product of the food marketing system is the absence of voices marketing moderation, balance: less carbohydrates, less salt, less saturated fats, less caloric intake. . . . We can hardly expect advertisers to promote reduced consumption. . . . It would be scapegoating to suggest that advertising alone has led to overconsumption. But it is not unreasonable to question whether massive advertising reinforces patterns of overconsumption and dwarfs the meager nutrition efforts of home and school.[1]

The release concluded that because of poor eating habits malnutrition is a problem in the United States "not only among the poorest of its citizens, but even among those who lack nothing."

Given these conditions, it is not surprising that demands have been made for regulation of commercials on children's television and for consumer education in schools. Guidelines have been issued for ads aimed at children.[2] They include the following:

[1]Michael Pertschuk, Federal Trade Commission Release, June 2, 1978.
[2]The Children's Advertising Review Unit, National Advertising Division, Council of Better Business Bureaus, 845 Third Avenue, New York City 10022, issues guidelines. Additional ones supplied by them are included in Activity CAD 3. Write them for a complete list.

Advertisements should avoid the contention that by possessing a product, a child will be more accepted by his or her peers or that by lacking it, he or she will be less accepted by his or her peers.

Ads should not mislead on perceived benefits such as acquisition of strength, popularity, and so on.

Prices should not be characterized as "only" or "just."

Ads should not urge children to convince parents or others to buy the product.

In this chapter, children survey both television commercials and print advertisements.

ACTIVITIES REQUIRING SPECIAL MATERIALS

Activities CAD 1–8 assume access is available to television set.
CAD 1: Watch with second hand.
CAD 6: Products for testing. (See also Chapter 5, Activities CS 27–30.)
CAD 11: Newspaper advertisements.

IMPLEMENTATION

Advertisements should be collected from newspapers, comic books, food packages.

Most activities can be completed independently by children viewing television at home. They may be homework assignments.

Since the primary goal is to aid children to view television advertisements critically, these activities may be ongoing ones with actual classroom time limited to discussion of findings and language activities (write ads, produce commercials).

EXTENSIONS

A critical look at television can be a natural outgrowth of this chapter. Consider the following approaches:

a. Have children analyze and record their personal viewing habits: total hours of watching, kinds of shows. Results can be compared, tabulated, graphed. Wider school surveys may also be made.

b. Recommend a weekend (or week) without television. Have children log substitute activities, reactions.

c. Review television shows from various perspectives: sexism, ageism; attitudes toward law, justice, equality; valued personal traits of men, women, youth.

(See also Media Unit Extensions, Part 6.)

EVALUATION

Check:

Accuracy of timing and percentages: CAD 1
Graphs, charts, reports: CAD 1–4
Quality of commercials, advertising copy writing: CAD 7, 9, 10, 13, 14, 15

Emphasis should be placed on children's growing ability to analyze advertisements critically.

ACTIVITY STARTERS

"What products have you seen advertised on television?" the teacher asked her class. She made a list of these. Then she questioned, "Which of these have you bought?" "Were you satisfied with them?" "Did they look like the products advertised?" "Could they do all the things they did on television?" Finally, she inquired, "Which advertised products do you wish you could buy?" From this introduction, a discussion about advertising ensued—how commercials create a demand for products, how exaggerated many claims are, and some of the techniques used to entice the listener. The class decided to monitor commercials and to become *advertising analysts*.

In another class, the teacher wished to impress the children with the frequency of commercials. First he asked that they time the length of individual commercials the preceding weekend. It was discovered that the average commercial lasts 30 seconds—the brevity surprised most students. He then urged the students when next watching television to walk out of the room for 30 seconds whenever a commercial appeared. (They could use a watch with a second hand or slowly count the seconds). After this experience, they did, in fact, become more aware of the *omnipresent* commercial.

One teacher decided to focus on the extent to which television, itself, dominated children's leisure time. She asked that for an entire weekend they go "cold turkey," that is refrain from viewing any television. Instead they were to record substitute activities during usual viewing periods. Many children were surprised at how difficult the assignment was and how few leisure activities they had developed.

ACTIVITIES ON ADVERTISING

How susceptible are you to advertising? Do you wish to buy all those products in television commercials and advertisements? Become more knowledgeable about advertising! You will learn to analyze and evaluate ads and even compose some of your own.

ACTIVITIES CAD 1–8: Start with television: Be a critical viewer.

CAD 1   Time those commercials.

Discover how many commercials you see in one week, how much television time they include, and the products advertised by recording the following information. You may keep a separate 3-inch-by-5-inch card for each program (see sample below).

(You will need a watch with a second hand for this activity.)

		Date:
		Name of Program:
		Total Time on Air:

COMMERCIAL INFORMATION*

Products Advertised	Classification (toys, food, clothes, etc.)	Length of Commercials (in seconds)

Total time devoted to commercials:

*Be certain to include lead-in and closing commercials.

Summarize the information on your cards. The data should include:

1. Percentage of time devoted to advertising. Does it vary for different programs? For half-hour and hour shows?
2. Most frequently advertised products. Also type of products.
3. Are the same products advertised on different shows?

Construct bar graphs showing the name of the program and the total number of minutes of commercials on each. Indicate the type of product by using a different color for each. You will need to make a separate graph for half-hour and hour shows.

CAD 2   Study techniques used in television advertising.

There are specific techniques used to convince the viewer to buy a product. These include:

1. Seductive language—words such as *new, improved, powerful, lasts longer, sensational offer.*
2. Inaccurate display of product—implying that it is larger than it is or has special powers. (For example, a basketball advertised on television was shown consistently going into the hoop when thrown by children. In fact, this was staged; the ball the children tossed into the air was not the one that dropped into the hoop.)
3. Satisfaction of needs—suggesting that users will be healthier, stronger, more popular, more attractive, and so on.
4. Endorsements—movie stars or sports figures may deliver the message implying that they actually use the product.
5. Cartoon figures—familiar ones or powerful giants may create an impression of special powers for product
6. Clever use of music—background music may suggest a mood, fast music for sports items, romantic music for cosmetics.

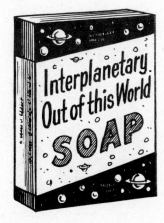

Can you find other techniques?
Try the following:

1. Select five television commercials. Analyze these for the advertising techniques employed. Compare your conclusions with other members of the class. Make a chart showing the commercial and class findings.
2. Select one commercial from this list that the entire class will view. (If a television set is available in the school, do this jointly.) See if you can identify all the techniques employed to convince people to buy.

CAD 3   Monitor commercials.

Guidelines have been suggested for commercials aimed at children. They indicate that the ads may be misleading if the answer to questions such as the following is *yes:*

1. Does the ad suggest that a child will be superior or more popular if the child owns a particular product?
2. Does the ad use the word "only" or "just" to describe price?
3. Does the ad urge children to ask parents or others to buy the product?
4. Are children shown using the product in ways that an average child couldn't?

These guidelines were developed by *The Children's Advertising Review Unit, National Advertising Division, Council of Better Business Bureaus, 845 Third Avenue, New York City 10022.*

Call their attention to violations of these guidelines. *(You may also wish to write for a full set of the guidelines.)*

CAD 4   Are television commercials sexist?

Do only boys play with action toys?
Do only girls use kitchen appliances?
Do only women cook food?
Is one sex depicted in a superior role?

Analyze commercials for examples of the above. Report on your results to the class. Identify the ones that appear most sexist, least sexist. List these.

You may wish to write to the manufacturer sharing your reactions.

CAD 5   Ask a professional.

Speak to your doctor or dentist about some advertising claims. Is one aspirin better than another? Do some toothpastes make your teeth whiter?

If possible, invite the professional to come to the class.

CAD 6   Be a product tester.

Duplicate the tests shown on television. Do you find the same results? Does a certain paper towel absorb more? Do certain diapers keep children drier? Do most people choose a certain product in a blindfold test?

Issue a report. Include the advertised claim, how you tested it, your results.

If your results differ, write to the companies and ask them to substantiate their claims. Tell them about your tests.

(See also Chapter 5, Activities CS 27–30 related to product testing.)

CAD 7 Evaluate products.

How healthy are the food products and soft drinks that are sold on television? Is there too much sugar in the cereal or drink? Should people be eating food of more nutritional value instead? (Refer to the previous chapter on shopping for more information.)

If you find a product being sold that you believe is not a wise choice for children, list your reasons and suggest possible substitutes.

Prepare a *commercial rebuttal.* In a group act out the original commercial, and then have an *evaluator* present the rebuttal.

CAD 8 Can politicians be "sold" to the public?

During a political campaign, analyze the television commercials for a candidate. What techniques are used to present the candidate? Who is in the commercial? What slogans are used? What is implied?

Discuss your reactions with the class. Find out, too, how expensive commercials are. How does this affect the ability of all people to run for office?

ACTIVITIES CAD 9–10: Now that you have learned to analyze commercials, write your own.

CAD 9 Produce commercials—three suggestions.

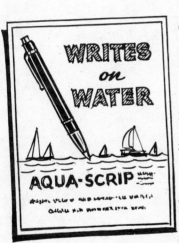

1. Invent a new product. It can be useless or even silly (a gadget to close a book after you have finished reading). Using some of the techniques described in the preceding activities, prepare a commercial that will make kids want to buy your product.
2. Sell an everyday object, such as a paper clip, a pencil, a ruler. Make your product sound extra-attractive.
3. Write commercials for nutritional products—fruit juices instead of cola drinks, fruits and vegetables instead of candies for snacks.

Dramatize your commercials in class. Ask the students to decide whether they would buy the product presented.

CAD 10 Produce timed commercials.

Most commercials last only 30 seconds. In that period they present a problem, a narrative, and end with a solution.

Can you produce a commercial that accomplishes this in 30 seconds? Have the class present a series of such commercials. They may do this during a change of periods or subjects. (One approach is to introduce the next subject with a commercial.)

ACTIVITIES CAD 11–14: Focus on print advertising: newspapers, magazines, comic books.

CAD 11 Collect and analyze printed advertisements.

Clip and mount them on construction paper or oaktag.

Categorize them by product being sold—clothing, food, toys, cosmetics, and so on.

Analyze each category:

1. Are there conflicting claims? For example, do two different brands of a product each claim to be the best?

2. What would the ads have us believe?
3. How can we tell if the statements are true?
4. Do the ads make you want to buy the product?

(In completing this, have groups work on different products, then exchange advertisements. See if reactions vary.)

CAD 12 Study techniques used in printed advertisements.

In *Activity CAD 2,* you learned some of the techniques used in commercials to induce you to buy a product. Here are some points to bear in mind when examining printed ads:

Who are the people in the ad? How are they dressed? What are they doing? Are they well-known? How might these factors influence the buyer?

What does the ad associate with the use of the product—glamour, status, power?

What else does the ad suggest—good health (or lack of it for failure to buy the product), comfort, romance, economy?

Prepare a bulletin board as follows:

Post an advertisement and next to it an advertising analysis calling attention to the techniques used. (For example, "the woman wearing the coat advertised is shown with a handsome man—appeal to romance.")

CAD 13 Write advertising copy.

Here are some tips!

1. Many ads use alliteration (words that start with the same letter), such as "crunchy cookies," "crispy chips." Products may have alliterative titles— "Hamburger helper." Find examples of these; then make up some of your own.
2. Study the names of products, and note other examples of how names can help sell them. (Perfumes, for example, called "Joy" or "Allure") Concoct names for new cereals, toys, cosmetics that you believe would attract buyers.
3. Research advertising slogans. Collect as many as you can from ads and television commercials. Note the vocabulary. Write advertising slogans for new products.
4. Invent a toy, a new cosmetic, a gadget.
   Using the techniques described, write an attractive ad for your product.

CAD 14 Write recruitment ads.

Select an historical event: Columbus' voyage, the pioneers' trip west, the first trip into space.

Write ads that might have been placed in newspapers attempting to recruit people for the event.

ACTIVITY CAD 15: Consider a different viewpoint.

CAD 15. Can advertising help the consumer?

You have been made aware that advertising can be misleading and should be scrutinized carefully. Now consider advantages for consumers as a result of advertising.

Complete this sentence:

Ads can help us to . . . .
Compare your answers with others in the class.

7
OTHER
CONSUMER
TOPICS

Consumer education has been described as *education for living*. Children are consumers and will remain consumers throughout their lives. The province of consumer education is broad. It impinges on societal values, on ecology, health, energy, and people's concern for the well-being of others. Numerous topics can be subsumed under the heading of consumer education. Shopping and advertising were discussed in the preceding chapters. Three additional topics are included in this chapter: basic economic concepts, rights and responsibilities, and money management. Economic concepts are frequently integrated with consumer education. As children become aware of prices, they become interested in factors that influence prices, note the effects of inflation, and are motivated to understand basic economic ideas. The other two topics were selected not only because they are fundamental to a study of consumerism, but because they also afford opportunities for developing reading and mathematics skills. The chapter concludes with general activities that can serve to culminate a unit on consumerism.

BASIC ECONOMIC CONCEPTS

What are needs and wants, products and services, some basic price determinants, and inflation? Activities in this section survey these.

TEACHER NOTES

BACKGROUND

Children are confronted daily with the subject of economics. Unemployment, recession, taxes and inflation affect their families and in turn affect them. The young child who no longer can afford his favorite candy bar on his limited allowance, and the teenager trying to save for a pair of boots that constantly eludes her because of its rising price, are both directly aware of inflation and economics.

One of the problems with teaching economics is that the subject is frequently confusing even to many adults. Hailstone notes that although "economics is considered to be a science . . . its laws are not universal or ironclad as the laws of the physical sciences."[1] Economists themselves disagree on fundamental questions: how to control inflation, the effects of a balanced federal

[1]Thomas J. Hailstones, *Basic Economics*, 5th ed., (Cincinnati, Ohio: South-Western Publishing Co.), p. 3.

budget, advisability of wage and price controls, and so on. However, there are less-complicated, basic concepts that can provide a foundation for the study of economics. These are the focus of the activities in this section. They can become part of the curriculum even in the early grades.

ACTIVITIES REQUIRING SPECIAL MATERIALS

CEC 7: Past copies of catalogs, newspapers, magazines

IMPLEMENTATION

The activities in this section may serve as an introduction to consumer education and be assigned prior to others in this part.

Teachers may further wish to integrate the activities with a more detailed unit on economics.

EVALUATION

Check:

Graph: CEC 2, 7
Visuals: CEC 1, 4, 7
Lists: CEC 3, 5, 6, 8

Key questions—Can students:

Distinguish between needs and wants, products and services?
Recognize some factors that shape wants?
Describe price determinants?
Define law of supply and demand, inflation?

ACTIVITIES ON ECONOMIC CONCEPTS

Investigate questions that concern economists in our society.

ACTIVITIES CEC 1–3: Analyze needs and wants.

CEC 1   Food, clothing, and shelter as basic *needs*.

It has been said that people *need* only food, clothing, and shelter.

Contrast the manner in which early people and people today satisfy these basic needs. You may do this by making models, drawings or dioramas of primitive and modern people's food, homes, and clothes. These should illustrate how much more complicated our needs have become.

In a class discussion, consider the effect of the following in shaping our needs:

Geography
Culture
Fashion
Neighborhood
Advertising
Television

Can you add others?

CEC 2   What determines your *wants*?[2]

Distribute the following questionnaire in class. Ask each member to select the two items in each category that he or she considers most important, numbering them *1* and *2*.

ANALYZING YOUR PREFERENCES

When you receive a new article of clothing, what would you prefer?

Fashionable item
One that friends will like
One similar to friends
Good quality
Easy laundering

When choosing a breakfast cereal, what influences you most?

Price
Taste
Nutritional value
Premium offer
Seen on television

When shopping for a new toy, whose advice would you be most likely to follow?

Friends
Parents
Television commercial
Teacher

How would you prefer to receive $10?

As a present
Work for it
Find it

Make a series of bar graphs illustrating the results of your survey. Have the class examine the graphs and write their conclusions.

CEC 3   Distinguish further between needs and wants.

Work with a small group on this. List ten items considered *needs* that may at one time have been thought of as *wants*.
Did the group agree on the items? Were there any "fuzzy" items?
Compare your lists with other groups in the class.

ACTIVITIES: CEC 4–8: Study more economics: prices, inflation, goods, and services.

CEC 4   What is meant by the *law of supply and demand*?

One factor that influences prices is the "law of supply and demand." This states that if products are in short supply and there is a large demand for them,

[2]Adapted from *Elementary Level Consumer Education* (Mount Vernon, N.Y.: Consumers Union of the U.S., Inc.), p. 6.

they will rise in price; conversely, if there is an oversupply of a product, it will tend to fall in price.

Imagine these situations:

A store has a large supply of posters related to a current television program. The program is canceled. What might happen to the price of the posters?

A store receives a shipment of a toy that is in short supply and very popular. Suggested retail price ranges from $3.29 to $4.00. At which price will the store be likely to sell the toy?

How does the cost of gasoline illustrate the law of supply and demand?

Now find examples of products that are expensive because they are in demand and conversely inexpensive because they are not. You may list these, bring in pictures, or make models of them.

CEC 5   What other factors influence price?

The price of a product is roughly determined by the cost of production (which includes materials, machinery, labor, factory, other expenses) and profit.

Pretend that you are a manufacturer producing roller skates. List all the things you can think of that might influence the price you place on those skates.

Try this, too, with a pair of designer jeans. What might determine its price?

CEC 6   Still other price determinants.

Activities CS 1–CS 5, CS 11, CS 17, CS 18 in Chapter 5 review still other factors that influence prices.

Make a chart of all *price determinants,* including information from CEC 5 and the activities previously noted.

Now pretend that you decide to make a Christmas tree decoration in your home and sell it to people in the community. How would you decide what to charge? Compare your projected price with those of other members of the class.

CEC 7   What is meant by *inflation*?

The word itself means *growing larger, swelling, expansion.* When applied to economics, it has a similar meaning—a steady increase in prices.

We are living in a period of high inflation—prices keep rising rapidly. Do you have any examples of this from your own experiences?

Compare the prices of ten items in an old catalog and a current one. Can you find the average percentage rise?

In the library copy down the prices of ten food items from newspaper advertisements ten years ago. What are the prices of these same items today? Can you find their average percentage rise?

Now select five more items, such as: the daily and Sunday newspaper, a popular magazine, a candy bar, the price of admission to a movie, the cost of a bus ride. Research their prices in the year you were born and compare them to current figures.

Find a means of depicting your investigation of inflation with charts and graphs.

CEC 8   Distinguish between goods and services.

Workers may produce either goods or services. *Goods* are tangible products that you can take away from a store, such as a toy, a soda. *Services* represent items done for you, such as a haircut, or taxi ride.

Can you find ten examples of goods and ten of services? List these on strips of paper and illustrate them.

RIGHTS AND RESPONSIBILITIES

Students need to be aware of their rights as consumers, but also that rights entail responsibilities. Both are included in the activities in this section.

TEACHER NOTES

BACKGROUND

There is a growing body of legislation—federal, state, and local—designed to protect consumers. But many consumers are not familiar with it, and even among those who are, many hesitate to exercise their rights. A vignette, suggested by the Consumers Union, illustrates this. It is titled "The Spoiled Pickles."

> An elderly woman mentioned to a consumer counselor that she had bought a jar of pickles that turned out to be spoiled. The cost of the pickles, 49 cents, was not an irrelevant sum to the woman, whose income was small. Yet she had not returned the pickles to the store for a refund, although she lacked neither energy nor incentive. . . .
>
> Asked why she had not returned the pickles to the store, the woman said she did not want to be embarrassed or made to look foolish by the store manager. The counselor explained that most managers refund money for spoiled foodstuffs without question, since they would in turn be reimbursed by the distributor. . . . [3]

The preceding incident reflects behavior typical of many consumers. What are the subtle psychological pressures that operate against our exercising our rights as consumers? Are we made to feel *cheap* if we return a defective item? The Consumers Union advises: "Teachers should be alert for student behavior that indicates a resignation to marketplace forces that appear beyond control. For example, a high school student may continue to pay for unwanted albums from a record club that ignores her cancellation letters; an adult may complain about his new car's poor performance but do nothing because 'all cars are lemons;' a college student may express concern about environmental problems yet refuse to take any action 'because you can't fight the corporate establishment.' "[4] Many of these attitudes start in childhood. Class discussions, role playing, and buzz sessions can help children clarify their feelings.

Closely related to rights are responsibilities. Children may not perceive of a relationship between their "innocent" stealing of a candy bar or magazine and the price of products, nor the cost of vandalism to a school district and the curtailment of after school sports. Consumer education should include discussion of shoplifting and vandalism as part of responsible consumer behavior.

ACTIVITIES REQUIRING SPECIAL MATERIALS

CRR 2: Samples of warranties
CRR 6: Mail-order catalog

---

[3] *Early Childhood Consumer Education*, (Mount Vernon, N.Y.: Consumers Union of the U.S., Inc.), pp. 61–62.
[4] Ibid., p. 62.

IMPLEMENTATION

Activities are more appropriate for upper-level students.

It is important to emphasize that rights imply responsibilities. Role-play correct consumer behavior when shopping, also how to protect rights effectively but quietly and respectfully.

EVALUATION

Check:

Classifications: CRR 2
Business letters: CRR 5
Filmstrip: CRR 7 and 8
Math, Poster: CRR 9
Booklet: CRR 10

ACTIVITY STARTERS

Read the case of "The Spoiled Pickles" to the class. Organize a discussion around the following questions:

What should the woman have done?

What price merchandise would you feel warranted "making a fuss"?

How would you feel about returning defective merchandise?

Have you ever tried to return something you bought? What was your experience?

Role-play returning the pickles. Stress respectful behavior. Note that being a wise consumer implies knowledge of rights and responsibilities, and it is these to which the next activities are directed.

ACTIVITIES ON RIGHTS AND RESPONSIBILITIES

What can you do if a product bought at a store or through the mail is defective? Be aware of your rights as consumers. Recognize also that consumers have responsibilities.

ACTIVITIES CRR 1–5: Learn about guarantees and how to proceed if merchandise purchased is faulty.

CRR 1   Is this product guaranteed?

A guarantee is a promise by the manufacturer, dealer, or store owner that a product will operate satisfactorily; otherwise, either the entire product or defective parts will be replaced. There are different kinds of guarantees:

Verbal: The store owner may say, "If anything goes wrong, bring it back; I'll fix it."

Written: Specify the length of time the guarantee will be in effect, also whether it is for parts and/or services. Some guarantees cover only certain parts; some do not include the cost of repairs. Note also who is responsible for the expense if the merchandise has to be shipped back to the manufacturer in another city.

Make a list of products and next to them whether you expect them to be covered by a guarantee and, if so, what should be included. Your list might include the following:

A candy bar
Hair dryer
Book
Toy
Crayons
Automobile

CRR 2 Classifying guarantees and warranties.

Guarantees in writing may be called warranties.

Try to collect samples of guarantees or warranties. They are most frequently included with purchases of electric appliances, wrist watches, automobiles. (Ask your parents or write to manufacturers for samples.)

Classify them according to the kinds described in preceding activity: length of time, extent of guarantee: parts (all or some), repairs, return shipping costs.

CRR 3 Is this bike free of structural defects?

What guarantee do you have a right to expect when purchasing a new bike?

Role-play requesting an appropriate guarantee from a merchant who offers you one you consider inadequate.

Have the class evaluate your consumer behavior. Was it logical, respectful, firm without being overly aggressive?

CRR 4 Consumers keep records.

What records are made of purchases *(sales receipt, guarantees, canceled checks, credit card charges)?* Can you see why it is important to keep these? For how long? Devise a filing system for maintaining these records and demonstrate it.

CRR 5 Consumers need records.

If merchandise that you have purchased is defective and there is no specific guarantee, follow the recommended procedure:

1. First return to the store where purchased (be certain that you have a sales slip or receipt).
2. If not satisfied, write a letter to the manufacturer explaining your problem.
3. If still not satisfied, write a letter to the local Better Business Bureau and Department of Consumer Affairs. (You can find their addresses in the telephone book.)

Practice this procedure. Pretend that you have bought an electric train and the motor is defective. The store owner refuses to replace it. Write a letter to the manufacturer requesting a new motor. What should the letter state?

Now pretend that the manufacturer ignores your request. Write a letter to the Better Business Bureau. What should this letter state?

Compare letters written by different members of the class. Which do you believe would be most effective?

ACTIVITIES CRR 6–8: Be aware of your rights when ordering merchandise in the mail.

CRR 6   Shopping by mail—1.

Many students order merchandise by mail through catalogs or other advertisements. It is convenient and can save money and effort. But you should take the following precautions:

1.   Read the description carefully. Do not rely on the picture of the item only. This may be misleading.
2.   Note the delivery time promised.
3.   Find out what the return policy is if merchandise is not as claimed or arrives broken.
4.   Unless the item is very inexpensive, do not send cash. Secure a postal money order or a bank check.
5.   Be certain to keep a copy of the order blank, the merchant's name and address, and the date you mailed your order.

To become familiar with these rules:

1.   Secure mail-order catalogs. (These are generally available during holiday seasons.)
2.   Cut out different advertisements. Work in groups. Have each group analyze the advertisement to see if any aspect might be misleading. Note the picture. What does it *not* show. How about the size of the item? Is the *return* policy clearly stated? Practice completing the order blank.

Try to find some of the advertised toys in local stores. How accurate was the ad? Should any additional facts have been included?

CRR 7   Shopping by mail—2.

The Federal Trade Commission has formulated rules to protect the consumer who shops by mail.[5] Publicize these to people in the school and community. Can you make a filmstrip and accompanying tape to explain them? (See instructions for filmstrips, Chapter 12, Activities M 6–10.) The filmstrip could be shown to other classes. Some of the rules are:

1.   You must receive the merchandise when the seller promises you will.
2.   If there is no promised time, the merchandise must be shipped no later than 30 days after your order is received.
3.   If "2" has not been complied with, you can cancel your order and get your money back, unless you agree to a new shipping date.
4.   If you request a refund, it must be mailed to you within seven working days after your request has been received.

CRR 8   Unordered merchandise.

What happens if you receive merchandise through the mail that you never ordered?

The answer—*you don't have to pay for it.*

Just be certain that you didn't order it and then forgot or that it wasn't ordered by a friend and then billed to you.

Publicize this information, too.

[5]For more complete information, write for free pamphlet: "Shopping by Mail? You're Protected." Consumer Information Center, Dept 627E, Pueblo, Colorado, 81009.

ACTIVITIES CRR 9–10: Consumers are responsible! They oppose vandalism and shoplifting.

CRR 9 What price vandalism?

Interview the principal and school business officer to find out if there has been any vandalism in the district and, if so, the cost. Ask for specifics, such as the price of replacing one broken window.

If vandalism is a problem in your district, organize a campaign against it. (In many communities where students have undertaken antivandalism campaigns, they have been effective.)

Compute what could be purchased for the money spent because of vandalism.

Make posters illustrating the above.

Investigate the legal aspects. In some communities parents may be legally responsible. Explain this.

If there is an example of a vandalized building, take a picture of it. Post the picture with an appropriate caption.

Recognize that vandals rob students.

CRR 10 What price shoplifting?

When is shoplifting *harmless*? Discuss this with the class. Is there any harm in stealing just one candy bar, an apple from the neighborhood store? Some children may regard these as harmless pranks, but the fact is that all shoplifting is *stealing*, and stealing is never innocent or harmless.

Undertake an educational campaign about shoplifting. Include the following:

When someone steals, someone else pays. The consumer pays for shoplifting by others. Interview the local store manager and write to companies that own department stores. Find out how much is added to the price of products to cover the costs of shoplifting.

Invite a law-enforcement official or a lawyer to the classroom to discuss penalties, possible consequences.

Prepare a booklet illustrating the facts you have learned.

MONEY MANAGEMENT

All children need opportunities to handle money and understand its value. Older children are capable of understanding more sophisticated money management concepts: budgeting, credit cards, borrowing, loan agreements, and contracts.

TEACHER NOTES

BACKGROUND

More and more people are purchasing goods on credit, frequently to the point where debt and interest payments become a financial burden. People may not understand the actual cost of interest and finance charges. For example, if a finance charge is stated in monthly figures (2 percent per month), to find the annual rate multiply by 12. A rate of 2 percent per month is actually 24 percent annually. If the rate is stated annually (14 percent per year), but is charged on the original cost of the purchase, the true rate is approximately twice the stated rate. Another point: stores may charge 1 percent or 2 percent interest monthly on past due accounts. These can add up to a substantial annual rate.

ACTIVITIES REQUIRING SPECIAL MATERIALS

CMM 2: Foreign currency
CMM 3: Visit to a bank
CMM 8: Watch with second hand or three-minute egg timer
CMM 10 and 11: May require contacting credit companies and banks
CMM 13: Loan agreements, contracts
CMM 15: Empty boxes or other containers for play store. Also used toys, books, magazines
CMM 18: Items for auction
CMM 19: Magazines

IMPLEMENTATION

A field trip to a local bank is recommended. (See CMM 3.)
A fixed amount of scrip should be put into circulation at any given period (CMM 14–22), and students should keep careful records of its use.

EXTENSIONS

The stock market may be studied. Students may decide to follow a particular stock; or each student may be given a hypothetical sum of money to *invest* in the market. The student will select stocks and note their value daily or after a given period.
Advanced students may proceed to a study of insurance and/or taxes.

EVALUATION

Check:

Chart: CMM 1
Math computations: CMM 2, 4, 6, 7, 9, 11, 15–22
Graph: CMM 5, CMM 19
Main ideas: CMM 13

Students may be assigned to read a contract critically.

ACTIVITIES ON MONEY MANAGEMENT

Become more knowledgeable about prices and ways of handling money. You will be taught to draw up a budget and to investigate credit, borrowing, and contracts.

ACTIVITIES CMM 1–4: Understand money values.

CMM 1   What does it cost?

a.   What do services cost? How much is a haircut? A car wash? A doctor's visit? A train or airplane ride to a designated point? Other services?

WHAT DOES IT COST?

	PRICE
Haircut	
Train Ride	
Bus Ride	
Doctor's Visit	
Shoe Repair	
Dry Clean Jacket	

Have members of the class research this information by asking parents and other adults and by contacting sources. Compare information. Does everyone pay the same amount for services?

Make a chart called "The Cost of Services." Next to each item, list the average cost as determined by the members of the class.

b. What do products cost? Bring in pictures of products or empty containers. Make a display by placing a card next to each showing the cost of the item. (Prices are investigated in more detail in section on shopping. This activity may be completed in conjunction with Chapter 5, Activities CS 6 to 15.)

CMM 2 Investigate foreign currency.

Collect as many samples of foreign currency as you can from teachers, parents, friends. Give each person a receipt for the money, and return it at the completion of this activity.

Compare the foreign currency to that of the United States. Note the size of the coins. Is size always related to value? What is on the coins—a picture, an emblem? Find out what it represents.

Make a currency converting chart. List the foreign coin and the equivalent United States dollar value. Check with a bank or local newspaper for current exchange rates.

CMM 3 Visit a bank.

Either with your parent or as part of a class field trip, visit a local bank.

Try to find out how cash withdrawal machines operate, how coins are stacked, where money is stored, how individual accounts are maintained.

Report on your findings to the class.

CMM 4 Practice computations with money and have fun.

Assign a price to each letter of the alphabet from 1 cent to 10 cents. Vowels should be priced higher because they are in short supply, as should consonants such as x and j.

Appoint a banker to keep the alphabet letters. Buy them as needed.

How many 25-cent or 30-cent words can you construct. The word must total the exact amount. Can you write a sentence worth exactly $1.00?

How much would your name cost?

ACTIVITIES CMM 5–8: All about budgets.

CMM 5 Do you receive an allowance?

How do you spend it?

See if you can remember how you spent your allowance this past month. Were you satisfied? Would you have preferred other expenditures?

Make a survey of how other members of the class spend their allowances. Which are the three most popular categories? Represent these on a graph.

CMM 6   Learn to budget.

Divide a sheet of paper into three columns:

Resources	Fixed Expenses	Anticipated Expenses and Savings
In this column include your allowance and any other income for the period covered.	Include any essential expenses.	Subtract your fixed expenses from your resources. This tells you how much you can plan to spend or save. In this column show how you expect to distribute your money.

Budgets may be prepared for a week or longer period. It is easier at first to plan for a short period (such as a week).

At the end of the budget period, compare your anticipated budget with your actual income and expenditures. If there is a difference, write in the actual figures in red.

Save your old budgets to help you plan the next ones.

CMM 7   Budgeting for a party.

If you had $5, $10, or $25 to spend on a party for your friends, how would you do so?

Decide how many people you would invite and prepare budgets for each amount of money.

CMM 8   Can you help the family budget?

Are you a telephone talker? Is your family telephone bill based on the length of time of each call?

Bring a three-minute egg timer into class or use a watch with a second hand.

Role-play telephone calls with friends in class holding each to no more than three minutes.

Use the timer at home to help you limit your calls.

Investigate telephone rates further. At what hours is it cheaper to call? What should you do if you reach a wrong number?

ACTIVITIES CMM 9–13: Examine some money management techniques.

CMM 9   Buying with credit cards.

Are you familiar with credit cards?

Do your parents hold any?

Investigate the advantages and disadvantages of making purchases on credit. List these in class.

Use the credit cards in class as suggested in Activity CMM 22.

CMM 10 Credit card penalties.

What are penalties for late payment? Check interest rates charged by different companies.

What is meant by a *credit rating*? Why might this be important?

What other penalties might occur for failure to pay bills?

CMM 11 Borrowing money.

If you needed to borrow $100, where could it be obtained?

Investigate differences in rates charged by a finance company, bank, credit union, private person.

How is interest computed? What is actually paid in interest if the annual rate on a loan is 20 percent of the full amount of the loan and the money is to be repaid in a year? Contact someone in a local bank to explain this.

CMM 12 Decisions on borrowing.

If your family would like a new television set that costs $350, which would you recommend: saving until you could afford it, borrowing money to pay for it, or financing the set with the company. Determine the actual cost of the set under each plan.

Determine the advantages and disadvantages of each, and defend your decision.

CMM 13 Learn to read contracts.

Secure blank copies of loan agreements from a bank and copies of contracts from contractors.

Working in groups, write down the main ideas.

Now have each student analyze a different paragraph.

Did you miss any important details?

ACTIVITIES CMM 14–22: Engage in money transactions.

CMM 14 Design a class scrip.

Make paper bills and cardboard coins of different denominations.

Distribute a fixed amount to each student each week to be used in the following activities.

CMM 15 Open classroom stores.

a. Start with a play store. Organize your store with empty containers. Be certain that there is a price on each. Devise a series of cards with specific shopping assignments and have students select one before they shop. Examples: Purchase three items that cost between 90 cents and $1.00. Buy an item that will serve as a snack for two. How much will each portion cost?

b. Open a toy store. Have students contribute used toys. (Some may have to be repaired.) Place a price on each toy and display. The class will have to establish rules for making purchases, since more than one person may wish to *buy* a particular toy.

c. Consider a book store. Students can donate books, comics, and magazines.

CMM 16   Receive pay for classroom jobs.

Draw up a list of all classroom jobs, including a description, salary, and duration of appointment. Give them fancy titles, such as in the following examples.

Ventilation Engineer: Will check all windows at the end of the day to be certain they are closed and that shades have been placed at approved level. Weekly salary $2.00. Two positions available.

Blackboard Maintainer: Will erase the blackboard during the day as required and wash board at the end of each day. Weekly salary $2.50. Three positions available.

Closet Control: Will examine clothes closets regularly to assure that clothes are neatly hung and miscellaneous items such as gloves, hats, boots are returned to owners. Weekly salary $2.00. One position available.

Other positions might include messenger, librarian, audiovisual equipment technician, interior designer (concerned with aesthetic appearance of room), sanitation engineers.

Post all the jobs, and then permit students to apply for them by completing an application.

Students are selected for the job by the teacher, student government, or a special selection committee.

CMM 17   Help pay for your education.

Here are more ways to use your class scrip:

1. Pay rent.
   Measure the area occupied by your desk. Pay 5 cents (or more) per square foot.
   You may also be charged a fixed amount for the use of your desk and chair and other facilities.
2. Pay taxes.
   Each person may be charged an educational tax.

CMM 18   Organize an auction.

You will need to collect items to be auctioned. They could be books or toys that classmates no longer need or that others contributed. Students may also make objects.

A few days before the actual auction, display all the items with their approximate value. Students should compute in advance the amount of money they have on hand and approximately what they are prepared to spend for an item.

Practice playing the role of an auctioneer; then select a person for the job, and go to it!

CMM 19   Satisfy fantasies.

Start by distributing a large amount of money to each student—from $10,000 to $100,000.

Research magazine advertisements for expensive items: cars, boats, trips, fancy clothes.

Make a fantasy book. Include ads, pictures, stories about how you would spend your money, but you must pay a class banker for every item you include.

Compare fantasies. Classify and graph items most frequently included.

CMM 20   Open a bank.

Open a class bank. You will need tellers and bankers. Your bank should be open at a set period each day. Have students deposit all their cash in the bank (and then make withdrawals as money is needed.) In turn, the bank should open an account for each and issue a numbered bank book indicating:

Deposits	Withdrawals	Balance

The bank will need to maintain careful records. Balances should be totaled regularly and checked against cash on hand. Statements should be issued to the students regularly.

A further activity: You may decide that the bank will pay interest on all money on deposit more than one week. Interest may be computed on a percentage basis, as in a regular bank, or on a sliding scale, depending on the amount of money on deposit.

CMM 21   Start a checking account.

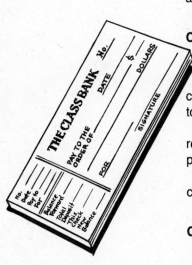

Have your class bank issue checkbooks (see sample form).

All money transactions should then be by check. Pay your bills by issuing checks, and in turn you will receive all payments in checks that you can deposit to your account.

Maintain an accurate balance in your checkbook. The bank should issue regular statements that must reconcile with your records. There should be a penalty for inaccurate figures.

A further activity: Have the bank charge each student 10 cents for each check used.

CMM 22   Organize a credit card company.

Design a card. Open an account for each person in the class. Cards and accounts should have the same number.

Use the credit cards to make purchases in class stores (see Activity CCM 15). Records of purchases should be prepared in duplicate—one for the purchaser and one for the credit card company to be posted to the person's account.

Bills should be prepared weekly and paid promptly.

Evaluate the experience. Which did you prefer: cash or credit? (See also Activity CMM 9.)

CULMINATING ACTIVITIES

Consumer education creates a link between school and home, school and the community. Involvement of parents can be the decisive factor in a successful project. Parents who are aware of the objectives of the study will collect empty boxes for the classroom, take children along on shopping trips, discuss prices with them, and help monitor advertisements. The community can be served by the school's publicizing consumer information, as suggested in activities below. These may be used in conjunction with the topics in this part or as culminating activities for a consumer curriculum.

ACTIVITIES CC 1–6: Summarize and apply your consumer knowledge.

CC 1   Build your vocabulary.

From the activities concluded, build a specialized consumer vocabulary. Words that might be included are *consumer, bargain hunter, credit rating, warranty, premium, installment plan.* Can you think of others?
Make a poster with the word, definition, and illustration.

CC 2   Write a series of "how-to" books.

You might include "how to shop for toys," "how to read labels," "how to save money on food shopping."

CC 3   Publish a newsletter to the community.

Tell what you have learned about television commercials or newspaper advertisements, or of your findings from product testing.
Indicate where you may have located a particular good buy and other results of price surveys.

CC 4   Find other means of publicizing information.

Consider filmstrips, radio skits, a community bulletin board, regular fact sheets.
Draw cartoons; invent puppet characters to tell your facts.
Invite parents to a consumer assembly. Dramatize some information.

CC 5   Organize a consumer fair

Demonstrate the activities included in this chapter.
Invite parents and members of the community.

CC 6   Consumers are environmentalists.

Recycle products. Make your own toys. Repair clothes. Find new uses for old jeans, outgrown clothes, unneeded toys.

RESOURCES FOR PART 2

Consumers Union of the U.S., Inc.
Educational Services Division
Mount Vernon, New York 10550
    Excellent publications available at low cost:
        Early Childhood Consumer Education
        Elementary Level Consumer Education
        Penny Power Magazine
    Request list of films and other resources

Consumer Information Center
Pueblo, Colorado 81009
    Request list of federal publications of consumer interest.
    Some are free, others low cost.
    Examples of free publications:
        #548G   The Confusing World of Health Foods
        549G   Computerized Supermarket Checkout

550G   Consumer's Guide to Food Labels
551G   Food Shopper Language
553G   Read the Label. Set a Better Table
554G   Your Money's Worth in Foods
562G   Food is More Than Just Something to Eat
565G   Nutrition: Food at Work for You
568G   Myths about Vitamins
577G   Cosmetics: The Substances Beneath the Form
573G   And Now A Word About Your Shampoo

Food and Drug Administration
5600 Fishers Lane
Rockville, Maryland 20857
      Request free curriculum materials.

Bureau of Curriculum Development
Board of Education of the City of New York
110 Livingston Street
Brooklyn, N.Y. 11201
      Curriculum Bulletin No. 14: Consumer Education.

Cornell University
Distribution Center/NYT
7 Research Park
Ithaca, New York 14850
      Consumer publications available at low cost. Write for list.

Action for Children's Television
46 Austin Street,
Newtonville, Mass. 02160
      Aims to improve television programs for children and sets standards for commercials on such programs.
      Write for information on publications, films.

THE
CLASSROOM
AS AN
ENVIRONMENTAL
AGENCY

The banner dominated the room. It hung across the entire back wall. On it the children had meticulously painted:

I HEREBY PLEDGE TO CONSERVE AND PROTECT
THE RESOURCES OF SPACESHIP EARTH

Every child in the class had signed the pledge.

"It's amazing how effective the banner is," the teacher explained as she noted the visitor's interest. "It serves as a constant reminder to all of us to conserve—water, paper, art supplies; to refrain from littering, to respect all forms of life. It has been interesting to me, to observe the change in children's attitudes since the subject was first raised. Our study of the environment," the teacher continued, "resulted from an event in the community. Cans of chemicals had been stored in a neighboring warehouse many years ago. It was recently discovered that the chemicals were leaking from the containers, posing a potential health hazard. One of the children reported the situation during a session on current events. The children were surprised that this could happen. It was evident that they had little understanding of environmental issues or options.

"I felt I could not ignore their interest in the subject and substituted a unit on air pollution for a previously planned one on space. We have gone on to study other environmental topics with gratifying results. Children have become conscious of how each can contribute to solving environmental problems, even at some sacrifice. It was recognized that each child who lets water run needlessly wastes a natural resource; each child who asks to be driven in an automobile when a bicycle could serve as well contributes to air pollution; and that everyone who smokes cigarettes adds a bit of pollution to the atmosphere."

In this class the topic had been motivated by a community problem and related to the children's own behavior with evident impact. This is obviously desirable. There is danger that environmental education will be presented in isolation or else in broad moral tones of good or bad, right or wrong, so that the ramifications are obscured. Children need to recognize the difficulty of coping with many environmental concerns and to identify those they are capable of affecting. There is a further consideration. It is essential that environmental education not be characterized by a *doomsday mentality*. The future can easily be depicted as bleak: a world with natural resources depleted, an atomic accident probable, mass starvation resulting from overpopulation, air and water polluted. To imply this is to destroy the future for children. The fact is that each generation has difficulties coping with change and visualizing an uncertain future. It is possible that the school children today will mature in a world with unparalleled advantages: food grown from the seas and cheaply in laboratories so that hunger is eliminated, different and more satisfying patterns of family life, homes with computers that alleviate the drudgery of housekeeping, elimination of war, discrimination, poverty; innovative measures of removing pollution from the environment, more leisure time and creative means of enjoying it; and transportation and appliances that require minimum energy to operate. If this is to occur, today's school children will be instrumental in shaping it. We can only offer them insight into both the dangers and the promises that lie ahead. What we cannot afford is to shut them out from participation.

OBJECTIVES OF ENVIRONMENTAL EDUCATION

Students will:

■ Adopt an environmental ethic based on the following concepts:

Interaction	All living organisms interact with each other and their environments, together forming an *ecosystem*.
Interdependence	All living things within each ecosystem are dependent upon each other for the quality of their lives and possibly even for survival.
Limitation	The natural resources of earth: soil, air, water, minerals are limited.
Distribution	The natural resources may be unevenly distributed throughout the earth.
Continuity	Nature has established conditions for the endless recycling of many natural resources.
Change	There is a constant process both of continuity and change as living things adapt to changes in their environment.
Survival	Survival of a species may depend on ability to live within the limited resources available on earth and to adapt to changes in its environment.
Rights and Responsibilities	All living things have a responsibility to other living things. No group has a right to deplete or despoil the natural resources of earth.

■ Behave in a manner that conserves and protects the natural resources of earth.

■ Become sensitive to their surroundings—to those aspects that promote well-being and those that inhibit it.

■ Gain in ability to use scientific process for investigating environmental problems.

■ Have opportunities to collect, record, interpret, and distribute data.

■ Broaden mathematics and language skills.

■ Become familiar with specialized environmental vocabulary.

■ Enhance self-concepts as active participants in matters affecting their future well-beings.

■ Learn to work cooperatively on common tasks.

■ Acquire an appreciation for the unique beauty of natural objects.

CURRICULUM INTEGRATION
Science

Environmental education can be integrated with each of the following major topics:

Our Growing Bodies and Living Things	Study effects on people of pollution, waste, overpopulation, radiation, soil erosion.
Air, Water, and Weather	Include water cycle and an investigation of air and water pollution.
The Earth	Study effects of pollution on atmosphere.

Social Studies

Integrate with a study of:

    Communities
    Economics: Cost of pollution and pollution-control equipment.
    Government: Responsible officials, anti-pollution legislation.

Mathematics

See special section on mathematics in the environment.

Language

Leads to vocabulary extension. Opportunities for research, reading for information, reporting, creative writing.

Art

See discussion of art in the environment in Unit Extensions below.

UNIT EXTENSIONS

A logical extension of the study of the environment is to provide children with sensory experiences designed to enhance their perceptions of their environment. They are then encouraged to express their reactions in painting, poetry, and writing. An effective approach is to take children for a silent walk outdoors once a week. Ask them to note the sights, smells, sounds, and feel of their surroundings. Some may tape the sounds and write about them on their return to the classroom. Others may paint a picture perhaps in one color that they believe best depicts what they have observed; or write a poem. Have them change their perspective. Describe the world from the eyes of an ant, a worm, a bird. Or they can write metaphors: the drop of water is a swimming pool . . . ; the leaf is an umbrella . . . ; or similes: the icicles are like sparkling diamond earrings. . . .

    Collages and constructions can be made from natural objects. Interesting ones can be collected. It is possible to preserve a spider web if it is handled carefully. Find a web that is on an area that can be sprayed with paint. Lightly spray white paint on the web; then place a dark piece of construction paper over it. The web should adhere to the paper because of the wet paint. A light coat of clear spray will help preserve it when the paint dries.

UNIT STARTERS

An important notion in environmental education is *trade-off* or *compromise*. It is essential that this be established as a basis for an understanding of the problems involved. For example, every new highway adds to air pollution and may destroy farmland, yet that highway may be necessary to transport people to jobs or bring food to the city. The notion of trade-off is of particular significance today as the country seeks new energy sources. Growing crops for gasohol seems to make good sense to lessen our dependence on oil, yet it may require large consumption of scarce water and may utilize acreage that could instead produce food for poorer countries. Substituting coal for oil to generate electricity is another example. Even with pollution controls, there is more danger of air pollution from coal than from oil.

To illustrate further the notion of *trade-off*, suggest that the students constitute themselves a legislative body charged with making the final decisions on a number of environmental issues. Each should be discussed in turn and then a vote taken. Start with the examples in the preceding paragraph, and ask: whether the highway should be built, land set aside to grow crops for gasohol, or coal substituted for oil in utility plants. Then pose the following questions:

1. You live in an area where there is a high incidence of unemployment. The local factory employs 200 people. It is a chemical plant and is known to spew potentially poisonous wastes into the air. There is a proposal before you to order the plant to close to halt pollution. The workers have appealed to you to vote against this proposal. How would you vote?
2. Automobiles are known to be a major source of air pollution. There is a proposal to ban the use of automobiles on weekends. It is suggested that people use mass transportation or enjoy leisure activities at home on Saturdays and Sundays. There is no question but that this would reduce air pollution. How would you vote?

8 AIR AND WATER POLLUTION

We seem to be living in a period of crises: economic crisis, energy crisis, environmental crisis. Each is real; each has impact on our students' lives. In this chapter two aspects of the environmental crisis are discussed, but first the dimensions of the problem bear review.

Many billions of years ago, the earth was formed—a mass rotating around the sun. From that mass, the earth as we know it evolved. Gradually, it differentiated into three components: land, water, and air. The land areas include inner and outer cores, a thick mantle, and an outer crust, each layer blending into the next, and becoming hotter the deeper it is. Water came to cover over 70 percent of the surface of the earth, and an atmosphere formed. At first the earth did not have an atmosphere. It is believed that it resulted from gases that escaped from rocks on the earth as well as the effect of the sun on plants. All life on earth exists in a comparatively tiny envelope of air, soil, and water that comprise the *biosphere*.

The biosphere is a self-contained, closed system. With the exception of the energy radiating to the earth from the sun, nothing else is added. There is no replenishment for wasted resources. No additional water or air reaches us. Fortunately, nature is a recycler, providing for an endless water cycle, and constant purification of air and water. However, as our technology advances and population increases, there is a danger that we could be depleting our resources and pouring more wastes into our land, water, and air than can naturally be purified.

This is a recent problem. For a long time, people lived in harmony with nature. Their lives did little to affect the balance in the environment. Modern people have undertaken to conquer nature, bending it to serve their needs, frequently despoiling it. In the past it seemed that the earth's resources were inexhaustible. Now suddenly as new technology has enabled people to harness the atom, develop powerful chemicals, burn ever-more fuels, there is a realization that the air and water can be poisoned, the planet overpopulated, and resources depleted to the point that there may not be sufficient food to feed the earth's population. This is the nature of the environmental crisis.

AIR POLLUTION

As the children prepared to leave the house, their mother reminded them, "Don't forget your air masks!" An impossible scenario? Not really; it might easily have occurred in Tokyo in 1970, when people wore masks outdoors to protect themselves from the harmful effects of air pollution. Many air pollution disasters have been documented: over 4,000 people died in London in 1952, when a mass of polluted air blanketed the city for a week. New York City reported serious incidents in 1953, 1962, and in 1966, when 168 pollution-related deaths were tabulated. In Los Angeles, there are periods when schools keep children indoors during lunch and recess to avoid exposure to thick smog. Examples abound, some less dramatic, but indicative of the seriousness of air pollution.

TEACHER NOTES

BACKGROUND

Air pollution can be said to have originated with the first people who burned wood or leaves releasing smoke into the air. But the smoke was easily assimilated; the effect negligible. Today, however, hundreds of pollutants pour into the air at a rate that seriously threatens to contaminate the atmosphere, leading environmentalists to charge that we are treating our air as a *garbage dump*. Pollution is a concomitant of industrial life caused by automobiles, buses, trucks, airplanes, power plants, incinerators, and factories.

Automobiles are among the worst offenders. Their exhausts fill the air with carbon monoxide, a poison that even in small amounts can cause nausea, headaches, blurred discrimination and vision. They also spew out hydrocarbons and lead particles—both damaging to the nervous system. Attempts to control automobile pollution have not been wholly effective. The control equipment cuts down emissions of carbon monoxide and unburned hydrocarbons but does not completely eliminate them. Further it loses much of its effectiveness if it is not checked regularly and properly maintained.

There are other sources of hydrocarbons in the air—incinerators that burn coal and leaves. When exposed to the sun, the carbons unite with nitrogen dioxide in the air to form a hazardous smog. The nitrogen dioxide is a by-product of factories that manufacture fertilizers and explosives. In the atmosphere it can frequently be detected by a strange odor and tendency to give the air a brownish hue. In itself it is a pollutant.

One of the most serious pollutants is sulfur dioxide. It taints almost everything it touches, causing surfaces of buildings to wear away, silver to tarnish, paint to erode; and it also impedes the growth of plants and impairs the respiratory systems of people. Sulfur dioxide is formed from the burning of coal and oil. Environmentalists fear that the energy shortage will result in wider reliance on coal and synthetic fuels, and that could mean increased amounts of sulfur dioxide in the air. Particularly disturbing is a new awareness that powerful chemicals like sulfur and nitrogen oxides can be carried in the air for hundreds of miles and fall as "acid rains" far from their original sources, polluting land and water where they come to earth.

Another recent source of concern is the buildup of carbon dioxide in the atmosphere from cutting the world's forests, burning fossil fuels, and the production of synthetic fuels. Carbon dioxide blocks the escape of radiation from the earth's surface into space, which could at its extreme lead to the melting of polar ice, shifts in wind and ocean currents, and changes in climate that could disrupt harvests around the world. No one is certain of the consequences.

Not all contaminants are gases. Industries release particles—ashes and soot. The small ones remain in the air, frequently combining with moisture to cause haze. They may also settle on clothing and buildings as dust and are breathed by people, irritating eyes, throats, and lungs.

It should be added that people pollute directly—smoking cigarettes, burning wood and leaves, using aerosol sprays. Air pollutants cannot be completely eliminated. But it is possible to achieve substantial reductions by restricting the use of high-pollutant fuels and installing devices that trap contaminants before they are released into the air. The price may be expensive, but far less expensive than the eventual cost of neglect.

ACTIVITIES REQUIRING SPECIAL MATERIALS

NAP 1: Vinegar or perfume or hair spray.
NAP 2: White cardboard.
NAP 3, 4, 8, 9: See details of experiments.
NAP 5: Cars on school parking lot; also additional materials for experiment.
NAP 7: Plants.
NAP 11: Children observe community.

IMPLEMENTATION

Activities can be combined with a science unit on *air*.
Start the topic by presenting the natural composition of air:

	Percent
Nitrogen	78.00
Oxygen	21.00
Argon	.93
Carbon dioxide	.03
Other gases	.003
Water vapor	.037

Children can demonstrate the existence of oxygen and water in the air.
NAP 5 requires children to check car exhausts. This should be carefully supervised.

EVALUATION

Check ability to experiment, collect, and analyze data: NAP 1–12.
Key questions:

What is an inversion?
What evidences do we see of air pollution?
What are some causes?
What can you do to help?

ACTIVITY STARTERS

One teacher lit a cigarette but did not smoke it. "What is being released into the air?" he asked.
Another showed the class a picture of smoke belching from a factory chimney. "Would you like to breathe that smoke?" she questioned.
In another class, the teacher mused, "I wonder what happens to the particles from our shoe heels and soles when they wear away? Or from automobile tires? Or wood that is sanded down?" The notion that tiny particles may collect in the air as a result of attrition and remain to pollute it was established. These examples led to a discussion of air pollutants.

ACTIVITIES ON AIR POLLUTION

Explore the presence of pollutants in the air, observe their effects, and then plan to fight pollution.

ACTIVITIES NAP 1–6: Investigate pollutants in the air.

NAP 1   Can we see gases that pollute the air?

Gases that pollute our air are released by cars, planes, factories, people. Just like the natural gases in the air, they are invisible, but we breathe them.

The following experiments illustrate that there may be a gas in the air that we cannot see. In each of these, we are able to smell the gas, but it should be borne in mind that most pollutants cannot be smelled.

Have a student walk out of the room. Another student should open a bottle of vinegar or perfume or spray some hair spray in a far corner of the room. As the first student returns, ask if he or she can see anything. Then have him or her walk to the corner and detect that something was indeed added to the air in the room.

NAP 2   Is the air dirty?

An easy way to investigate this is to place a piece of white cardboard outdoors. Cover half with a piece of wood or sturdy paper. After a few days, remove the covering and compare both parts. What do you find? Do you see any evidence of dirt in the air?

NAP 3   Examine particles in the air.

You will need:

Vaseline
Waxed paper
Heavy cardboard or pieces of wood
Covered jar
Microscope and slides (optional)

To proceed:

1. Spread a thin layer of vaseline on a few sheets of waxed paper about 2 inches by 4 inches.
2. Place one piece in a covered jar. This will be your control.
3. Staple the other papers to heavy cardboard or wood so that they will not blow away. Place them outdoors in various locations where they will remain undisturbed.
4. Retrieve the papers in a week.

What has adhered to them? How do they compare with your control? Use a magnifying glass to look closer. Are there common particles on each piece? Where do you think the particles originated? Which area was more polluted? What conclusions can you draw?

If microscope slides are available, repeat this experiment by placing slides which have been coated with a thin smear of vaseline in different areas. When you collect the slides, investigate them under a microscope.

Discuss your findings in class.

NAP 4   Test a hypothesis about particles.

Formulate a hypothesis as to whether the number and kinds of particles will vary in different parts of the school, such as the furnace room, the classroom, cafeteria, school kitchen, halls. Be as specific as you can.

Write your hypothesis and reasons for it.

Now repeat the procedure in the previous activity, placing slides or papers in each of the locations.

Collect your data; observe; draw conclusions. Has your hypothesis proved accurate? Write up the experiment, using the following headings: *hypothesis and rationale, procedures, findings, summary.*

NAP 5   Do cars pollute?

You can find out by checking cars in the school parking lot.

Staple a piece of white cardboard smeared with vaseline to a long stick. Hold the stick so that the cardboard is about one foot from the exhaust pipe of the car, parallel to the back of the car. Have the owner start the car and let it run for a few minutes. Be certain to stand to the side of the car, not to breathe in the fumes, and not to touch the pipe.

Check the cardboard. If a car is particularly "dirty," call it to the attention of the owner; it may need adjustment.

Note: In this activity you are only testing for carbon particles, but there are gases released that can be hazardous. To avoid inhaling exhaust fumes, you may wear a handkerchief mask.

NAP 6   Cigarettes also pollute.

Smoking not only pollutes the atmosphere, it also *pollutes* our bodies. Cigarettes can lead to lung cancer, shortness of breath, irritation of nose and throat, affect heart and blood pressure, and shorten life span.

Note the warning on a pack of cigarettes!

Write to your local Board of Health or American Cancer Society for information on cigarette smoking. Request statistics, such as rate of lung cancer among smokers vs. non smokers.

Discuss reasons why people smoke.

An important extra: Mount an antismoking campaign. Make posters for school and community, urging young people never to start smoking. Give reasons for this that you believe will be convincing. (You might interview former adult smokers for the reasons they stopped.)

ACTIVITIES NAP 7–10: Determine some of the effects of air pollution.

NAP 7   How does pollution affect plants?

Grow two plants from seeds. Tie plastic bags around each. In one bag insert a *pollutant,* such as aerosol spray, cigarette smoke.

Compare the two plants. What do you observe?

NAP 8   Does air pollution affect clothing?

You can research this by noting the effect of pollution on nylon.

You will need discarded nylon stockings or panty hose (not the stretch or mesh type) and a few sticks.

Cut the hose into equal pieces about 9 inches by 9 inches (or 23 × 23 centimeters). Staple the pieces onto two sticks so that the nylon is stretched between them and will stay in place. Do not stretch the nylon too tightly.

Place your sticks in as many different locations as you can: busy streets, garages, gas stations, near the school. Be sure to keep one indoors as a control.

Inspect your nylon samples regularly for any breaks in threads, holes, runs. Compare the samples from different areas.

If you can, obtain 35-mm. slide mounts.[1] place pieces of nylon in the mounts, and then repeat the above. When you collect the samples, you can project them onto a screen to inspect them.

Summarize your findings in writing.

NAP 9 What is an inversion?

a. To understand an inversion, you need to establish two premises:
  1. That hot air rises. This can be graphically demonstrated: Place a balloon over the top of a soda bottle. Immerse the bottle into a pan of hot water. You will note that as the air in the bottle heats, it rises to fill the balloon.
  2. That the air closer to the ground is generally warmer than the air higher up. Think of a picture of a snow-covered mountain peak in the summer to illustrate this.

b. Usually each day as the warm air close to the ground rises, it carries some of the pollutants that have accumulated in it away into the atmosphere above. Occasionally, however, a layer of cold air is trapped under a warmer one. The cold air close to the ground cannot escape, and, as a result, the pollutants in the air also remain close to the ground. This is called an *inversion*. Inversions are responsible for many of the air-pollution disasters that have occurred over the years. In the United States they are more frequent in Southern California.

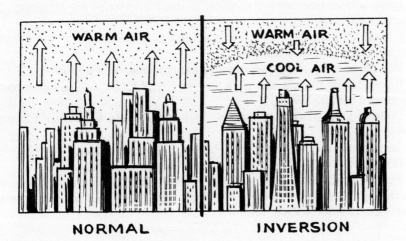

c. You can simulate an inversion:
  1. You will need two jars equal in size. Place one in the refrigerator or in a pan of ice cubes and the other in a warm spot.
  2. Remove the cold jar and fill with smoke (from a candle or cigarette to simulate pollutants). Place the warmer jar upside down over the colder one so that the jars' lips meet.

[1]Photograph supply houses carry these, or you can use mounts from discarded color slides.

Note that the smoke does not rise into the top jar.

You may wish to repeat this experiment to observe what will happen if both jars are the same temperature.

NAP 10   Why is an inversion dangerous?

Here's a research project:

Investigate the effects of inversions in London in 1952, Donora, Pennsylvania in 1948, New York City in 1966. There were other instances you may discover.

Report your findings to the class orally or by graphic illustration: roller movie, filmstrip, poster.

ACTIVITIES NAP 11–12:   What can you do about pollution?

NAP 11   Become aware of air pollution in your community.

Take a pollution inventory.

Walk through the community observing signs of pollution (smoke from factories or chimneys, car exhausts, incinerators, planes, buses, trucks, open burning of leaves). If you have a camera, photograph these and post them on a bulletin board with an appropriate heading. ("They are dirtying the air we breathe!")

NAP 12   Fight air pollution.

All of us can enlist in the fight against air pollution. Here are some suggestions:

Find out the local, state, and federal laws on air pollution by writing to local health officers, United States Environmental Protection Agency, environmental groups in your community.[2]

Invite a local environmental officer to class to discuss the legislation and how you can help.

Report examples of excessive air pollution (dark smoke pouring from a factory) to the local health office.

Walk or bike instead of requesting a car ride whenever possible.

If your family owns a car, urge that it be kept tuned and pollution-control equipment be maintained.

Write to local officials requesting that certain streets be closed to traffic during weekends.

Reduce use of aerosol sprays. (Research reasons for this.)

Don't start smoking and urge that your friends follow this rule!

Publicize facts about air pollution—bulletin boards, displays of results of preceding experiments, posters, filmstrips. Help make your school and neighborhood a cleaner place to live!

AIR SHOULD BE CLEAN!

PEOPLE BREATHE ABOUT 3,500 GALLONS OF AIR EACH DAY.

---

[2]Also contact groups such as The National Wildlife Federation, 1412 16th Street, N.W., Washington, D.C. 20036; League of Women Voters, 1730 M Street, N.W., Washington, D.C. 20036.

WATER POLLUTION

The same water that we use today has been here since the earth was formed. It is a finite resource, circulating in an endless cycle of evaporation and condensation, from the surface of the earth to the atmosphere, and back again to the surface. In the process many of the impurities in water are eliminated. Recently, however, scientists have warned that we are polluting our water faster than it can naturally purify itself.

TEACHER NOTES

BACKGROUND

About 70 percent of the earth's surface is covered with water; without it the earth would be unable to sustain life. But the bulk of the water lies in the oceans, which in their natural, salty state cannot be used for drinking or irrigation. The remaining water must be shared by ever-increasing populations. Each person in the United States uses about 180 gallons of water per day for drinking, washing, bathing, growing and preparing food, and flushing toilets. New technology demands more water, but improper planning permits it to be squandered. Even more serious, however, is the fact that our existing resources of water are being contaminated so that many are becoming worthless for drinking or for supporting marine life, which we depend upon for food. Lakes and rivers are open sewers into which are dumped every manner of waste—domestic, industrial, and agricultural. One need only observe the shores of beaches or lakes to see visible signs of this: bottles, plastic containers, cans, tissues, oil from spills, even fecal matter.

There are also the less visible pollutants—chemicals and metals such as lead, zinc, mercury, nickel, and other wastes—over 50 potentially dangerous industrial agents routinely discarded into the water. Their effects have not been completely documented, although some have created known problems. Mercury is an example. Mercury is absorbed by the plants and tiny animals in water, which are later eaten by small fish, which in turn are eaten by larger fish, such as swordfish and tuna. The mercury accumulates in the tissues of the larger fish as a result of the huge quantities of the smaller fish they eat. When people eat the fish, they are susceptible to mercury poisoning. A number of instances of mercury poisoning have occurred in Japan, and more recently around the Great Lakes regions in the United States.

The list of potential pollutants can be expanded: add agricultural wastes, runoffs from pesticides, fertilizers, and animal remains, and poisonous chemicals stored in the ground that leak into the water table below. Still another factor is thermal pollution. Plants, particularly nuclear-powered ones, use large quantities of water for cooling and then return the heated water to the source, upsetting the natural environment of the fish. It is interesting that a rise in water temperature of just five degrees can kill off trout and salmon. There is a danger that thermal pollution could mean the end of the salmon population in the northwest United States.

But the problems do not end there. Common household detergents contain an array of chemicals, particularly phosphates, that can have a devastating effect. Phosphates stimulate the growth of algae in water, and as they decay, they deplete the oxygen supply. The suds in detergents create problems, too. They are decomposed by bacteria in the water that compete with the fish for oxygen. As oxygen is exhausted, fish suffocate.

It is a frightening picture, but the process can be reversed. It will take a vast educational campaign and the expenditure of huge sums of money, less however, than the hidden cost of water pollution. Teachers may well ask: Will children ever know a Hudson or Mississippi River open for swimming, Great Lakes stocked with fish, the pleasure of shellfishing in local waters, and safe drinking water in every village?

ACTIVITIES REQUIRING SPECIAL MATERIALS

NWP 1: Children are asked to inspect local bodies of water.
NWP 2, 8 to 13: See details of experiments.
NWP 3: Water from different areas in community.
NWP 4: Oil.
NWP 5: Plants and fertilizers.
NWP 7: Old magazines.

IMPLEMENTATION

Activities can be combined with a unit on water or weather.
Integrate with a study of the water cycle (evaporation, condensation, precipitation).

EVALUATION

Check ability to experiment and to collect and analyze data.
Key questions:

What are some of the causes of water pollution?
Why is water conservation necessary?
What can you do to help?

ACTIVITY STARTERS

The teacher filled a glass with water. "Do you believe that this very water could at one time have been used by Lincoln to wash his beard?" he questioned. This discussion led to a comprehension of water as a limited resource, endlessly recirculating through the ages.

Another teacher took two glasses of water. In one she dissolved a teaspoonful of sugar; in the other, a teaspoonful of salt. "Which would you drink?" she inquired. "Can either of these waters be described as 'polluted'?" she pressed. "What should be added to water to describe it as polluted?" The purpose of this discussion was to establish a definition of *water pollution*, as the presence of any substance in water that prevents it from being used for an intended purpose, such as drinking, recreation, agriculture, or to support fish and wildlife.

ACTIVITIES ON WATER POLLUTION

Examine indications and causes of water pollution, methods of purification, and finally learn to conserve.

ACTIVITIES NWP 1–7: Become aware of water pollution.

NWP 1   Signs of water pollution.

The water on earth is fast becoming polluted by people and industries carelessly tossing garbage into it or permitting toxic substances to run off into it.

If you live near a body of water, inspect it for signs of pollution: debris, sewage, oil drops, detergent suds, odors. Where is the waste originating? Check the shore, too. Is it kept clean?

Bring back visible signs of pollution and make a display. Label it with the date and place collected and with a heading such as "Are You Polluting Our Water?"

If a particular industry is responsible, check with the local health officer to see if any environmental regulations are being violated.

NWP 2   Are you a polluter?

Garbage or scraps of food thrown into a lake can remain to pollute it. You can demonstrate this by collecting some scraps of leftover food—banana peel, cores of fruit, coffee grounds, bits of meat. Place these in a jar with some water; seal the jar. After a week open the jar and observe the contents. Smell them, too.

Compare the results of your experiment with what might happen to bodies of water if people threw debris into it.

NWP 3   Impurities in water.

Collect water in small jars from different areas in your community: pond, lake, stream, puddle, gutter. (Do not include drinking water.)

Shake the jars well and place a small amount in different dishes. Permit the water in the dishes to evaporate. What is left? How do the samples from different areas compare?

Keep careful records of your observations.

NWP 4   Oil spills on water.

From time to time we read of an oil tanker that has accidentally spilled oil into the water. Power boats, too, occasionally drip oil. Though some of this is cleaned, a residue remains to foul the beaches.

To demonstrate the difficulty of removing oil from water, try the following. Partially fill a large baking pan with water; then carefully pour oil over the surface. Try to "clean" the water. Experiment with different absorbent materials. Compare results. Which removed the oil best? Was all the oil removed by any?

NWP 5   How can fertilizers pollute?

Prepare two containers (plastic cups, lunch milk containers) with equal amounts of soil. Plant two seeds in each. Place both in a sunny spot and water regularly. Add fertilizer to one of the plants in accordance with the directions on the fertilizer. Which grows better?

What do you think happens to plants in water when large quantities of fertilizer run off into them? Why might this be a problem?

NWP 6   How do detergents pollute the water?

Investigate the effects of detergents on water. Why have counties, such as Suffolk County in New York State, banned the sale of detergents? Write to the county health officer to find out.

NWP 7 Suffocated fish—a sign of pollution.

Streams, rivers, ponds contain bacteria, which are nature's sanitary engineers. They decompose the wastes in water keeping it clean. They require oxygen for their work.

When there are too many pollutants in the water, the bacteria multiply and exhaust the oxygen in the water faster than it can be replaced. Without oxygen, fish suffocate.

You can illustrate the effects of pollution on different species. Cut out pictures of fish, birds, and animals from magazines. Mount each on a poster and pretend it is expressing concern with water pollution. For example, a fish might be saying, "I can hardly breathe in this water it is so dirty."

Display your posters.

Poster illustrating effects of water pollution on fish. (Courtesy Rushmore School, Carle Place School District, Carle Place, N.Y.

ACTIVITIES NWP 8–14: Experiment with methods of purifying water. Keep careful records of each of these.

NWP 8 Purifying water by sedimentation.

Water may contain undissolved particles. If the water stands undisturbed, these will tend to settle to the bottom, leaving cleaner water above. The settling of particles (or sediment) is called *sedimentation*.

Illustrate this by adding a handful of sand to water, mixing it, and letting it stand. Note that the sand will eventually settle.

Experiment with different materials: mud, soil, clay, ashes. Use containers with equal amounts of water. Add the same quantity of different materials to each container of water. Time to see how long it takes for each item to settle. Chart the results:

SEDIMENTATION CHART

Material	Time Added	Time Water Clear	Settling Time

NWP 9 Purifying water by coagulation.

Some of the smaller particles in water may not settle by sedimentation. In coagulation, a gelatinous mass, called a "floc," is formed in the water by the addition of aluminum sulphate (also called filter alum). The particles adhere to this mass, which in turn slowly settles to the bottom.

To demonstrate coagulation, you will need a pinch (less than a teaspoon) of alum. Add this to one of the containers in the preceding activity that may not have completely cleared. Note how this purifies the water further.

NWP 10   Purifying water by filtration.

Line a funnel with a coffee filter, a few thicknesses of tissues, or paper toweling. Pour muddy water through the filter. What do you observe?

Note that commercial filters generally use sand and charcoal as filters.

NWP 11   Purifying water to remove dyes and odors.

None of the preceding activities remove dissolved substances in water. Activated carbon or charcoal (a few pieces of charcoal briquets pounded until they are powdery may be substituted) will absorb foreign dyes and odors from water. The dyes tend to adhere to the charcoal. Activated charcoal may be obtained from a tropical fish store.

To observe how the charcoal removes dyes:

Line a funnel with a filter. Add a few pieces of charcoal. Pour water to which a food coloring or ink has been added through the funnel. What do you notice? Try also to add the charcoal directly to the water. Mix thoroughly; then filter. Any difference?

To observe how the charcoal removes odors:

Add equal amounts of bleach to two containers of water. Repeat the preceding experiments with one container. Compare it with the unfiltered one.

NWP 12   Purifying water by evaporation.

Traces of dissolved substances may still remain in the water after the preceding steps. You can check for these by pouring small quantities of water that has been *purified* into shallow dishes. Expose the water to the air (a warm spot will speed the process), and note whether any residue is left in the dish after the water has evaporated.

NWP 13   Purifying water by disinfection.

To purify drinking water further, add very small quantities of chlorine. This destroys any harmful microorganisms.

Examine the effect of chlorine on microscopic organisms. You will need household bleach (this contains chlorine) and some pond water.

Place some pond water on a slide, and study it until you find some moving organisms. Add a drop of the bleach to the water. What happens to the organisms?

NWP 14   Water for human consumption.

Find out the source of your community's drinking water. How is it purified for home consumption?

Perhaps you can visit a water-treatment plant.

Investigate also: Who determines when water is safe for drinking? What standards are used? How about water being safe for shelling? For swimming?

Write to or invite a local water engineer to the class to explain this.

ACTIVITIES NWP 15–17: Water is a *finite* resource. Conserve it!

NWP 15   Billions and billions of gallons of water.

It has been estimated that each person in the United States uses about 180 gallons of water per day for drinking, washing, bathing, growing and preparing food, flushing toilets, and so on.

Estimate the following for each day:

How much water the people in your class use.
How much water the school population uses.
How much water the people in your town or city use.
How much water the people in your state use.
How much water the people in the United States use.

NWP 16   From drips to gallons.

Little drips from leaky faucets can add up to substantial wastes of water. Prove it as follows:

1. Set a faucet to produce a slow, steady drip of water as when it leaks.
2. Collect the amount of water that drips in one hour.

Now be a mathematician:

1. Multiply the total number of ounces collected by 24 to find out the daily ounces wasted. Multiply the daily amount by 365 for the yearly waste of water.
2. Since there are 128 ounces in a gallon, to determine the number of wasted gallons yearly, divide the total yearly ounces computed above by 128.
3. Compute also the number of wasted quarts.

NWP 17   Conserve water.

The supply of water in the world is limited.
Enlist in the fight against polluting it.
Brainstorm with members of the class to devise methods of conserving it. Make an "I Can Save Water" poster showing methods of conservation, such as:

Do not permit the water to run when you are brushing your teeth.
Occasionally shower instead of bathing.
Call attention to leaky faucets.

Enlist the support of parents, members of the community in your campaign.

9
OTHER ENVIRONMENTAL TOPICS

The pollution caused by the gases discharged into the air or the liquids that run off into our streams may not be apparent, but a trip along our highways readily reveals another form of pollution, *waste*. Waste accumulation poses a major threat to the environment. This problem, along with other environmental concerns, is explored in this chapter. The chapter closes with a special section devoted to environment-related math activities.

WASTE DISPOSAL

Litter, garbage, trash, solid waste, refuse—call it what you will—the fact is there may soon be no room left on earth for it. We now throw away over a ton of garbage each year for every man, woman, and child.

TEACHER NOTES

BACKGROUND

Our society has been described as a "throw-away" society. Products are built with a "planned obsolescence." Appliances, cars, furniture, clothes are bought, used, discarded, replaced with regularity. Billions of tons of plastics are manufactured annually to be used only once. And the mounds of garbage grow throughout the country. Included in the garbage each year are 85 billion cans, 40 billion glass bottles, 44 million tons of paper, 5 million tons of plastic, 200 million tires, 1 million abandoned cars, 10 million tons of appliances, 200,000 tons of copper, 1 million tons of aluminum, and 20 million tons of leaves and grass. The statistics increase annually as our population expands.

It is estimated that by 1985 it will cost us 12 billion dollars just to collect and store the waste. The sad fact is that much of it is valuable. It could be recycled or burned for energy. But at the moment it keeps accumulating. We throw garbage *away*, but in fact, it will not *go away*. In the past much of the trash was *biodegradable;* that is, it was naturally decomposed by microorganisms in the soil and remained to enrich it. Nature provided a recycling process. But gradually we have begun to manufacture products that are *nonbiodegradable*, that cannot be naturally recycled, such as detergents, aluminum wrap and pans, and plastics. Plastics are a particularly interesting case in point. They are virtually indestructible. No one knows with certainty how long that plastic container we dump in our trash basket will be around. Some estimate 100 years, but it could be much longer. And no method has been devised for safely disposing of chemical wastes or the ultimate question: What to do

135

with radioactive wastes from nuclear plants? They are said to have a life of anywhere from 25,000 to 150,000 years.

Currently, our solid wastes are disposed of primarily in dumps, sanitary landfills, or incinerators. Each involves health hazards. The majority of trash in this country is thrown into open dumps that attract rats and insects, pollute the air and water, and make surrounding areas unattractive for real estate. Poisonous chemicals leak from them into underground water supplies or into the atmosphere. Burning them pollutes the atmosphere.

Sanitary landfills involve compacting waste, covering it with fresh layers of earth, and eventually using the resulting soil. Although hailed as an advanced method of disposal, the fill has not always been managed properly and may not be as *sanitary* as the name implies. The third method, burning waste in incinerators, may also be a hazard. Incinerators have frequently operated with inadequate pollution-control equipment, and as a consequence billions of pounds of pollutants have been released into the air.

A growing concern is sewage disposal. In coastal areas, sludge, which is treated sewage, is dumped into the oceans, creating a potential future problem. In New York City, a shortage of sewage-treatment plants has led to raw sewage being tossed into the Hudson River, making it unfit for fish or recreation. Much of the sewage sludge in other parts of the country is buried in waterways or brought to landfill sites where there is a danger that it may eventually leak poisons into the underground waters.

Faced with the enormity of the problem, solutions, at best, are partial. But environmentalists note that the sooner they are attempted, the more amenable the problems will be to correction. The first imperative, they urge, is recycling of waste. Valuable materials are rotting in our garbage dumps. Metals are a particularly apt example. The United States now imports more than half of all its aluminum, nickel, tin, chromium, tungsten, manganese, and platinum. By 1985 it is projected that we will import more than half our iron and lead. Yet recycling could save 30 percent of many of the metals now lost in production, use, and disposal. As an added bonus, recycling metals saves energy. For example, it requires about 25 percent more energy to produce aluminum from ore than from scrap, eight times more energy to mine and produce copper than to recycle it.

Other products, too, could be recycled. Our forests are being denuded, yet paper can be saved. Oil is in short supply, yet most of the oil that is regularly changed in automobiles is discarded. Fifty percent of used motor oil is recycled in Europe; here, only 10 percent. Compost to enrich soil can be produced from solid waste. For that matter, much of the garbage could be burned as a source of energy. This possibility is receiving increased attention.

There are impediments to recycling. An outmoded tax structure makes it cheaper for industries to use virgin materials than recycled ones. They receive tax breaks, depletion allowances on raw materials, that do not apply to recycled ones. Further complicating the picture are freight rates that discriminate against recycled materials.

On a personal level, people need to become aware of the need to conserve, reuse. Here children can contribute. They can be educated to acquire ecologically sound attitudes.

ACTIVITIES REQUIRING SPECIAL MATERIALS

NWD 6: Outdoors.
NWD 7: Suggests inventory of garbage at home. This may be a sensitive area in some families.

NWD 14, 16, 17: See details of experiments.
NWD 15: Proposes a compost heap in schoolyard, if feasible.
NWD 18: Best completed at home.

IMPLEMENTATION

Activities NWD 2–7 suggest inspecting trash. Sanitary ways of handling this should be discussed.

MODIFICATION

Waste Inventory form may be too difficult for some children. It can be simplified by instructing children just to inventory a few items.

EXTENSION

Plan art activities using junk.
Maintain ongoing *Recycling Chart,* on which children list all examples of personal recycling.

EVALUATION

Check:

Accuracy of waste inventory data.
Research: NWD 8, 9, 13, 18.
Understanding of term *biodegradable* and its implications.

Note evidence of attitudinal changes: Are children less apt to waste supplies? Are they sensitive to problems of litter and garbage?

ACTIVITY STARTERS

The activity starters are designed to impress children with the enormity of the waste disposal problem.

One teacher held up a soda can. "How many of these do you think are thrown away each year?" she asked. She wrote the figure 85 on the board and suggested the children tell her how many zeros to add. With each zero, she stopped and had the children read the numeral. The total of 85,000,000,000 was impressive. She repeated this procedure with other statistics, too. (See background notes.)

Another teacher asked the children to collect and bring to class all the bottles and cans that their families discarded on a given weekend. These were then lined up, end-to-end, around the room. The length of the pile was computed and recorded. The stack was then placed side-by-side and the area occupied recorded. The bottles and cans were taken to the school yard and placed randomly about, as they might be in a dump. This area was recorded.

Various calculations from the preceding data were encouraged—estimated space required to store bottles and cans discarded by these families in a week, month, year; space required for total families in school in a week, month, year; for total families in city, etc. By concentrating on just these two items, the teacher was able to impress the children with the enormity of the waste disposal problem.

> # ACTIVITIES ON WASTE DISPOSAL
>
> Learn why our is called a "throw-away" society. Analyze our waste, where it is discarded, and possibilities for recycling and conservation.

ACTIVITIES NWD 1–7: What is thrown away?

NWD 1   Many words describe it.

We now throw away over a ton of garbage each year for every person in the United States. (You can compute some interesting mathematical statistics from this. For example: How many tons of garbage will members of your class throw away in ten years?)

Many words are used to describe the things we throw away. How many can you discover? (Consult a thesaurus for help: *trash, garbage, litter, waste, sewage, junk, disposables, refuse—incidentally, it is said to be called refuse because we refuse to deal with it further.*)

Start a booklet on waste. Make this information your first page.

NWD 2   Take an inventory of solid waste.

In the next few activities, you will be directed to survey some of the things that are thrown away in class, school, home, and your neighborhood.

You will classify the information on a form, such as the one illustrated in Figure 9.1. You will be directed to examine each piece of waste to determine whether you believe it could have some further use.

Organize teams. Decide which areas each will survey. Be equipped with large plastic bags, and if any waste is to be handled, wear gloves.

Keep records of all your findings and conclusions in your "Waste Booklet." (See preceding activity.)

SOLID WASTE INVENTORY

Place Found _____ Date _____

Items (Indicate number found of each)	Total Number Found	Possible Further Use (Indicate how many could have more use)	Total with Further Use
Bottles			
Jars			
Cans			
Paper bags			
Plastic bags			
Miscellaneous paper			
Plastic containers			
Aluminum trays			
Food remains			
Clothes			
Furniture			
Appliances			
Boxes			
(Add others as you find them.)			

Figure 9.1   Sample form.

NWD 3   What is thrown away in class?

Empty the class trash basket toward the end of the school day.

Using your Solid Waste Inventory Forms, place a check mark next to everything you find. If there is a large amount of paper, you may wish to add additional categories of paper—notebook paper, construction paper, duplicating paper.

Examine the items carefully. Could any have been used further? For example, look at the discarded paper. Were both sides used? Was the whole of the paper used? Could parts of the unused portions be cut off and stapled together to make a memorandum pad? Are there paper or plastic bags that might still be serviceable?

Summarize your data, and write or discuss your conclusions.

NWD 4   What is thrown away in the cafeteria?

Organize teams of students to note the trays of children as they finish their lunches. List all the uneaten food.

Estimate: If the discarded food was combined, how many sandwiches, pieces of fruit, containers of milk, lunches would they total?

If it is feasible, wearing rubber gloves, inventory the contents of one trash basket. Record the items other than food on your Solid Waste Inventory Form.

NWD 5   What is thrown away in the school?

Ask the school custodian if your class may examine one can of school trash. Record the contents on your Solid Waste Inventory Form.

Find out how many cans of school trash are discarded daily. What is their weight? Can you estimate the weight of trash in a month? A school year?

NWD 6   What is thrown away on or near the school grounds?

Working in teams, record the litter you find on the school grounds or a square block near it.

You may do this in one of two ways. 1) Each team may assume responsibility for counting one type of litter (bottles, cans, paper); or 2) each team may investigate one small area. It should not be necessary for you to touch the waste in order to count it; a long stick can be used to separate the trash.

Enter your data on your Waste Inventory Form when you return to class.

NWD 7   What is thrown away at home?

On your Waste Inventory Form, keep a record of what is discarded at home during one week.

From individual records have the class compile one large class list.

The statisticians in your class may want to compute other totals: Assuming your class is typical, what is thrown away by all families in the school in a week, month, year.

ACTIVITIES NWD 8–9: What happens to the waste?

NWD 8   Methods of disposing of waste.

The three most common methods of disposing of solid wastes are:

Dumps: Tossing it into dumps
Landfills: Packing it closely, covering it with soil, and reusing the new earth
Incinerators: Burning it

Find out which method is considered most desirable and any problems associated with each.[1]

NWD 9   Which methods are used in your community?

Investigate the following questions:

1. How is solid waste disposed of in your community? In your school?
2. How is the material transported to the disposal site?
3. What happens to it there?
4. Are there any garbage disposal problems identified?
5. What does it cost your community (or city) to dispose of garbage?
6. How is sewage disposed in your area? It may be possible for you to visit a garbage disposal site or sewage-treatment plant.

(For answers to these questions, interview school custodians and building superintendents, and write to local offices, such as County Health Department, Environmental Office, Planning Commission, Sanitation Department, and government officials—council president, mayor.)

ACTIVITIES NWD 10–19: It's smart to recycle and conserve! Explore ways of doing this.

NWD 10   Review your Solid Waste Inventory Forms.

Evaluate your findings. What items were most frequently discarded? How many could have further use?

Plan how to publicize your findings to the school and community.

Suggest means of conservation. See activities that follow.

NWD 11   New uses for junk.

Choose all the items on your Waste Inventory Forms that you indicated could have further use, and describe possibilities. (Many library books suggest art projects with junk.)

Organize a contest for the most creative uses for discarded bottles, plastic containers, bits of cloth, newspapers, magazines, milk containers, plastic drinking straws.

NWD 12   Organize a "junk fair."

The fair will be an exhibit of products made from items normally discarded. Have each member of the class participate (or open it to the entire school). Awards can be given for the most creative project.

Contact local newspapers and radio and television stations to publicize your fair.

NWD 13   Let's save a tree.

It has been estimated that it takes 17 trees to make one ton of paper. Forty-four million tons of paper are thrown away annually.

How many trees must be destroyed to make those 44 million tons?

[1]Write for "Curbing Trash," League of Women Voters Education Fund, 1730 M Street, N.W., Washington, D.C. 20036.

Why are trees important to people? There is concern about an accumulation of carbon dioxide in the atmosphere. How could cutting down trees contribute to this?

And a More Extensive Activity: Protect your community's trees.

a. "Have you helped a tree today?"

Mount a campaign to make the community conscious of its trees. Prepare posters and ask permission to have them placed in local stores. Urge people not to litter or permit dogs to excrete on trees. Suggest they keep the soil around trees clean and that on hot days they give trees "a drink."

Take a walk and check the condition of the trees in your area. Do what you can to help.

b. Adopt a tree.

A class can contribute to the community and receive educational benefits from adopting a tree. Identify a tree near school and care for it. First clean up any litter around it; then carefully loosen the soil. Water it regularly and fertilize occasionally. Seal any cracks with tree paint.

Observe *your* tree. Note seasonal changes. Keep careful records of dates: when first leaves appear in the spring, when all leaves are out, when leaves begin to change color, when all leaves have fallen off.

Make leaf prints and rubbings from *your* tree by placing a thin sheet of paper on the bark and rubbing lightly with crayon.

Write stories about it: Who lives there?

Try to find out when it was planted.

If you have a camera, photograph it weekly.

Select one branch. Note when the first leaf appears on it in the spring, and the last falls off in autumn.

NWD 14   Recycle paper.

Paper can be recycled instead of wasted. You can recycle paper right in the classroom as follows:

You will need:

A page of newspaper (tabloid size)
Egg beater or electric blender
Mixing bowl (if you are using a blender, the blender container is fine)
Two tablespoons of wallpaper paste or laundry starch
Cake pan
Square of window screen
Water
Waxed paper
A glass or jar

To proceed:

1. Tear the newspaper into shreds and cover with one cup of water. Let it stand for about one hour.
2. Beat the paper with an egg beater or in an electric blender until it is a creamy pulp. (Do not make it too thin.)
3. Dissolve the wallpaper paste or laundry starch in water, and then add to the pulp. Mix well.
4. Place the screen over the cake pan, and pour the mixture onto it. Spread it out on the screen.

5. Cover with waxed paper, and roll the jar over it to eliminate the water. Remove the waxed paper, and allow the fibers to dry. When dry, peel the paper off the screen.

Your paper will be a grayish color because there was ink in the newspaper. You can also make recycled paper from other used papers—towels, napkins, construction paper.

NWD 15   Nature is a recycler.

One hundred years ago, waste was not a problem. Not only were there fewer people on earth, but our ancestors did not throw away as many things. Furniture lasted a long time, clothes were handed down, refashioned, or even made into quilts, and most of the food was grown locally, so there was less need for packages. Later when our grandparents shopped in stores, they usually brought their own packaging. To obtain cream, they would bring a metal container; for fruits, a shopping bag.

The waste consisted chiefly of natural materials. As this was buried in the ground, bacteria in the soil decomposed it and *recycled* it into nutrients that plants need for growth. Thus there was a natural recycling process. This can best be illustrated by studying a *compost* heap. Leaves and grass and other natural discards (coffee grounds, vegetable and fruit skins) are piled together. When these are combined with soil, the resulting mix is a valuable nutrient for plants and vegetables.

If there is an area available on your school grounds, secure permission to make a small *compost* heap. (If you have a school garden, the resulting soil will be valuable.)

Study the heap over a period of time. Check its temperature. What happens to the discards? Record observations weekly.

NWD 16   Is it biodegradable?

Substances which are naturally broken down as in the activity above are considered *biodegradable.* Certain products manufactured by people cannot be decomposed and recycled naturally. They are termed *nonbiodegradable.* An example of the latter is *plastics.*

Test for biodegradability.

Compare what happens to a piece of newspaper and a piece of plastic when each is buried in soil.

Fill two equal containers with soil and "plant" equal-sized pieces of newspaper in one and plastic wrap in the other. Keep the containers moist.

After a month dig up your plants and compare.

Repeat this experiment with other natural and people-made products, such as cotton and nylon, wool and acrylic. Which is biodegradable?

NWD 17   Plant a waste garden.

If there is room in your school yard, you can conduct the preceding experiment on a much larger scale.

Choose an out-of-the-way plot of ground. Dig holes about one foot deep, and plant both natural and synthetic products. Some items you might include are: pieces of fruit, cookies, leaves, vegetables, cotton, wool, plastic containers and wrap, aluminum foil, nylon, dacron, and polyester. Water your "garden" daily. You will need a marker over each plant so that you can remember what you buried. Every two weeks dig up the plants and check their conditions.

Keep careful *biodegradability* records.

NWD 18   Is that packaging essential?

You have noted in preceding activities that many materials used to wrap items, such as aluminum foil and plastic wrap, create disposal problems.

Examine packages. How many have unnecessary packaging? For example, is a food product wrapped in more than one container (a bag and a box)? What is currently sold in plastic that could be put in a paper bag instead? How much of the packaging is merely a way of making an object look more expensive (toy items that could be in bags instead of boxes—see Chapter 5, Activity CS 5)?

Start a wasteful packaging chart, as follows:

Product	Unnecessary Wrapping (specify)

NWD 19   How you can help.

In addition to tips mentioned in the preceding activities, environmentalists suggest the following. Some you can do personally; others can be brought to the attention of your parents and people in the community.

Use both sides of paper.

Be prepared to return bottles to store. Buy drinks in returnables.

Conserve paper use.

Take a reusable shopping bag to the store. Tell the clerk you will not need a paper bag.

Reuse wrapping paper, plastic bags, foil.

Urge that your community recycle garbage and personally cooperate. Find out if trash can be burned for energy.

Invent new uses for throwaways.

PUBLICIZE WHAT YOU HAVE LEARNED!

OVERPOPULATION, RADIATION, SOIL AND LAND USE, AND NOISE POLLUTION

The following is an overview of additional topics that might be included in a study of the environment with suggestions for the kinds of activities that relate to each.

OVERPOPULATION

The current population of the earth is about four billion human beings. It is projected that early in the next century it will increase to seven billion and keep doubling every 35 years. The population explosion places an increasing strain on the world's resources and the quality of life. People will need food, housing, energy, transportation, and recreational facilities. But as important, behavioral scientists have warned that close living creates physical and emotional stresses that can cause serious strains.

A number of research projects can aid children to analyze the nature of the population explosion:

1. What are the populations of the major countries on earth? What were they 50 years ago? 100 years ago?
2. What are the populations of the major continents?
3. Where is the population increasing most rapidly? Most slowly? What can you conclude from these statistics?
4. Investigate the *life expectancy at birth* at present and 100 years ago. How does the life expectancy of men and women in the United States differ? How do both compare with countries in other parts of the world?

RADIATION

People have always been exposed to a certain amount of radioactivity from the sun and outer space. But it is only recently since they have begun to tamper with the structure of the atom that additional radioactive fallout has been released into the atmosphere and water. There is no question but that radiation can be hazardous. In large doses it can cause cancer and genetic damage and seriously interfere with other bodily functions. What is not clear is what constitutes a *large* dose. Some believe that any increase in radiation exposure is potentially injurious.

Radiation is measured in units called *rems* and *millirems*. The latter is equal to 1,000 rems. People are exposed to about 130 millirems annually from natural sources plus about 77 millirems from nuclear and electromagnetic technology. Radiation comes from X rays, color television sets, microwave ovens, and other products, but the major concern is the radiation released by nuclear plants, both those that manufacture atomic weapons and power. Their nuclear reactors release small amounts of radioactivity into the atmosphere. They also accumulate radioactive wastes. Disposal of the wastes constitutes a major problem inasmuch as they may remain radioactive for 25,000 years and more. There appears to be no safe way to bury them. Finally, concern exists with the safety of nuclear plants. The near-disaster at Three Mile Island in Pennsylvania has led to a reevaluation of the control systems at nuclear plants.

Combine this topic with the study of nuclear energy, utilizing activities from Chapter 3.

SOIL AND LAND USE

A billion-dollar expressway stretching from the city to rural areas across former potato fields; a modern housing development and shopping center replacing cabbage and lettuce patches, built to accommodate ever-increasing populations. Signs of progress? "More likely signs of shortsightedness," environmentalists would be apt to reply, questioning, "If we continue to pave over our arable land, where is the food to come from to feed those same populations?"

Less than 30 percent of the surface of the earth is covered by land. Of this only a small portion can be defined as *soil*, an area capable of producing vegetation. And not all the soil is available for growing food. Some of it lies in deserts or other areas so dry that it would require constant irrigation for cultivation; some is covered with trees; some is required for pasture.

All soil is derived from rocks. The action of air, wind, and water on rocks causes them to decompose, split, chip, and finally break down into the powdery substance we call soil. To this substance is added organic matter from the plants and animals that die, decay, and become part of the soil. The process takes thousands of years. It is primarily the top layer of soil, topsoil, that is valuable for cultivation. Since it is closest to the surface, it is this layer that can most easily be depleted. About 200 years ago, topsoil in the United States averaged nine inches deep. Today it is estimated at six inches. It is destroyed through erosion: water washing it away, wind blowing it away. When trees and grass are cleared from an area, the open soil is more susceptible to erosion from wind and rain. Soil is also exhausted through thoughtless farming methods that fail to replace fertilizers in the soil or utilize scientific methods of planting.

Soil is classified as a renewable resource. Plants remove nutrients from the soil as they grow; but when they die, they fall back into the soil. Their remains are broken down by worms and bacteria in the soil, replenishing it. However, there is a danger that humans will deplete the soil faster than it can be recycled by nature.

Possible activities relating to soil and land use include:

1. Investigate the school plot and home: what was on the land 50 and 100 years ago? Indicate changes in land use.
2. Study how soil is formed, erosion, and methods of preventing it. Demonstrate by simulating conditions in plastic boxes. Analyze different kinds of soil.
3. Research the *dust bowl* in the United States in the thirties.
4. Research action of earthworms on soil; secure some for the classroom. Place some in a container with soil; set up a control container with no worms. After one month check to see which soil retains water best.

NOISE POLLUTION

Noise has been defined as *unwanted sound*. Its definition is largely subjective. A whisper in a quiet classroom may provoke a teacher to remark to a group of children, "You are being too noisy," whereas fans of a blaring rock group may resent the band being described as *noisy*. To many, noise is just a nuisance—a loud radio that interferes with sleep, city traffic, or a jet plane flying overhead that disturbs conversation. Yet the fact is that noise is a serious pollutant whose effects on our health are still to be assessed. It is known that repeated exposure to loud sounds can impair hearing; harm the nervous system; produce fatigue, insomnia, and high blood pressure; and interfere with other bodily functions.

Just as the pollutants in air and water are not always discernible, noise may be so much a part of the environment that people are unaware of it. It has been described as the most pervasive pollutant, a constant intruder particularly in the city, but one to which many have grown accustomed. Fear has been expressed that the frequent exposure of young people to loud music may take a heavy toll on their physical well-being.

A study of noise pollution may be combined with a unit on sound or introduced with some basic concepts about sound:

> Sound is caused by vibrations that travel in waves through the air. We hear because, as sound waves reach our ears, the eardrums vibrate, and the inner ear converts the vibrations into nerve messages.

Activities should be directed towards aiding children to perceive their constant exposure to sounds, both wanted and unwanted, and to recognize that even the former may have damaging effects. Possible activities include:

1. Classification of sounds: noisy, quiet, pleasant, unpleasant, scary, soothing, familiar, unfamiliar, and also piercing, startling, explosive.
2. Measuring sound: children research decibel levels.
3. Sound mufflers and amplifiers (test various ones).
4. Research effects of noise and methods of combating noise pollution. (See also audio activities, Chapter 12)

MATH IN THE ENVIRONMENT

The outdoor environment, whether urban or suburban, is a natural mathematics laboratory, a setting in which children can practice a variety of math skills. Children are naturally curious about their environment, eager to explore it and by exploring it to gain a sense of familiarity with it. Teachers can encourage children to view their surroundings from a mathematical perspective—estimating and measuring distances, sorting, classifying, and counting natural objects.

No matter what the mathematics unit, teachers can reinforce learning by a period outdoors. Even young children can establish one-to-one relationships by counting pebbles or blades of grass, can compare their shadows; investigate concepts such as "bigger than," "heavier than," and "taller than;" and can search for natural shapes. Older children can graph, compute statistics, gather data, and measure angles.

To illustrate the potential for reinforcing mathematics by venturing outside the classroom, 14 activities are presented here. They are arranged sequentially—those for young children first. With the exception of NME 10, they require only measurement materials.

ACTIVITIES ON ENVIRONMENTAL MATHEMATICS

Venture outside your classroom into the school yard or playground and apply your mathematics skills to study your environment.

ACTIVITIES NME 1–5: Investigate your environment to find sets, count, and classify.

NME 1   Sets in the environment.

You will need pieces of string.

Go into the school yard. You have 15 minutes (*time may vary*). Collect objects in the environment to form as many different sets as you can with the cardinal number six (*number may vary*).

As you collect the members of each set, place a piece of string around them.

How many can you find?

NME 2   Classify objects in the environment.

Look for objects with the following common attributes:

Color
Shape
Texture: rough, smooth, soft, hard
Weight: heavy, light
Breakable or unbreakable
Or a different attribute that you determine

To proceed:

1. Before you leave the classroom, agree on a particular attribute to be observed. Now go outdoors for a specified period of time. Identify all such objects. List them.
2. Bring as many back to the classroom as you can. Make a display: "Objects in our Environment." Separate them by attribute and label each group.

NME 3   Go on a *scavenger hunt*.

Prepare a series of cards with different categories: artificial, once living but now dead, seeds, objects smaller than 10 cm., those with attributes noted in preceding activity, and so on. Divide into teams. Give each a card and a specified period of time. See how many each can find.

NME 4   Investigate a leaf.

Give each child a leaf and a piece of graph paper.
Prove the leaf is *symmetrical*.
Find the area of the leaf. Find its height and width at the largest points by using graph paper.

NME 5 How many different ways can you classify leaves?

Divide into groups. Give each group a packet of leaves chosen at random from the environment.

Note how many different ways they can be sorted and classified.

This can be repeated with pebbles or other natural objects.

ACTIVITIES NME 6–10: Practice measurements and computations, and construct a trundle wheel.

NME 6 Measure by pacing.

Estimate a distance of three meters. Place a marker at that point.

Now estimate how many steps you will need to reach it.

Close your eyes and take those number of steps. How close was your estimate. Compute any difference.

NME 7 How long is your pace?

Walk a given number of steps (5, 8, 10, 12).

Determine the size of each step by measuring the distance covered and dividing by the number of steps.

NME 8 Unusual measurements.

Work in groups. In a given period (15 or 30 minutes), have each group collect unusual measurements outdoors: length of a worm, size of a crack, depth of a hole, shadow of an ant.

Record your results, and make a large chart in the classroom displaying the information.

NME 9 Practice computations on the playground.

Draw a rectangle on the playground with numerals. (The numerals will vary with the ability of the children.)

Each child, in turn, must throw a pebble into the required number of spaces to total a given number. For example, young children will need to total *ten,* using diagram A; older children may need to total *100,* using diagram B.

0	9
8	7
6	5
4	3
2	1

Diagram A

15	25
23	37
20	30
12	13
9	16

Diagram B

You may add rules; for example, you must achieve the total with a specified number of tosses.

(*Note:* Other operations may be substituted for addition.)

NME 10 Construct a trundle wheel.

A trundle wheel is a calibrated wheel attached to a handle, which is used to measure distances on the ground. It can be made as follows:

1. Cut a circle from a piece of heavy cardboard (or lightweight plywood, if available) with a diameter of 11.465 inches. This will give a circumference of one yard. (For a wheel with a circumference of one meter, you will need a diameter of 12.22 inches.)
2. Calibrate your circle: starting with zero, draw lines dividing the yard by 3-inch intervals, noting each foot (or in the event of a meter, note decimeters).
3. With a bright red magic marker, indicate the starting and ending points of the measurements on the rim of the wheel so that it can be easily seen when the wheel is rotating.
4. Drill a ¼-inch hole in the exact center of the circle.
5. Attach the circle to an old broomstick (or similar-size stick) with a screw and nut (or nail and cork) in such a manner that the wheel is free to rotate.
6. To measure a distance, place the point marked "Zero" on the beginning spot; walk your wheel, counting off the number of turns until you reach the finish line.
7. The trundle wheel can be employed to measure various distances: the length, width, and area of the playground; the size of a neighboring city block; the area of one portion of the sidewalk (are all portions equal?) perimeter of the school yard or building.

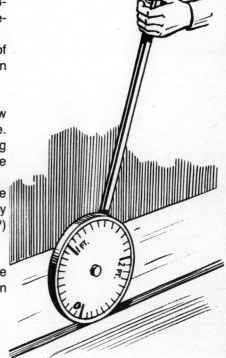

In each instance, you will improve your math skills if you first estimate the distance, then actually compute it, and finally record the differences between your guesses and actual measurements.

ACTIVITIES NME 11–14: Practice more advanced measurements.

NME 11   Become acquainted with your shadow.

A shadow is an image or figure cast by an object blocking light. Outdoors our shadows are created by blocking the light from the sun.

You can become better acquainted with shadows, practice measurements, and learn more about the changing position of the sun by investigating the following problems:

How can you lengthen your shadow? Shorten it? Make it look wider? Narrower?

What is the length of your shadow? Compare it to your actual height. Do this with a group of children of uneven heights. Have each stand in the same spot, facing the same direction, and make a chart showing their heights and the length of their shadows. Analyze the data you have collected. Can you draw any conclusions?

NME 12   Find the height of a tree by measuring your shadow.

Stand parallel to the tree so that you and the tree cast shadows in the same direction.

Have a classmate measure your height and the length of your shadow.

Now measure the length of the tree's shadow.

In geometry we learn that the triangle formed by you and your shadow will be proportional to the one formed by the tree and its shadow:

$$\frac{\text{Your height}}{\text{Your shadow}} = \frac{\text{Tree's height}}{\text{Tree's shadow}}$$

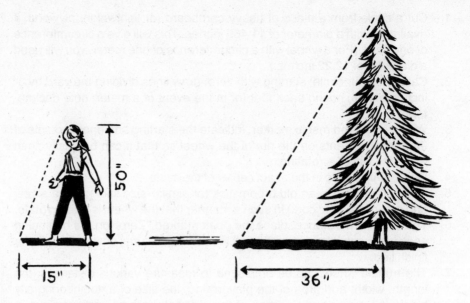

To find the height of the tree:
Multiply your height by the length of tree's shadow. Divide the product by the length of your shadow. The result is the height of the tree.
See illustration.

In the illustration, the height of the tree would be computed by multiplying $50'' \times 36'' = 1,800''$. Divide 1,800 by $15'' = 120''$ (or 10 feet), which is the height of the tree.

NME 13   Other measurements with shadows.

You can measure the height of a flag pole, a telephone pole, a building, and other objects by comparing the shadows they cast to yours. Follow the directions outlined in the previous activity.
Shadows other than those cast by people can also be used to measure heights. Design a "shadow stick" for this purpose.

NME 14   Investigate a small plot.

Work in groups.
Each group should select a grassy area 6 inches or 15 centimeters square. Outline the area with string. Investigate the area very carefully. Use magnifying glasses, if available.
Find out all you can about your plot: how many blades of grass or other covering, average height of each blade, any insect population, what kind of soil (coarse, sandy, crumbly), colors.
Record all your findings. Compare the observations of the different groups. What is the average number of blades of grass in each plot? Kinds of insects?
You might try to repeat this investigation in a different spot, such as a neighboring park.

RESOURCES FOR PART 3

Air Pollution Control Association
4450 Fifth Avenue
Pittsburgh, Pa.
    Write for "A Dictionary of Air Pollution Terms."

Environmental Action Coalition
156 Fifth Avenue
New York City 10010
    Films and publications available.

Environmental Protection Agency
Office of Public Affairs
4th and M Streets, S.W.
Washington, D.C. 20460
    Excellent publications available. Highly recommended: "Your World, My World:
    A Book for Young Environmentalists."

Izaak Walton League
1326 Waukegan Road
Glenview, Illinois 60025
    Request "Clean Water—It's Up to You."

League of Women Voters
1730 M Street N.W.
Washington, D.C. 20585

McDonald's Corporation
One McDonald Plaza
Oak Brook, Illinois 60521
    "Request Ecology and Energy Action Pack" (Spirit Masters)

Mobil Oil Corp.
150 E. 42 Street
New York, N.Y. 10016
    Request "A Primer on Air Pollution"

The University of the State of New York
The State Education Department
Albany, N.Y. 12234
    Request "Energy and Scarcity. Environmental Education Instructional Activities,
    K–6."

National Wildlife Federation
1412 Sixteenth St. N.W.
Washington, D.C. 20036
    Request list of Conservation Education Publications.

PART

THE
CLASSROOM
AS A
CAREER
BANK

"*Xylophonist* saved the day," the teacher informed the visitor pointing to a large chart on the bulletin board. On it all the letters of the alphabet were listed, and next to each, job titles beginning with that letter. Over 200 titles had been recorded. "We wanted an entry for each letter," the teacher continued, "but had difficulty finding one for the letter 'X'. Finally a student suggested *xylophonist*, which was confirmed in the dictionary, and our goal was met."

The chart had been started as an introduction to a unit on career education. "Most children's knowledge of occupations is limited to those of their immediate families," the teacher explained. "I wanted them to become aware of the large variety of career possibilities in our society. The activity has had many peripheral benefits," he noted. "By researching job titles, students have increased their vocabularies and gained spelling and dictionary skills. And as a next step," he continued, "I will ask students to research individual careers in depth, further reinforcing their language skills."

Career awareness, as practiced in this class, is but one facet of career education. Most programs also include self-awareness and preparation. Self-understanding is clearly essential if children are to realistically assess their life goals and aspire to roles consistent with their abilities, free from preconceived limits. Students need also to be prepared with the intellectual and occupational skills that will permit them to have genuine career choices. They need to acquire a respect for work. They must also be prepared with adaptive skills to enable them to cope with a rapidly changing future in which most will have a number of careers in their adult lives.

OBJECTIVES OF CAREER EDUCATION

Students will:

■ Acquire an attitude of respect and appreciation for the contributions of different workers to society and for the dignity of constructive work.
■ Develop an awareness of their own special talents, interests, abilities, and personal goals, enabling them to make satisfying career choices.
■ Gain the self-confidence necessary to aspire to careers uninhibited by stereotypic barriers.
■ Acquire information about many specific careers and have increased career options.
■ Be better prepared to achieve personal fulfillment in their future work.
■ Recognize the commonality of all people and the uniqueness of each.
■ Learn methods of studying the future.
■ Become aware of the rapidly changing world in which they live, and gain in ability to adapt to it.
■ Recognize that careers require special skills and training.
■ Learn specific techniques of finding a position.
■ Learn to apply information to new situations.
■ Improve basic skills through application.

CURRICULUM INTEGRATION

Science

Integrate self-awareness with health, study of human body.
Note careers associated with current scientific fields and projected future possibilities, such as new careers in *energy*.

Social Studies

Include in units dealing with family life, social and economic organization.

Relate geography, history, economics, natural resources, and politics to people's work.

Note, too, specific careers associated with government.

Mathematics

Specific problems can be devised relating to salaries: hourly, weekly, monthly, annual and lifelong earnings.

Compare average salaries in different occupations.

See also probability formulas developed in conjunction with future studies.

Language

Language is a key area for integration with career education. Students research career information, interview, report, increase vocabulary, and spelling skills. They write letters, employment ads, complete applications. Career booklets are maintained.

Career material can be used specifically to improve reading comprehension.

Art

Design uniforms, tools. Illustrate booklets, reports.

Make collages, mobiles, media presentations.

UNIT EXTENSIONS

1. Establish a career learning center. Include picture file, activity cards, and books related to careers.
2. Consider a *career day*. Students may dress in the mode of a selected career, such as white surgeon's coat, pilot's cap, business suit, athlete. Information about different careers may be placed on tables and an accompanying tape, prepared in advance by the students, be available to the visitors.
3. Select a "Career of the Month." Have the class investigate one career each month. Collate all the information gained into a booklet.

10
CAREER
EDUCATION

Children are exposed to career education throughout their lives. They hear about the work of their parents and other close adults, observe the workers in their communities and the athletes and performers on television. Parents and teachers stress "good work habits," and endeavor to instill a respect for work. Children are subject to other influences, as well. Societal values affect career goals. During the era of Watergate, a survey of teenagers revealed that more aspired to be *rock stars* than *President of the United States.* Sex stereotypes maintain their hold. A 1979 Gallup survey of teenagers noted that most "career categories chosen by boys and girls remained divided very much along old sex-oriented lines."[1] Two exceptions were noted: medicine, now the first choice of girls but the third of boys, and computers, which was the tenth choice of both groups. The first five choices of each sex were as follows:

Boys
1. Skilled worker (carpenter, plumber, electrician, etc.)
2. Auto-diesel mechanic
3. Medicine
4. Professional athlete
5. Engineering

Girls
1. Medicine
2. Secretary
3. Nursing
4. Fine arts
5. Teaching

Gallup also concluded that there was frequently little relationship between the careers selected in school and students' actual later work. "The fact that the fourth most common category among boys was professional athletics indicates that the teens may have been overly optimistic."

Career education programs in elementary schools vary from those concerned primarily with community helpers to comprehensive units that integrate many areas of the curriculum. In this chapter career education is viewed from three perspectives: self-awareness, career awareness, and future studies.

SELF-AWARENESS

As children today enter the world of work, job satisfaction will largely depend on the match between the demands of their careers and their personal interests and aspirations. It is essential that children begin to clarify these traits in themselves at an early age.

[1] George Gallup, "Careers and Modern Technology," *Newsday* (March 19, 1980), Part 11, p.2. Report of telephone interview with cross-section of 1,012 teenagers, 13 to 18 years old, in October, 1979.

TEACHER NOTES

BACKGROUND

In the classroom self-awareness can be fostered through a dual approach: one expressing the commonality of all people; the other, the uniqueness of each individual. Recognition of people's basic similarities leads to increased acceptance of their personal differences.

Abraham Maslow's hierarchy of basic needs provides a useful starting point for an understanding of shared characteristics. He considered the following basic:

> Physiological needs (such as hunger, thirst)
> Safety
> Belongingness and love
> Self-worth
> Self-actualization
> Cognitive (thirst for knowledge)
> Aesthetic (desire for beauty)

He further theorized that the early needs pressed most for satisfaction, and it was only when they were satisfied that the next were able to emerge, adding that when people were denied fulfillment of their needs, they were more likely to behave antisocially.

Although the actual terms used in Maslow's hierarchy may be too complex for young children, each can be analyzed on children's levels. Discussions will stress *similarity* of needs regardless of backgrounds. As each term is noted, concrete examples should be solicited from the children. An open, accepting environment is essential to the activities in this section.

Following a foundation of common needs, children can explore their own *specialness*. At this point, respect for individual differences is stressed. Each person shares common characteristics but is also *unique*. No two people look exactly alike (not even identical twins). Each person has special feelings; each perceives things a little differently because each has different experiences. The activities that follow aid children to examine their *individuality:* their likes, dislikes, interests, characteristics, emotions, and reactions. Children have at times been made to feel that their concerns or interests were of little consequence. The objectives of this section are just the opposite: to aid children to recognize that their patterns are worthy of recognition and that the best preparation for rational choices in life lies in self-understanding.

ACTIVITIES REQUIRING SPECIAL MATERIALS

None require special materials.

IMPLEMENTATION

Activities RSA 15, 16, 21, 22, and 26 require group participation. All others are completed independently.

Teachers may schedule regular class meetings to share ideas, as described in *Background* notes.

EXTENSION

Physical differences can also be observed and tabulated.
Teachers may wish to continue regular classroom meetings.[2]

EVALUATION

Culminating activities (RSA 28–32) should be checked rather than individual ones.

Seek affective changes: Are children clarifying their own attitudes, values, feelings? Does classroom atmosphere reflect a growing respect for each person?

ACTIVITIES ON SELF-AWARENESS

The following activities are designed to help you recognize more about yourself and your classmates. Keep a record of your answers. At the end of this section, a number of different ways are suggested for you to summarize them. You may decide to survey members of other classes and children of varying ages to see how they would answer these same questions. Construct bar or circle graphs to illustrate the results of your surveys.

ACTIVITIES RSA 1–17: Explore your likes, dislikes, interests, characteristics.

RSA 1   What is your favorite . . . ?

Food
Song
Sport
Subject
Movie
Activity

RSA 2   Which is your favorite television program?

What type of program do you prefer: sports, crime, situation comedy, comedy, movie, documentary, soap opera, other?

RSA 3   Which is your favorite kind of book?

Do you prefer to read about sports, mystery, travel, history, romance, adventure, science fiction, biography, other?

---

[2]See Jack Canfield and Harold Wells, *100 Ways to Enhance Self-Concept in the Classroom* (Englewood Cliffs, N.J.: Prentice-Hall, 1976).

William Glasser, *Schools without Failure* (New York: Harper & Row, 1967). Also activities such as Magic Circle, available from Human Development Training Institute, El Cajon, California.

RSA 4   Whom do you admire?

If you could be like any person alive today, who would it be?

RSA 5   What would you change?

If you could change any three things in the world today, which would they be?

RSA 6   What are you proud of?

Think of something you have done that made you feel good about yourself. What are you proud of?

RSA 7   What would you buy?

If you had $100 to spend, what would you buy?

RSA 8   What are your likes and dislikes?

List five things you like best and then five you dislike most. Now put them in order of importance from one to five.

RSA 9   What do you enjoy?

What did you do this past month that you enjoyed the most? The least?
Complete this sentence: "If I could do whatever I wanted for a whole day, I would . . . "

RSA 10   How do you like to spend your time?

Check one from each column:

A	B
Alone	With others
At home	Away from home
Indoors	Outdoors

Active	Passive
Playing games	Constructing something
Reading	Watching television
In school	Away from school

RSA 11   Do you have a hobby?

Hobbies are any activities that people do in their spare time. You may not have thought about your baseball card collection as a hobby, but it can be classified as such. Hobbies can be fun and even profitable. Many people have started coin or stamp collections in their youths that later proved profitable.

The most common hobby of young people is collecting: comic books, baseball cards, matchbook covers, labels, dolls, stamps, coins, postcards, bottles and autographs. Arts and crafts and sports are other popular hobbies.

If you have a hobby, note what it is. If you don't, choose one that you think might interest you.

RSA 12   Think about a friend.

What do you like most about that person?
What traits do you value most in people? Check the five most important:

Loyalty	Smart
Willingness to share	Trustworthy
Fairness	Honest
Strength	Will follow your ideas
Leadership	Liked by others

RSA 13   What is your best characteristic?

What do you like best about yourself? Least? What one thing would you change?

RSA 14   Do you have responsibilities?

Make a list of all the responsibilities you have at home and in school.
Analyze them and decide whether you believe you have too many, just the right amount, or not enough.

RSA 15   How do you work with others?—1.

It is more difficult for a group to make a joint decision than for one person to do so alone.

The following permits you to analyze your group behavior:

Divide the class randomly into groups of six. Present this problem to each group. "You may have one hour free time. The group must decide how to spend the time, but whatever choice is made will be binding on all the members; each must do the same. You have ten minutes to decide."

How did the group make the decision? Were they able to agree? What role did you play in the group? Did you contribute to any solution?

Try this again with other problems and with different members of the groups.

RSA 16   Working with others—2.

Change the composition of the group, and this time pose more complicated problems:

How would you weigh an elephant?

If you could do three things to improve the human body, what would they be?

Again the only requirement is that the group agree on one answer in a limited period of time. Note how you work with others to resolve problems.

RSA 17   What will you expect from a job?

Each of the following is a reason for people working:

Fame
Prestige
Economic security
To keep busy
To help others
To get rich
Personal satisfaction

Select the three that you believe would be most important to you. Survey the class and graph the results.

How do your choices compare with others in the class?

ACTIVITIES RSA 18–24: Think about your feelings.

RSA 18   Feelings affect us physically.

Think about your emotions and how they affect your body. What happens to your heartbeat when you are scared? Have you ever felt sick because you couldn't face doing something like taking a test? Have you become "red with anger"?

Can you think of any other *physical* signs of *feelings*?

RSA 19   Analyze your feelings.

What makes you happy? Sad? Angry?
When do you feel most frightened? Lonely?

RSA 20   How do you react to feelings?

Complete the following:

When I am sad, I . . . .
When I am happy, I . . . .

Substitute *angry, frightened, lonely* for *sad* and *happy,* and complete the sentences.

RSA 21   More about your reactions.

How do you react to the following?

You are not invited to a friend's party.
You have an argument with your best friend.

The baseball game you were supposed to see is rained out.
You believe you have been punished unfairly.
Your brother (or friend or sister) has broken a favorite toy.

Role-play these situations with different members of the class demonstrating how they might react.

RSA 22 How do you manage conflict?

Conflicts are natural. People cannot always agree. Explore alternative methods of reacting to conflict. As these are discussed, analyze which you prefer.

Work in groups on this. Have each group write a potential conflict on a card. These might include:

1. There is only one ball, and two groups wish to play kickball during recess.
2. Someone cuts in front of you on the lunch line.
3. A student takes your pencil without permission.

Have another group take one of the cards, role-play the conflict and at least two possible solutions.
The rest of the class should evaluate the solutions.

RSA 23 Do you like to take chances?

Pretend someone offers you $10. You can either take this or toss a coin: heads would result in your receiving $20 instead; tails would result in your receiving *nothing*.
Which would you choose?

RSA 24 Do you wish you had the courage to . . . ?

Is there something you would like to do but do not feel you have the courage to do? What is it?

ACTIVITIES RSA 25–27: How do you make decisions?

RSA 25 Are you a *decision maker*?

Which of these decisions do you make?

What time to go to bed?
What time to get up?
What clothes to wear?
How to spend free time?
When to do homework?

If you do not make these decisions, which do you feel you could capably make? Are there other decisions you believe you should be making that you do not?

RSA 26 How would you resolve these?

a. How would you make a decision on each of the following?
    1. Two good friends each invite you to their homes for the same day.
    2. There are two television programs scheduled for the same hour both of which you would like to see.

3. You are permitted to choose a gift, and there are two toys you really want.

b. You can add to the above with similar conflicts, but also consider more difficult ones:
1. You have broken a glass that your mother cherished. She specifically asked you not to use it. Should you tell her or try to hide it?
2. You find a $5.00 bill on the playground. Should you keep it or turn it in to the school office?

Discuss with the class how other members would resolve these and other tough decisions.

RSA 27   Do you consider the consequences of your behavior?

Select one of the problems described in the preceding activity. List the possible alternative solutions, the consequences of each, and then decide on your behavior. You may do this by completing the Decision Tree.[3]

Decision Tree

State the problem _____
What are the alternatives?   1) _____ 2) _____ 3) _____

What are consequences of each   1) _____ 2) _____ 3) _____
alternative?

Your decision _____

ACTIVITIES RSA 28–32: You should be more aware of yourself now as a *very special person.*

Present some of this information by completing one or more of the following activities.

RSA 28   Make a booklet titled "A Very Special Person."

Include as many facts about yourself as you can. In addition to the answers to the questions posed in the preceding activities, you may wish to draw a picture of yourself and family; write a short autobiographical sketch, and add physical characteristics—your measurements, sample of your fingerprints and footprints, lock of your hair, and so on.

RSA 29   Create a collage.

Cut out pictures from old magazines that illustrate your likes and interests. Put them together into a collage.

RSA 30   Consider a mobile.

On a wire hanger, dangle objects, pictures, or words that tell about you.

RSA 31   Prepare a media presentation.

Read Chapter 12 and make a filmstrip, slide show, or photo essay that best represents you.

[3]Adapted from "Civic Responsibility," Merrick Public Schools, Merrick, New York.

RSA 32 Try an acrostic.

Using your name, fill in words that tell something about you. For example:

C hoosy
H ates peanut butter
R eads about sports
I s always late
S arah is best friend

CAREER AWARENESS

Butcher, baker, candlestick-maker—these are the careers envisioned in an old children's rhyme forecasting adult roles. If written today, the rhyme might well read "programmer, astronaut, aerodynamics engineer." Tomorrow, interplanetary transporter . . . ? It is difficult to define which careers will be available for our students.

TEACHER NOTES

BACKGROUND

"If current trends continue, 25 percent of the kinds of jobs that exist today will not exist in ten years, and 25 percent of the jobs ten years from now will be ones which do not exist today."[4] Machines will increasingly assume routine tasks; sophisticated communication networks may permit people to work at home, technological advances may enable them to work beneath the oceans or in outer space. With this vision of the future, career awareness implies more than an investigation of specific careers. Equally pertinent is awareness of the multiplicity of career options in our complex society and job-related skills. In this section, students are directed to collect information about careers, study how jobs are obtained, and practice skills related to applying for positions.

ACTIVITIES REQUIRING SPECIAL MATERIALS

RCA 1, 19, 20, 23, 24: Newspapers and magazines.
RCA 3: Interviews of parents or close relatives.
RCA 4: Yellow Pages (telephone directory).
RCA 6, 7, 18: Interviews of working adults.
RCA 17: See details of assembly line.

IMPLEMENTATION

RCA 6 and 7 can be simplified for use with younger children.

EXTENSION

See suggestions in Activities RCA 26–30. These can be maintained all year.

EVALUATION

Check children's ability to interview and organize data, and identify and classify careers.

[4]Draper L. Kauffman, Jr., "Futurism and Future Studies," pamphlet, National Education Association, 1976, p. 33.

Review children's writing: RCA 21–24.
Check specifically lists and charts: RCA 2–6, 7, 9–11, 14, 18, 19.
Culminating activities: RCA 26–30.
Math: RCA 31.

ACTIVITIES ON CAREER AWARENESS

You will investigate people's careers and attitudes toward their work. You will discover how people find jobs and different means of classifying them, and you will practice working on an assembly line. Suggestions for summarizing your data conclude this section.

ACTIVITIES RCA 1–8: Collect information about different occupations.

RCA 1   Maintain a class career file.

Clip pictures from magazines and newspapers of people working. Mount each on construction paper, and add a title identifying the person's job.

RCA 2   What work do people do in your community?

Together with members of your class, note all the jobs that are performed right in your own community. Start with the school community.

List the jobs on a chart labeled "People at Work in Our Community." If you have a camera available, photograph some of the people at work to illustrate your chart.

RCA 3   Parents work.

What is the work of your parents or close relatives? Have each member of the class secure this information and then summarize it. Which is the most common line of work?

RCA 4   Still more jobs: the Yellow Pages.

Examine the *Yellow Pages*. How many positions can you find that are suggested by the advertisements? List them.

Now from this list and the jobs you have identified in the preceding activities, select five jobs that you think would interest you the most.

Divide a piece of paper into five parts, write the title of one of the jobs on each part, and note the reasons for your choices (sounds exciting, interesting, think it pays well, important, and so on.)

File this paper. At the conclusion of this section, review your choices, and note whether any have changed.

RCA 5   Identifying jobs by products.

Have a student write the name of a common object on the board—a dress, a pencil, a piece of paper, a book, a woolen coat.

Now have the class brainstorm all the jobs involved in creating that object.

Here's an example of some associated with producing paper: tree farmer, lumberjack, sawyer, transporter, paper mill worker, salesperson.

How many occupations are associated with constructing a new house? Can you find 25?

RCA 6   Interview people about their work.

Interview five people using the following questionnaire. You may record the answers in writing or on tape. Try to select people who have interesting occupations.

After you have completed the interviews, analyze the answers, and present a summary to the class.

Would you be interested in choosing any of the occupations discussed? Explain your reasons in a small group discussion or in writing.

SAMPLE OCCUPATION QUESTIONNAIRE

1. What is your occupation?
2. How many years have you worked at this occupation?
3. What are the main responsibilities?
4. Does it require any special training or education?
5. Does it require any special traits (such as patience, enjoy working outdoors)?
6. Does it require continued training?
7. What do you like most about your work?
8. What do you like least about your work?
9. Would you prefer to work at a different occupation, and, if so, which would that be?
10. Have you held any other jobs that you liked better? If so, which?
11. Would you say that jobs in this field tend to be low-, average-, or high-paying?

RCA 7   Job satisfaction.

Now interview as many additional people as you can to collect data on job satisfaction. Ask each person to complete one of the following forms, checking the appropriate box. The person's name need not be included.

JOB SATISFACTION FORM

Title of job:	Satisfied with Job	Dissatisfied with Job	Partially Satisfied with Job
Woman			
College Graduate			
High School Graduate			
Didn't complete H.S.			
Man			
College Graduate			
High School Graduate			
Didn't complete H.S.			

If dissatisfied or partially satisfied, indicate the chief reason for this:
_____
_____

You will now have collected some interesting statistics. Summarize and publicize these to the school community or local newspaper. Include:
Who appear to be most satisfied with their work:

Men or women?
Those with which level of education?
Those in which job (divided by men and women)?
What is chief reason for dissatisfaction?

What other conclusions can you draw?

RCA 8   Play "What's My Line?"

Have one person pretend that he or she has a particular job. Members of a panel (or the entire class) ask questions of that person to try to guess the job. Only questions that require a "yes" or "no" answer are acceptable.
Ten questions are permitted. If the panel cannot guess, the person wins. If someone guesses the job, that person tries to stump the panel by selecting a new occupation.

ACTIVITIES RCA 9–17: More ways to think about jobs; analyze and classify them.

RCA 9   Classifying jobs: goods and services.

Some people work at jobs that produce goods *(dress manufacturer, steel worker)*. Others offer services *(plumber, doctor, entertainer).* Some may do both *(seamstress who repairs clothes and also sews new ones).*
Classify your picture file of occupations (see Activity RCA 1) in three columns: *Goods, Services, Goods and Services.* Add other occupations to the columns as well.
(See also Chapter 7, Activity CEC 8.)

RCA 10   Analyzing occupations.

Here are other ways of analyzing and classifying occupations:

1. How many jobs can you name that depend on specific geographic location?
2. How many that are affected by weather conditions?
3. How many require working outdoors?
4. How many require working at night? Or weekends and holidays?
5. How many require working alone?
6. Can you think of other classifications?
7. Secure a long roll of paper, such as is used for adding machine tape. Cut off strips, and on each strip list jobs in the different classifications.

RCA 11   Occupations and the five senses.

Some jobs require greater facility in one or more of the five senses (taste, touch, sight, smell, hearing). Can you identify these? (For example, taste-cook, touch-doctor, sight-bus driver, smell-utility worker, hearing-nurse.)
Which would a surgeon require?
Compile lists of jobs related to each of the senses.

RCA 12   Occupations and clothes.

Some jobs require special uniforms. You can illustrate these in a number of ways. Make paper dolls or puppets. Dress each in different *work clothes,* such as overalls, nurse's uniform, bathing suit. Identify the occupations by giving each puppet a name: "Chris, the construction worker."

Design work clothes (use paper or fabric remnants). Have classmates guess the occupation.

Consider, too, a class fashion show with each student dressed as a different worker. Have the class decide which occupation is being portrayed.

RCA 13   Hats tell the story.

Some jobs require special hats *(sports helmet, miner's hard hat with lights, police caps.).*

As in the preceding activity, dress puppets in special hats, or make a display of hats.

Can members of the class identify the occupation from the hat?

RCA 14   What do they need to know?

Some jobs require people with training in a particular subject. You can classify these as follows: On a bulletin board, place some charts titled: *They Need to Know Math, They Need to Know Science, They Need to Know Geography,* and so on.

Under each heading, list as many occupations as you can.

Keep adding to the charts as members of the class think of other occupations.

RCA 15   Many occupations require special tools.

Make a display of tools. You can include pictures, drawings, or tools you have made from clay.

Identify the jobs that would require these.

RCA 16   Invent a new tool (or machine).

Some inventions have created new industries. Read about Eli Whitney and Elias Howe for examples of these.

Invent a new tool (or machine), and tell what it could do.

RCA 17   Working on an assembly line.

Some jobs require working on *assembly lines;* that is, in large factories products are assembled by each person adding a part as it moves along a line of workers.

You can simulate this in the classroom. Select a product for the class to manufacture, such as a paper bag puppet. Make a model of the puppet. In an assembly line all the finished products look exactly the same, so your puppets will all be copies of the model.

Now accumulate all the parts you will need (bags, buttons for eyes, glue, wool for mustache or hair, and so on). Put these in the center of a table.

Have a group form an *assembly line* around the table. Each person will be responsible for adding only one part to the paper bag as it is passed around the table from one person to the other.

Manufacture six puppets, and time yourselves to see how long that takes.

You can compare this process to manufacturing without an assembly line. Again accumulate all the parts. This time have each person complete an entire puppet by himself or herself. Time the process.

Repeat this with other products (an animal, sailboat).

Can you understand why large factories that produce thousands of the same objects would organize assembly lines?

What are some of the advantages and disadvantages of working on an assembly line? Which do you prefer?

Children work on an assembly line constructing globes. (Courtesy of Westorchard Elementary School, Chappaqua, N. Y.)

ACTIVITIES RCA 18–20: Investigate how people find out about available positions .

RCA 18   How did you find out about your job?

Interview as many working adults as you can. Ask them the above question.

Summarize all the answers secured by you and other members of the class on a page called "Sources of Jobs."

Make this the first page in a booklet in which you will keep information from this and the activities that follow. The booklet might be called: "Finding and Applying for Work."

RCA 19   "Help Wanted."

Available jobs are frequently advertised in "Help Wanted" columns in newspapers.

> CLERK-TYPIST $200
> Must type 60 wpm
> Experienced with figures
>   Caldwell Co.
> Call 717–3600 for appt.

These ads always indicate: Type of job
Skills and experience required
How to apply

They sometimes also include: Name of employer
Salary

Find this information in the sample ad above.

Now try the following:

Working with a group, secure the Help-Wanted columns from your local newspaper. You need only one day's ads.

Note which positions are being advertised and how many of each. Summarize the ads as follows:

Position (Title)	Number of Ads for that Kind of Title	Requirements Stated	Salary (if Noted)

Study your data to determine the following: Which kinds of positions are most frequently advertised? Which appear to require the most training? What are the average weekly, monthly, yearly salaries shown?

RCA 20   What is an employment agency?

Look for advertisements placed by employment agencies in your newspapers. How do they differ from those in Help-Wanted columns?

Find out some advantages and disadvantages of securing a job through an employment agency by interviewing some adults.

Share your information with the class.

ACTIVITIES RCA 21–25: Practice applying for a job.

Learn to complete applications, write résumés, prepare for interviews, and advertise for work.

RCA 21   Complete a job application.

Employers frequently ask that persons applying for a job complete an application. Figure 10.1 illustrates a sample application form.

Pretend you are applying for a position that you could actually hold: newspaper deliverer, baby-sitter, gardener, dog walker, and so on, and complete the application accordingly.

Here are explanations of some of the headings on the form to help you complete the application:

Position desired: Try to be specific. Use actual job title. If you wish a temporary position, state this.

Date Available: Again be specific. If it is a summer job or for after-school hours, note this.

Education: If you have attended more than one school, list all. Just the month and year that you started and finished are sufficient. When listing the school you are now attending, show the starting date, and in the column marked "To," write *Present.*

Job Experience: Any previous job you have held is important. If you have been a dog-walker, plant-sitter, baby-sitter, and so on, include this information. It indicates that you are serious about working.

Hobbies and Interests: Don't assume that your interest in sports, scouting, or music is unimportant. They contribute to making you a well-rounded person. If you play an instrument, make models, or paint, be certain to mention this, too.

Miscellaneous Information: In completing an application, you are asking an employer to choose you for the job instead of someone else. Anything that is special about you should be stated. Here is the place to tell that you are a member of the student government or class president, or that mathematics is your favorite subject.

References: Write the name of three adults who will be willing to say that you should be hired for the job. They should be people who have known you for awhile, but *not* relatives.

A Final Point: Your application must be neat and accurate. Practice writing your answers before you actually put them on the form. Check the spelling of doubtful words.

JOB APPLICATION FORM

Name _____

Address _____

Telephone Number _____ Date of Birth _____

Position Desired   Date Available

Education:
Schools Attended   **From**   **To**

Job Experience
Employer   **Type of Work**   **Dates**

Hobbies and Interests:

Miscellaneous Information:

References:
Name   **Address**   **Occupation**
1.
2.
3.

Figure 10.1 Sample form.

RCA 22   Learn to write a résumé (pronounced rez oo māy).

A résumé is composed by you. It includes similar information to that included on the job application form, but starts with a blank sheet of paper on which you arrange the information. Practice writing one.

RCA 23   Answer a newspaper "Help-Wanted" ad.

Select an ad that you find interesting. Pretend that you are an adult, qualified for the position. Write a fictitious letter applying for it. Decide which qualifications you will need, and include them in your letter.

After you have completed your letter, read it carefully. If the employer receives a great many letters, is there any reason for choosing you? Can you add anything that would call attention to you in a constructive fashion?

Exchange letters with your classmates. In small groups, discuss which letters would be best received. Why?

RCA 24   Write a "Situation-Wanted" ad.

Find the *Situation-Wanted* columns in your newspaper. You will note that people advertise for work.

Think of a job you might like to have on weekends or after school. Draft an ad you might place.

Keep it short. Fifteen words or even less.

Here's an example:

> BABY-SITTER. Sat. nights only.
> Dependable, experienced
> Excellent refs. Call 331–7000

RCA 25   Role-play a job interview.

Have one member of the class role-play an employer and another a job applicant.

The employer should review the applicant's *Job Application Form* or *Résumé* in advance, and questions should be based on these. For example, the employer may say, "I understand you mowed lawns last summer. How many did you mow?" "Or I see you are interested in sports. What do you play?"

The applicant will need to pay attention to the following:

Appearance: You will want to make a good impression. Be dressed neatly and be aware of good posture.
Speech: Answer questions clearly.
At the interview: Be prepared to say why you want the job. Describe any experience that makes you qualified. You may ask questions about working conditions—salary, hours, responsibilities. But give the employer an opportunity to ask questions first.

ACTIVITIES RCA 26–31: Summarize your career information.

RCA 26   Acrobat to zoologist.

Construct a career dictionary. Make a book of large sheets of blank paper held together with ring binders. Letter each page in turn from A to Z.

List as many job titles as you can on each page. Can you find at least one title for each page? Consult the dictionary, newspapers, telephone Yellow Pages, and employment advertisements for suggestions.

Illustrate the pages.

RCA 27   Start a career library.

Have each member of the class research one different career in greater depth. Sources of information include people working in the career, professional associations, labor unions, United States Employment Services.

Write a report on the career you researched. Include:

1. Any special training or traits required.
2. Description of work and chief responsibilities.
3. Working conditions.
4. How is career apt to change in next ten years.
5. Average salary.
6. Reports of interviews with those working at career. (See Occupation Questionnaire and Job Satisfaction Form, Activities RCA 6 and 7).

Accumulate the reports of each of the class members, and file them in a "career library." Keep adding to this library as the class continues to research information.

RCA 28   Dramatize your career library.

An author, Studs Turkel, wrote a play that was produced on Broadway called *Working.* In it characters described their work in skits, song, and dance.

Using your career library for information, have groups of students select a particular career and dramatize it. They can dress for the job (if a uniform is required), act out some of the responsibilities, tell about the important features, and write a song or dance about it.

RCA 29   Add a media section to your library.

Make a filmstrip, slide show, photo essay, or movie describing "A Day in the Life of a . . ." Focus on different careers: teacher, doctor, local officeholder, and so on.

(See Chapter 12 for media directions.)

RCA 30   The vocabulary of careers.

Maintain a dictionary of words related to careers. Include *salary, employer, employee, blue-collar worker, white-collar worker, professional, paraprofessional, skilled worker, unskilled worker, résumé, reference, bonus.*

Add others as you find them.

RCA 31   What do people earn?

In a listing of salaries, some are shown weekly; others, monthly or annually. It is important to be able to compute these so that accurate comparisons of earnings can be made.

To do this, use three different cards. List at least five salaries on each.

Card 1:

If your weekly salary is:	Monthly Salary	Annual Salary
$200		
350		
etc.		

Card 2:

If your monthly salary is:	Weekly	Annual Salary
$1,000		
1,500		
etc.		

Card 3:

If your annual salary is:	Weekly Salary	Monthly Salary
$10,000		
15,000		
etc.		

Now find out the United States minimum hourly wage. (You can call the local office of the United States Department of Labor or a trade union office.) If a person works 40 hours per week, what would be the minimum weekly, monthly, and annual wage?

Here's another problem. If a person worked 45 years at an average salary of $300 per week, what would that person's lifetime earnings be? (Substitute other salaries and periods worked for additional statistics.)

FUTURE STUDIES

Toffler accuses schools of facing "backward" rather than "forward"[5] He claims the curriculum focuses on the past with "a thin sliver of the present. And then time stops. The school is silent about tomorrow. . . . It is as though there were no future."[6] Yet, he argues, "If our children are to adapt more successfully to rapid change, this distortion of time must be ended. We must sensitize them to the possibilities and probabilities of tomorrow. We must enhance their sense of the future."[7] Career education is, in fact, future education; it is education in the "possibilities and probabilities of tomorrow" when children will be ready to assume careers.

TEACHER NOTES

BACKGROUND

Although children may daydream about their adult roles, studies have shown that their future orientation is indeed weak. Asked to draw pictures of themselves in the past, present, and future, children tend to be stymied by the future. Their past and present drawings may be rich in detail, but future depictions are vague. Yet career education relies upon children's ability to project into the future, to envision changes in careers and their own life-styles, and to examine issues that will affect their later lives.

[5]Alvin Toffler, *Future Shock* (New York: Random House, 1970), p. 343.
[6]Ibid., p. 362.
[7]Ibid., p. 363.

Kauffman[8] recommends an "Alternative Futures Approach" to future studies. Since no one can predict what the future will actually be like, knowledge about what is possible rather than certain needs to be explored. Freedom of choice is dependent upon analysis of alternative options. He suggests three steps in *forecasting* the future:

1. Examine the past for trends as a possible basis for what lies ahead.
2. Research expert opinion through articles, books, and interviewing people. A questionnaire can be drafted on a particular topic and distributed to various groups.
3. Assemble the information into a group of potential "scenarios" so that students come to see that there are alternative ways of viewing the future.

Kauffman concludes:

The most important outcome of the alternative futures process is not the set of scenarios, but rather the experience which students gain in a whole way of looking at the future. If, as a result, they acquire the habit of looking ahead, of evaluating alternative possibilities and their consequences, and of trying to find a balance between influencing the future and adapting to it, they will have taken a major step toward gaining better control over their own lives in an uncertain world.[9]

Relating this approach to career education, children first examine careers in the past, note how they have changed in the present, research information about current careers and trends, and then project "potential scenarios" for themselves in the future. The activities that follow first introduce the general topic of future studies and then relate this to future careers.

ACTIVITIES REQUIRING SPECIAL MATERIALS

RFS 3: Two coins.
RFS 4: Dice. Colored disks (or similar objects).
RFS 5: Baby pictures of students.
RFS 7: Old catalog or newspaper.
RFS 8: Suggests survey of neighborhood.
RFS 10 and 11: Interviews with adults.

IMPLEMENTATION

These activities constitute an introduction to future studies. *Futurism* can be incorporated into many curriculum areas: energy, environment, history.

The topic lends itself, too, to creative writing and to teaching probability formulas in mathematics.

EVALUATION

Check:

Graphs: RFS 2, 4.
Records RFS 3, 4.
Reports, drawings, media: RFS 1, 5–7, 9, 10–13.

Look for signs of increased understanding of *future* in the sense described by Kauffman above.

---

[8]Kauffman, op. cit., pp. 11–16.
[9]Ibid., p. 16.

ACTIVITIES ON FUTURE STUDIES

Project into the future: make predictions; study probabilities; note changes.

ACTIVITIES RFS 1–4: Is it probable?

RFS 1 Predicting the future.

Future events can be considered:

Certain
Probable (likely to happen)
Chancy (unpredictable)

Divide a sheet of paper into three columns headed by each of the above. Write your prediction for the following in the appropriate column.

Day of first snowstorm this winter.
Temperature tomorrow at 3:00 P.M.
Outcome of a sports event to be played this weekend.
Day of the week on which your birthday will fall in 1990.

Compare the way you classified these with others in the class. Did all agree? Now add two other predictions to each column.

RFS 2 More predictions.

Which of these do you think will be true by the year 2025?

1. Automobiles will not require gasoline to run.
2. Travel between the earth and the moon will be available for most people.
3. There will be no schools—education will take place in homes with computer instruction, and so on.
4. People will routinely live to be 100 years old.

Compare your predictions with classmates. On what were they based? What information may have aided you in making these?

It is interesting to survey other people to see how they would answer these questions. Summarize their predictions by age. Graph all your results.

RFS 3 Probability and chance.

You will have noted that the outcome of many future events is governed by both probability and chance. For example, in a sports event the team with the better players will generally win (probability), but some unforeseen circumstances may occur, such as a star player becoming ill (chance) to change the result.

Analyze probability and chance further. Toss a coin. Does it land *heads* or *tails?* The result is *chance.* However, if you toss it a large number of times, it is *probable* that an equal number of *heads* and *tails* will appear. The results can be predicted mathematically. The greater the number of tosses, the greater the probability of a particular outcome.

Test this. Toss a coin 100 times, then 200 times. Record the numbers of heads and tails.

RFS 4   More probability exercises.

a.   Organize into teams to do this. Have each team roll a pair of dice 100 or more times and record the totals of the numbers that appear as follows:

Possible Totals	Frequency of Each

(List 2 to 12.)

Now have each team summarize results in a graph. (See illustration.)
   The probability is that *6, 7, 8* will appear more frequently and that *4, 5, 9, 10* will appear more than *2, 3, 11,* or *12.* Can you find an explanation for this?

b.   Place first equal, then unequal, numbers of colored disks in a bag. Predict in each case the probability of a particular color being picked from the bag.

   Here's an interesting statistic: In a group of 24 people, it is likely that two will have the same birthday. To check this you will have to survey a number of groups of 24.

ACTIVITIES RFS 5–9: People change; styles change; neighborhoods and cities change. Sometimes the past is a clue to the future.

RFS 5   How will I look?

   Try to secure a picture of yourself as a baby. Examine yourself closely in a mirror.
   Which features seem to have changed the most?
   How do you think you will look ten years from now? Estimate your height, weight, how you will wear your hair.
   Write about this, or you may draw a picture depicting this.

RFS 6   What will I be doing?

   When thinking about the future, it is obvious that it is easier to predict events that will occur at a near date than farther away. Try the following:

1.   What will I be doing on Saturday one week from today?
2.   What will I be doing on Saturday one month from today?
3.   What will I be doing on Saturday one year from today?
4.   What will I be doing ten years from today?

   Make a class folder for each of the above: a week, a month, a year, ten years. In a week and month, check your predictions for the early dates. Ask the school principal to file the folders for the one year and ten years away. Open the first in a year. Perhaps you can return to the school ten years from now to open the second. In one school, students did this and were surprised at some of the things they had written.

RFS 7   Styles change.

   Try to secure copies of an old Sears-Roebuck or similar catalog or else newspaper advertisements of ten or 20 years ago.
   Analyze the changes in hair styles, clothes, manner of dressing.
   How do you think styles will change ten or 20 years from now?

Draw pictures of the way people will look. You might also wish to make clothes for paper dolls showing your ideas.

RFS 8   Neighborhoods change.

Look for signs of change in your neighborhood: a new building, new sewers, roads, trees. Any changes in the population.

Try to imagine what the neighborhood will look like at some future date. Compare your ideas with others in the class.

RFS 9   Future changes.

List ten important things that you think will be different in the twenty-first century than they are now. You may include anything: family life, education, transportation, energy sources, communication.

Compare your list with others. Summarize the ideas by creating a chart entitled "Life in the Twenty-first Century" as predicted by Class ____.

ACTIVITIES RFS 10–13: Careers in the future.

RFS 10   The changing world of careers—1.

First interview a working adult. Ask how his or her type of job has changed in the past ten (or more) years. Any new equipment? Different settings? Other changes?

Now interview a retired person. Ask what job changes he or she has seen. Report results orally or in writing.

RFS 11   The changing world of careers—2.

Talk to a doctor, nurse, printer. If possible, invite one to the class. Trace how different the job of each is compared with ten, twenty years ago. Summarize the changes.

RFS 12   The changing world of careers—3.

From information gained in Activities RFS 10 and 11, try to project into the future. How will each of the jobs you have discussed above change in the future? For example, can you describe how a doctor might practice medicine at some future date?

RFS 13   The changing world of careers—4.

What new careers will exist in the future that do not now exist? For example: spaceship hostess, rocket driver, laboratory food farmer.

Can you think of five? Make a filmstrip or roller movie illustrating the most interesting.

RESOURCES FOR PART 4

United States Department of Labor
Bureau of Labor Statistics
Occupational Outlook Service
GAO Building
Washington, D.C. 20210

> The United States Department of Labor publishes the *Occupational Outlook Handbook* which lists hundreds of different occupations.

> Reprints relating to specific occupations can be purchased separately at nominal cost. The reprints include: nature of work, job qualifications, advancement prospects, employment outlook, earnings, and working conditions.

> The complete *Handbook* can be obtained from Superintendent of Documents, U.S. Government Printing Office, Washington, D.C. 20402.

Job Information Center
United States Civil Service Commission
1900 E. Street N.W.
Washington, D.C. 20415
> Information on jobs in the federal government

Reading and Writing on the Job by Ruth D. Handel and Eleanor S. Angeles
New York: Scholastic Book Services, 1979
> Contains good background material for a career unit.

New York Life Insurance Co.
Box 51
Madison Square Station
New York, N.Y. 10010
> Publishes a number of individual career booklets.

Contact also local insurance company offices, labor unions, trade associations, chambers of commerce, and local companies for information on careers in community.

THE
CLASSROOM
AS A
PUBLISHING
HOUSE

The sign on the classroom door read, "Pawpaw Publishing Company." When questioned about the name, the children explained. Pawpaw is the colloquial name for the papaya fruit that grows profusely in the West Indies. A Jamaican child, recently admitted to the class, had informed them of this. The students were intrigued with the word and had unanimously voted to adopt it for their publishing company.

This particular class chose different organizational formats every few months. "I continue with my regular curriculum," the teacher stated, "but each format gives the work of the class a special cohesiveness, a special interest. Most important it permits me to emphasize a basic skill. In a *publishing company*, writing is the focus. Previously, we had organized as a consumer bureau, and mathematics was primary. In this period, I find the children writing constantly. They write in their spare time in class; they write at home. They suggest ideas for books; they research material. And because their writing is *published*, there is an added incentive for accuracy in spelling, punctuation and grammar."

Organizing the classroom as a publishing company, as this teacher found, is an excellent format for developing writing skills. It provides *practice, purpose*, and *pleasure* in writing, three factors that contribute to growth in writing ability. It implies a particular concern and respect for children's writing, both individual and collaborative. It requires only that a class' writing culminate in finished work—neatly written, carefully edited, and collected in a bound book or other final form.

OBJECTIVES OF PUBLISHING UNIT

Students will:

- Be motivated to write by having a real purpose for writing.
- Develop an awareness of varied kinds of publications.
- Practice spelling, grammar, and punctuation in context.
- Extend vocabulary.
- Improve reading and math skills.
- Research information about their communities.
- Record oral histories.
- Gain in ability to express themselves in writing prose and poetry.
- Learn interviewing techniques.
- Become acquainted with publishing as an industry.
- Be able to produce quality greeting cards.

CURRICULUM INTEGRATION

Part 5 can be integrated with every area of the curriculum. Students can *publish* books as part of their work in all subjects.

UNIT EXTENSIONS

1. Maintain a permanent publishing center in your classroom. It should contain papers of various sizes and colors, pens, crayons, magic markers for illustrations, dictionaries—both commercial and made by the children. The center should also contain activity cards with directions for poetry

forms (see Chapter 11, Greeting Card Activity PGC 8), story starters and other writing activities. In addition, there should be instructions for bookbinding and the necessary materials, so a child is free to bind any work of which he or she is proud.

2. Introduce a new *publishing* focus each month, such as a class paper or community directory.

11
PUBLISHING: BOOKS, JOURNALS, GREETING CARDS

The publishing company approach to motivating writing has many advantages, as noted in the introduction to this part. To institute this format, consider the following steps:

1. Acquaint children with the work of publishing companies. Have them search for the names of publishers in their books. Categorize them. Which texts or trade books are published by each?
2. Suggest that the class select a name for their company.
3. Schedule election of officers. Instead of a class president, there should be an editor-in-chief, one who is able to review copy and correct spelling and grammatical errors. Other possible jobs are managing editor, news editor, features editor, production manager, business manager, reporters, artists, photographers. The responsibilities of each should be defined in advance.
4. With the company organized, permit the students to select their initial projects. Numerous ones are possible: books—fiction and nonfiction, magazines, catalogs, directories, calendars, greeting cards, newspapers, comics and manuals. It is advisable to select no more than two as classwide concentrations, although individual children will undoubtedly write additional stories and poems for publication.

Throughout this book, there are suggestions for children's writing, both creative and as culminations of their research. In this chapter three additional projects are presented as examples of publishing activities: writing and binding books, cultural journalism, and designing greeting cards.

WRITING BOOKS

TEACHER NOTES

BACKGROUND

Even young children can write books. They can draw pictures and dictate stories to the teacher or another adult. They can write on a theme or relate an experience. These stories may be collected and bound and become the child's *beginning readers*. Because personal stories assure a match between the children's speech and the text they are expected to read, they permit children to make accurate predictions as they read and to feel comfortable with the syntactic structures of the readers. This has been identified as an aid to learning to read.

Older children can write a variety of material. They can publish anthologies of poetry, short stories, or reports, or research material for books of special interest. The books may be made part of the class reading center or be donated to the school library or to other classes. (Younger children enjoy reading books written especially for them by older children.) Some with wider interest may be sold to the people in the school or community. The bound books may also be presented as gifts for special occasions—Mother's Day, Father's Day, birthdays.

ACTIVITIES REQUIRING SPECIAL MATERIALS

PWB 15: See requirements for bookbinding.

IMPLEMENTATION

Before starting this topic, aid the students to understand the organization of a book. Suggest that they analyze books—page by page, noting the title page, placement of author's name and publisher, copyright information, table of contents.

Students should be encouraged to plan the format and layouts of their books in advance. This will require attention to the following:

Size and Shape   Encourage experimenting with different formats for books. For example, size and shape may reflect the contents. A tall book (about 10 inches by 5 inches) may be appropriate for Paul Bunyan tales; small books (7 inches by 5 inches) or wide ones (6 inches by 8 inches) for personal stories. Books can also be in the shapes of fish or animals, such as snakes, dogs, lions; or objects, such as trains or houses. When using odd shapes most of the left-hand margin should be kept in a straight line. This will make it easier to bind the book later.

Paper   Supply various colors of paper and ink. The inside pages need not all be in the same color. Colors can express the mood of the text: dark papers for *spooky* stories, blue paper for sad stories, and brown and orange for autumn tales. Different paper and ink combinations, such as white ink on black paper can be effective.

Layout   The first page of the book should have the title, author, year of publication, and name of publishing company. A dedication page and a table of contents may follow.

Authors should decide how much copy each of the other pages will contain, where the illustrations will appear, and whether the pages will be framed. A border of a straight line, block of color, repetitive geometric pattern, or miniature design can be drawn around each page. Leave a margin of at least 1¼ inches on the left side of the pages to facilitate binding.

Illustrations   Illustrations can match the text or be mood pieces to enhance the atmosphere. They may be incorporated into the text or appear on separate pages. They may be drawn by the author or a collaborating "artist." Where illustrations are on the same pages as the text, the placement of them should be varied.

Type Face   Some books will be improved if they can by typed. Others can be satisfactorily completed in the children's own writing. The appearance of the book can be perked up by varying the formation of initial letters. These can be enlarged, written in a different color, or *illuminated*. Illuminated lettering was used in handwritten manuscripts years ago. Some are truly works of art. They are most commonly made by decorating the inside of capital letters with patterns or designs or by setting the initial letter into a background design. Many libraries have examples of early manuscripts that include illuminated lettering.[1] (See illustration.)

EXTENSION: PUBLISHING CHILDREN'S WRITING

If a child has written a piece of exceptional quality, consider submitting it to a newspaper or magazine. Submissions should be neatly typed and include name, address and age of author. Send them to one publication at a time. A copy should be kept by the author as some publishers will not return material because of the large number received. To avoid disappointment, children should be aware that each publisher receives a tremendous volume of contributions and can only accept a few. The chances of any one piece being printed are slight.

The following publications have indicated that they will accept contributions from children subject to the specifications noted. Some local newspapers and magazines may also do so.

Publication	Publisher
Child Life. Short stories (up to 600 words), poetry, jokes, art	The Saturday Evening Post Youth Publications 1100 Waterway Boulevard P.O. Box 567B Indianapolis, Indiana 46206
Jack and Jill. For children ages 8 to 12. Stories and articles (no longer than 500 words), poetry, letters, art.	
Children's Playmate. For children ages 5 to 8. Poetry, jokes and riddles.	
Cricket. Stories (200 to 2000 words) articles (200 to 1500 words) poems (no longer than 100 lines)	Cricket P.O. Box 100 La Salle, Illinois 61301
Know Your World Extra. Will accept only jokes.	Xerox Education Publications 245 Long Hill Road Middletown, Connecticut 06457
Highlights. Original stories, poems, and drawings. A note must be included from parent, guardian or teacher stating that work is original. Drawings must be in black on white paper. Also riddles and jokes. These need not be original. Will also publish a story starter or unfinished story several times a year and publish responses.	Highlights for Children 803 Church Street Honesdale, Pennsylvania 18431

EVALUATION

The initial step in evaluation of children's writing should be completed by the children themselves—self-evaluation. Teachers should insist that children

[1]See also Carol B. Grafton, ed., *Historic Alphabets and Initials* (New York: Dover Publications, 1977). Contains examples of decorative letters.

proofread their work. To facilitate this, post a checklist with questions for the children to answer as they proofread.

SELF-EVALUATION

Have I checked the spelling of unfamiliar words?
Have I used complete sentences, paragraphs where necessary?
Have I varied the forms of the sentences?
Should I insert colorful adjectives?
Did I punctuate correctly?
About the content:
   Do I have an interesting beginning?
   Is my story well-developed?
   Is the plot clear?
   Does my story end at a proper point?

If the story is to be rewritten for publication, it may not be necessary for the child to rewrite it at this point, just to indicate corrections.

Teacher evaluation will consist of two aspects: technical (grammar, spelling, and punctuation) and contents. In some instances, it may be advantageous to have the teacher's reactions on a separate form rather than on the child's paper. Forms for this purpose can be prepared in advance. They will contain the following headings with space for notations under each:

Overall Comments
   When possible, a positive reaction should be included, such as "I like main idea."
Areas of Possible Improvement
   Sentences that are unclear; structure repetitive.
   Form, character development, style, language, use of modifiers.
Techniques Requiring More Attention
   Spelling (note key words misspelled).
   Grammar.
   Punctuation.

ACTIVITIES ON WRITING BOOKS

Be authors: Write and then bind your books. The books can be written by individual students or be collaborative efforts.

ACTIVITIES PWB 1–14: Here are fourteen book ideas to get you started.

PWB 1   Write mystery stories.

Organize a mystery story workshop.

First you will need a fictional detective. Have the class invent one. Decide sex, age, name, description, personality, style of solving problems.

Now you will need to create adventures for your detective. Again you may do this collaboratively, or members of the class may write complete sequences.

Before you start:

Analyze mystery stories. Read the first pages of as many as you can. How does the author set the mood? You might practice writing first pages.

Note the author's techniques for maintaining suspense, for providing clues.

Outline your plot. Is the story interesting? Is your solution plausible? Have you given your readers all the clues available to the detective? Was the ending obvious?

You should now be ready to write your stories.

PWB 2   Invent superhuman characters.

Write of the adventures of: "Superant," "The Bionic Child," or one class' character, "The Incredible Bulk."

Read about Paul Bunyan and his giant blue ox, Babe.

Write your own *tall tales*.

PWB 3   Write fables.

a.   Read *Just So Stories* by Rudyard Kipling for examples.

Now write how the elephant got its trunk, the zebra its stripes, the camel its hump, the kangaroo its pouch. Invent more of these: how trees came to lose their leaves in winter, bears decided to hibernate, spiders developed eight legs (instead of the six common to insects).

b.   Now read about a different kind of fable—one that teaches a lesson—by reading *Aesop's Fables*. Aesop was a Greek slave who explained people's actions by telling stories about animals. His stories always ended with a lesson. Imitate Aesop in your writing.

Write fables to illustrate a proverb, such as:

The grass is always greener on the other side of the fence.
A bird in the hand is worth two in the bush.
Slow but steady wins the race.

PWB 4   Be biographers, autobiographers.

Compose a class book of autobiographies.

Or write a biography of a famous person. Research the life of the person, and select an incident to describe.

Or write a biography of a parent, a grandparent, someone in the community, a friend.

PWB 5   Compile sensory books.

a.   Write of strange and familiar smells.

Write of the times you have smelled cookies baking, perfume, hair spray, gasoline.

Or have a bag with garlic, onion, mothballs. Reach in and smell one. What comes to mind?

b.   Write of strange sounds and sights.

Write of scary ones, happy ones, distorted ones, puzzling ones, unexpected ones, silly ones—and of purple grass, yellow cows. . . .

c. Write about feelings.

How does it feel to walk in the rain?
To stand in the wind?
To lie in the sun?

d. Paste different fabrics in your book: corduroy, silk, velvet, burlap. Close your eyes, touch them, and write how they feel and of what they remind you.

PWB 6   Publish a book of hobbies.

Survey members of the school, including teachers and all other adults. You may either personally interview them or send letters requesting information about hobbies or collections.

(An exhibit of "unusual collections" at one school included yogurt tops, matchbook covers, chopsticks, bottle caps.)

Describe the most interesting hobbies or collections in your hobby book.

Consider, too, sponsoring a hobby fair at which collections can be displayed and your book distributed or sold to cover expenses.

PWB 7   Publish a calendar with novel information.

In which month do the swallows return to Capistrano? Which month is National Peanut month? In which month was Harriet Tubman born? The answer to each of these is "March."

Research information about other months. (The encyclopedia lists key events under each month.)

Or write a story related to each month. In January, write about a snowstorm, in February, about the ground hog or Washington or Lincoln. Collate the stories into a "literary calendar."

PWB 8   Publish a book of names.

What is the most common first name, last name in school?

What is the most common first name of parents, grandparents? Note how "styles" in names change.

What is the origin of different names?

Include anecdotes as to why a particular first name was chosen.

PWB 9   Publish an art book.

Paint in the style of a noted artist—Van Gogh, Seurat, Mondrian.
Write a short introduction about the artist and include paintings.

PWB 10   Publish a comic book.

Design a comic book character. Write a series of comic strips.
Learn images used by comic writers.

PWB 11   Publish a holiday book.

Select a holiday—New Year's Day, Christmas.
Research how this is observed around the world.
Research other holidays in the encyclopedia.

Also write to the Cultural Affairs Officers of foreign embassies for information about unusual celebrations in their countries, such as, Children's Days in Japan. (The United Nations publishes a booklet about many of these.)

PWB 12   Organize a children's literature workshop.[2]

(In this activity, older children will write books for those in younger grades.) Examine picture books from your school library.

Note that many rhyme. Note the vocabulary, style of writing, simplicity of plot.

Write a children's book for a younger class. Or have different members of the class select specific children in younger grades. Write books specially for them, using their names in the stories.

PWB 13   Publish a community directory.

Research the stores, libraries, banks, industries in your community. Here's how it was done in one school.

The Doherty Elementary School in Andover, Massachusetts, published a community directory entitled *The Yellow Pages of Doherty.* Children of all grades collaborated in the project with the cooperation of the school Parent-Teachers Association.[3]

Each child accepted an assignment to visit a neighborhood site. Parents accompanied and supervised the children during their visit. At each visit, the children interviewed the owner or responsible employee and asked about the work of the organization and any interesting facts.

The children then wrote reports about their visits. Parents helped compile, print, and distribute the finished book. (See Figure 11.1 for a sample directory page.)

PWB 14   Research the history of the school.

When was it built? What was previously on the site? How was the name determined? What is its significance? Who was the first principal? Are there any well-known graduates?

Interview the principal, graduates, and school board members for information.

Compile your facts in a bound booklet for presentation to the school library.

ACTIVITY PWB 15: Learn to bind books in the classroom.

Each of the books described in the preceding pages may be bound in the classroom. (You will find the process easy to follow. Since it does not require pages to be stitched in advance; individual pages can be corrected before binding.)

---

[2]This is an excellent activity for older children with reading difficulties, permitting them to read and write easy books.

[3]It is interesting to note two of the goals of the project described by Lois Haslam, Doherty School principal: (1) to apply "the basic curriculum skills to a learning situation not bound by the parameters of a school building" and (2) to enable parents to "share a strong mutual responsibility with teachers for both the selection and implementation of an educational project."

Towne Deli

500 people eat at the Deli every day.

Food comes from 30 distributors.

The owner makes all the pies himself.

They use left-over ham for salads.

They make the "Lee" famous sandwich.

The Board of Health wrote a letter saying that they were the cleanest place in town.

—Grade 2

Tax Collector

The tax collector has two jobs, tax collector and treasurer. He does not travel much. He works from 8:30 to 4:30 on weekdays. He likes every part of his job, collecting money, and seeing people. There's nothing bad about it. He is very busy and doesn't have much slack time. A man named Dick Bowen hired him. He started this job in 1966. Five people work for him. He hired 3 people and 2 were already there. He said this was his best job and he loves it.

Grade 5

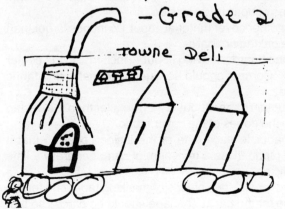

Figure 11.1 Sample Page from "The Yellow Pages of Doherty." (Excerpts from "The Yellow Pages of Doherty," published by students at Doherty School, Andover, Mass. Reprinted with permission.)

PWB 15.   Instructions for bookbinding.

You will need:

Cover material: Either fabric or contact paper
Masking tape
Oaktag or cardboard
Construction paper
Rubber cement or glue
Scissors
Stapler
Pages to be bound

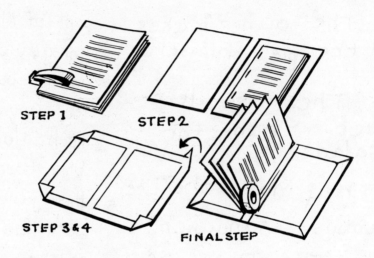

STEP 1   STEP 2

STEP 3 & 4   FINAL STEP

To proceed:

1. Staple inside pages together down the left-hand side, about ¼ inch from the edge.
2. Cut two pieces of oaktag or cardboard, ¼ inch larger than the inside pages. Lay the two pieces of board side by side.
3. Cut one piece of fabric or other cover material about 1½ inches larger than the combined size of the oaktag or boards.
4. Glue the cover fabric to the boards, leaving about ¼ inch free in the center for the spine of the book. Corners should be glued diagonally, and fabric turned up around boards.
5. Cut two pieces of construction paper about ¼ inch smaller than the oaktag but large enough to hide the edges of the cover fabric.
6. Glue the construction paper to each side of the inside cover so that it masks the edges of the fabric. (Use a minimum of glue; generally a little around the edges is sufficient.)
7. Attach inside pages to cover with two pieces of masking tape, one for the front of the book and one for the back. The tape should be placed so that part of it covers the staples of the inside pages and the other covers the edge of the construction paper.

CULTURAL JOURNALISM

TEACHER NOTES

BACKGROUND

In communities throughout the country, children are acting as "historians" recording the culture, roots, folklore, and history of their areas that might otherwise remain unnoted. The concept originated in a rural area of northeast Georgia where the first magazine devoted to cultural journalism, *Foxfire*, was published back in 1967. *Foxfire* now has subscribers throughout the country and books devoted to its methods.[4] It has spawned cultural journals in many other schools.

Whereas many of the journals are slick, printed, quite expensive publications, unpretentious projects have also been produced by children at all grade levels. They serve as a bridge to the past, aiding children to gain an appreciation of their own and others' cultural heritage. They also reinforce language skills as children interview, listen, speak, identify main ideas and write for publication. A cultural journalism project requires identifying older residents and those with unique backgrounds in the community, interviewing them, and reporting their stories.

Students inquire about earliest memories, childhood experiences, when the people arrived in the community. They ask what the community was like in those days, about shopping facilities, transportation, food, occupations, salaries, and hobbies. They are also interested in legends, superstitions, home remedies, anecdotes, ethnic customs, rites associated with courtship, marriage, and birth of children. They explore games, chants, rhymes, crafts, and popular songs.

The publication may focus on just one of these aspects or on a few. Much will depend on the age of the children. For example, a class of seven-year-olds published a history of transportation based on interviews. Older children have published slick magazines that were living histories of their communities and were sold. A cultural journalism project can be a real service to a community, and provide children with an appreciation for different cultures, their own roots, and an identity with the past. This has been the experience of those who have attempted such projects.

A magazine titled *Lagniappe* (an old Louisiana French term meaning "something extra") is published by fourth grade children at Chamberlin Elementary School, Port Allen, Louisiana. The heritage of the children is mostly Afro-American and Cajun French. The school's racial mix is 60 percent black, 40 percent white. Tom Arceneaux, the class teacher, describes the mix: "We have the black culture and the Acadian culture. We have an Italian and we just got a Yankee, a little girl from New York." "The importance of *Lagniappe*," he adds, "is that each child is made to feel its culture and heritage are important."[5] The magazine includes stories about cooking local dishes, catching, cleaning and cooking frogs, old-fashioned playthings, home activities (butter-making, quilting, soap-making), school life, ghost stories, and home cures. The children conduct most of their interviews on tape.

[4]For more information on publishing a journal such as *Foxfire*, see Pamela Wood, *You and Aunt Arie* (Nederland, Col.: IDEAS. 1975).
[5]Interview with Tom Arceneaux. *Sunday Advocate* (Baton Rouge, La., December 10, 1978), p. 6B.

Each step in developing a cultural journal is described in the activities that follow.

ACTIVITIES REQUIRING SPECIAL MATERIALS

PCJ 3 and 4: Tape-recorder may be desirable.

IMPLEMENTATION

Interviews may be conducted with parents and grandparents, asking each about their memories of their own parents and grandparents; or with people in the community. People can be invited to come to the classroom or in some cases actually visited by students (parents' help is required for transportation). Where a personal interview is too difficult to arrange, it may be possible to send a blank tape with written questions so that a person's answers can be recorded.

EXTENSION

Activities PCJ 6 and 7 may be viewed as an extension of cultural journalism projects or can be completed independently.

EVALUATION

Evaluation will be based on written material and also children's ability to conduct interviews, research information, and transcribe data.

ACTIVITIES ON CULTURAL JOURNALISM

You will learn to be an *historian,* to interview people about the past, and to publish their stories. Here is the procedure.

ACTIVITIES PCJ 1–5: Publishing a cultural history.

PCG 1   Identify your topics.

Decide what particular aspect of the past you wish to investigate. You may concentrate on one theme or select a few.
Possible topics:

School: What it was like, size and composition of class, organization of the
day, subjects studied, discipline, homework, hours, teachers.
Games
Superstitions and beliefs
Transportation
Holidays: how celebrations differed
Family customs
Responsibilities
Leisure time activities
Work

Local food: how prepared
Home remedies
Dating, courtship, marriage

Or more general topics:

Recollections of the past
The community in bygone days
Key events in people's lives
Earliest memories
Arrival in the community

PCJ 2 Identify your sources.

Compile a list of people to interview:

Relatives: parents, grandparents, great-grandparents, oldest living relative.

Community residents: older people living in the community. If there is a nursing home in the community, it might be possible to write a letter inquiring whether a resident at the home would agree to be interviewed. There may be members of an historical society or other community residents who would have information.

PCJ 3 Prepare for the interview.

a. Determine where the interviews will take place.

1. In school: people may agree to come to class.
2. In yours or a relative's home.
3. At resident's home.

You will need to arrange for transportation to bring the person to class or the students to the interview. Are there parents available to help?

b. Decide whether you will tape the interview. This may help you remember what was said, but you will need permission in advance.

c. Draw up a list of questions in advance. Here are some that have been used:

1. What were times like when you were a child?
2. What kinds of things did you do when you were a child?
3. What did you like to do most?
4. What was school like?
5. Did you have dates?
6. How did you meet your husband or wife?
7. How is life different today?
8. What is the most important change you have seen?
9. What advice would you give young people today?

If you are concentrating on a specific theme, you will also need to include questions relating to it.

d. Distribute assignments. Some interviews will be completed individually; others, particularly if they entail a visit to a person, may be in teams. Be certain team responsibilities are clear. Who will take notes, ask questions, take pictures (if any)?

e. Practice interviewing classmates.

PCJ 4   At the interview—five rules.

1. Listen! Let the person talk.
2. Don't stick to your original questions if something more interesting is discussed.
3. Be prepared with some key phrases if the person is relating an experience: *How did that happen? When was that?*
4. Think about that person. How would you describe her or him to a friend?
5. At the conclusion, be certain to thank the person for participating.

PCJ 5   Writing the information.

The interviews may result in individual books (see Figure 11.2) or in a class collection.

Each person will have to write the report of his or her interview. Young children may dictate a report to their parents or teacher.

In writing the story, try to tell it in the person's own words, as in these excerpts:

Interview with Carla Lugo Parkinson

One of the family traits was compassion. They were just very trusting. They trusted everybody, and were very generous. When somebody came to my grandfather with a sad story that they had a family and they didn't have any money or any place to live and they didn't know what they were going to do, he would say, "I'll give you a piece of my property. We'll go and build you a little house and I'll give you a few head of cattle and some grain." We would set them up; he was doing that all the time. . . . Another family trait is that we live to be very old. Also, the men don't lose their hair.[6]

The following is in a different style:

Interview with Goldie Hickox on the topic of Boyfriends and Fun

I declare! Boyfriends! When the boys went to see you, they'd come right there in my daddy's house. They didn't get out in automobiles and go off. Course in them days there weren't no cars no how. But we had different ways of having fun. Yeah, we had cane grindings. . . . We had candy pulls. We'd boil candy at the syrup boil. Then they'd gather up, just the young folks and pull that taffy and enjoy yourself. And we'd play games. . . . [7]

Exploring Ethnic Heritage

Sixth graders in a school in Valley Stream, Long Island, collaborated on a project that first was displayed in a "Museum of Ethnic Heritage" they organized at their own school and later shown at the American Museum of Immigration at the base of the Statue of Liberty. The project was originally part of a social studies unit on social organizations, but later involved all areas of the curriculum. The students started by exploring their own backgrounds to find out from where their ancesters came. Forty-two percent of the children were of Italian heritage. The students learned that the original immigrants had arrived in the United States at Ellis Island.

[6]Excerpt from interview by Suva Intermediate School students, Bell Gardens, Cal., published in *Long, Long Ago,* Spring, 1979, p. 3. Michael Brooks, advisor.
[7]Excerpt from interview by Ken Trowbridge, Lynn Roberson, Jay Kaufman and Kay Gayner, published in *Ebbtide,* Frederica Academy, St. Simons Island, Ga., Winter 1979, p. 7. Bill Coursey and Jim Wardlow, advisors.

The children had to
sweep the floors.
The children had to
shovel the snow.

The children had to help do hard work.
They had to carry wood for the stove.
They had to carry water into the
school.

Figure 11.2 Kindergarten children dictated and illustrated these stories following a visit to the class by a retired teacher. Stories became part of a bound book, *School in the Old Days.* (Courtesy James Harris, Thomas Jefferson Elementary School, Wausau School District, Wausau, Wisconsin)

Sometimes the school was dark inside.
They didn't have electric lights.

Her school did not have a heater. They had an old stove.
The school was always cold.

The project soon developed into a study of immigration to the United States, a history of Ellis Island, and of the Statue of Liberty. Extensive research was conducted and portrayed.

The class made graphs indicating statistics on immigration, read and wrote reports on Ellis Island and interviewed elderly relatives. From their accounts, they wrote diaries as they might have been kept by the immigrants, and published a mock newspaper of 1886, the year the statue was dedicated. In addition, they painted a mural, made a quilt, and created a 1900s diorama of the Lower East Side in New York, where many of the immigrants had lived. The exhibit they prepared also included memorabilia loaned to them by the immigrants.

Although the cultural journalism projects described in PCJ 1 to PCJ 5 also explore ethnic heritage, the following two, PCJ 6 and 7, focus more specifically on this topic.

ACTIVITIES PCJ 6–7: Digging into roots.

PCJ 6 Who am I?

Fill in your own family tree. Note the sample of a completed one on the next page (Figure 11.3). Interview your parents and grandparents, and see how far back you can go.

Find out all you can about your ancestors. What were they like? Where did they live? When were they married? How many children did they have? What was their work?

PCJ 7 Who lives in this community?

Investigate the ethnic background of the people in your community. Are there newly arrived immigrants? Where did they come from? How did they get to the community?

Try to arrange to interview them.

You might wish to publish information about immigration as the Valley Stream students did.

GREETING CARDS

Quality greeting cards can be produced in a classroom; cards that will be appreciated more than commercial ones because they are made personally.

TEACHER NOTES

BACKGROUND

Children who learn to make cards acquire a valuable skill. Sending a card for an appropriate occasion—a birthday, an anniversary, or as a "thank-you" for a gift—represents an act of thoughtfulness that is much appreciated. Yet the cost of commercial greeting cards makes this gesture difficult for young children. They can avoid the expense by making their own cards. Designing greeting cards can be a legitimate classroom activity.

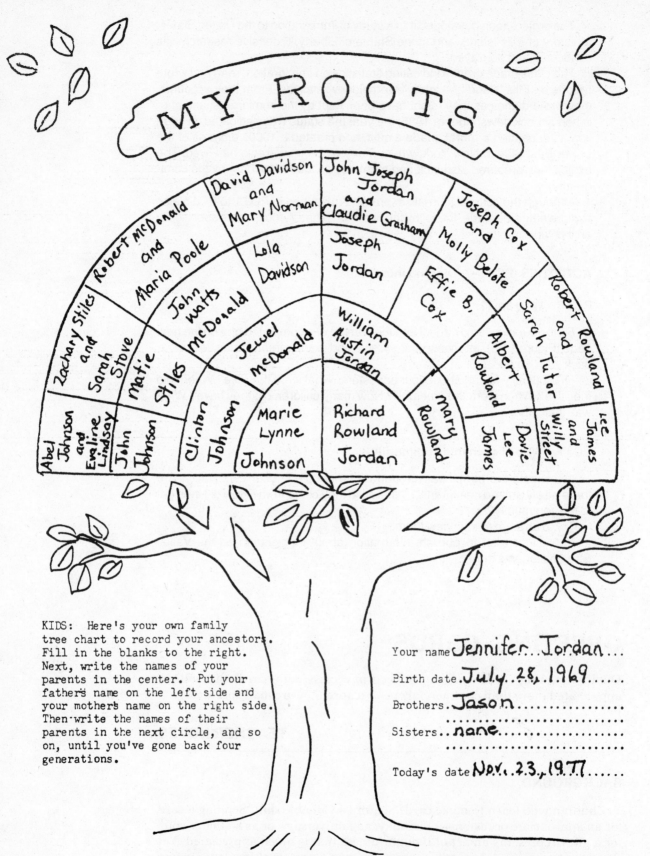

MY ROOTS

KIDS: Here's your own family tree chart to record your ancestors. Fill in the blanks to the right. Next, write the names of your parents in the center. Put your father's name on the left side and your mother's name on the right side. Then write the names of their parents in the next circle, and so on, until you've gone back four generations.

Your name Jennifer Jordan
Birth date July 28, 1969
Brothers Jason
Sisters none
Today's date Nov. 23, 1977

Figure 11.3 Sample Family Tree. (Reprinted from "Activities for a Study of Our Community and Its Past," published by Third Grade Students of Chickamauga Elementary School, Chickamauga, Georgia.)

Academically, the process has many benefits. Since greeting card messages are frequently written in short poems, they are an excellent stimulus for poetry writing, permitting children to follow structured forms. These can be helpful to children who have limited experience writing poetry. Further, if the cards are sold, practice in mathematics results. This section includes instruction for designing and selling cards and poetry forms.

ACTIVITIES REQUIRING SPECIAL MATERIALS

PGC 1–7, PGC 10: Paper in different colors. A 20-lb. bond paper is superior to construction paper for cards.

Art supplies: Glue, paint, also natural objects, felt, burlap, wire (see individual activities for details).

PGC 2: Flowers, grass or leaves, newspaper, heavy book.

PGC 4: Bright light (as from filmstrip projector).

IMPLEMENTATION

Have the children collect old greeting cards. Classify them by theme: invitation, holiday, get well, thank you, and so on, and also by message: humorous, sentimental, general.

Discuss the formats: which appear to be most attractive and the attributes of each.

Practice making some cards with the class. After that most children can work independently.

EXTENSION

Consider a permanent greeting card center in the classroom where children can work independently to make greeting cards in free time.

Encourage cards for a classmate's birthday or illness and special occasions—birth of a brother or sister.

EVALUATION

Quality of cards will depend on maturity and ability of youngsters.

ACTIVITIES ON GREETING CARDS

Design greeting cards and write messages. Consider selling your cards.

ACTIVITIES PGC 1–7: Cards for all occasions.

PGC 1 Start with an interesting shape.

Try miniature cards with a tiny pressed flower and an appropriate message, such as "Enormous wishes come with this tiny card."

Fold the card accordion style or as a house; doors can open for the message.

Consider the shape of a Christmas tree, Hanukkah menorah, a heart for Valentine's Day, flower petals, or an animal.

PGC 2 Pressed flower cards.

Pressed flowers add a lovely, delicate touch to a card. Paste them to the front; outline with a geometric pattern (see illustration), and that is all the decoration you need.

You can also make note cards or note paper by adding a pressed flower to small cards.

To make pressed flowers, you will need:

Flowers (whole or petals), grass or leaves
Newspaper
Heavy book

To proceed:

1. Gather material for pressing. Petals of a flower or single blossoms with a stem may be used. They should not be thick.
2. If possible, gather plants during a sunny day so they will be dry.
3. Before pressing, arrange the plant as you wish it to look when dry. You will not be able to change the shape later.
4. Lay the plant flat between eight thicknesses of newspaper—four below and four above.
5. Place the newspaper into the middle of a heavy book. You may add a few books on top for more pressure.
6. Check the plant daily. If the newspaper is damp, gently move the plant to dry paper.
7. The flower should be dry in about a week.
8. Remove the pressed flower and glue onto the front of the card. Pressed flowers break easily. Handle them carefully.

PGC 3 More unusual covers.

a. Print the cover.
   Sponges, vegetables, linoleum, corrugated paper—any object with a natural design or upon which a design can be etched can be used for printing. Dip into water color and press onto the card.
   Try leaf prints: They can be made by tracing—lightly rubbing crayon on a piece of thin paper placed over the leaf, spatter printing with a small sponge or toothbrush around a leaf resting on paper, pressing carbon paper onto the underside of the leaf, or lightly painting the back oi the leaf with shoe polish or water color and then transferring the design to paper.
b. Etch a design.
   Lightly sketch a design on the outside of the card; then outline it with glue. Sprinkle soap flakes, coffee grounds, jello powder, birdseed, almost any object onto the glue. Shake off excess. Objects will stick to the glue for an interesting effect. For winter season, soap flakes or absorbent cotton will create the image of snow.
c. The print can be framed by cutting a window in the cover of the card, leaving a border of about ¾ inch all around. Use the cutout piece for your design. Replace this piece by pasting a sheet of paper the same size as the front of the card onto the back to hold it in place.

PGC 4 Silhouette faces.

Silhouettes can be produced by placing a piece of black construction paper on a dark wall or blackboard.

Have a child sit sideways in front of the paper, and shine a light (such as one from a filmstrip projector) onto the child's profile. Another child traces around the outline with white chalk.

Cut out the silhouette, and mount for a personalized greeting card.

PGC 5   Banner cards.

Sew a message in felt or other fabric onto a piece of burlap. Staple the burlap to a dowel or stick to which string has been attached for hanging.

Roll up the banner and present.

PGC 6   Roller movie cards.

A roller movie in a small box, such as one used for jewelry, makes an interesting card.

Make small holes in the sides of the box about ½ inch from top and bottom. Insert toothpicks or small sticks through the holes.

Draw a message and roll it onto the toothpicks.

PGC 7   Figures as cards.

Figures may be made of wire, papier-mâché, or decorated boxes.

The figure should carry a small piece of paper with the greeting, or it should be painted on.

ACTIVITIES PGC 8–9: Write messages in poetry and prose.

Note that a poem on your card need not refer to a specific occasion. It may celebrate nature, a season, or just express a mood. Inclusion cf the poem will add a touch of beauty to your card.

PGC 8   Forms of poetry[8]

a.   Couplets and triplets. As suggested by the title, couplets are two-line poems that rhyme; triplets three-line poems that rhyme.

> *First Snow*
> Snow makes whiteness where it falls
> The bushes look like popcorn balls.
>> Stacy Pieper
>> Grade 5

> *Birthday*
> Know you had a birthday due
> So here's a wish just for you.
> Hope that all your dreams come true.

b.   Quatrains are four lines with an *abab* pattern

> *Spring*
> Spring is time to jump and shout
> The trees wish they could hop
> And flowers pop up bright and stout
> I want to spin, like a top.
>> Maura Martin
>> Grade 4

[8]All the signed poems on this and the following pages were written by children at the Rushmore Elementary School, Carle Place, N.Y.

c. Limericks have five lines with the rhyming pattern *aabba.* Lines three and four are shorter than the others.

> *New Year's Resolution*
> There once was a terrible lad
> Who vowed he'd no longer be bad
> He'd try every way
> To do a good deed a day
> But alas he was too much a cad.

d. Cinquains are also five-line poems but require no rhyming.

First line: one word title
Second line: two words describing the title
Third line: three words describing action associated with the title
Fourth line: four words or a phrase expressing feelings about the title
Fifth line: one word synonym or reference to the title

> *March 17th*
> Green
> Soda bread
> Saint Patrick, shamrock
> Four leaf clover, shillelah
> Irish
>> Meredith Miller
>> Grade 3

> *Spring*
> Spring
> Flowers, children
> Blooming, growing, laughing
> Carefree days go by
> Life.

e. Haiku and senryu are Japanese poems similar in form, but haiku refers to nature whereas senryu utilizes other topics. They are three lines each, totaling seventeen syllables: the first and third lines contain five syllables, the second, seven.

Haiku: The warm sun shines down
            It soothes the plants and flowers
            Like a kind mother.

Senryu: Isolated soul
            All alone on the desert
            Never to come back
                        Peter McEntegart
                        Grade 5

f. Tanka is similar to haiku but adds two more lines for a total of five. The syllable pattern is 5, 7, 5, 7, 7. None of the lines rhyme.

> Silent mother bird
> Giving her babies some food
> Feathers glistening
> Against the dew-dropped straw nest
> Forming a radiant sight.
>> Peter McEntegart
>> Grade 5

g. Acrostics are poems in which the first letter of each line when read vertically spells a word.

The Desert	*Mom*
Dried and hot	Multitude of moods
Echoing with sand	Offering love, help, care
Scorched and sunburnt	Murmuring support.
Everlasting heat	
Rain at last	
The sun will come again.	
Beth Lellis	
Grade 4	

h. *Up and down* poems start with one word; the second line has two words; the third, three; the fourth, four; the fifth; three; the sixth, two; and the seventh, one again.

Seasons
Winter
North winds
Blowing, raining, snowing
Oh cool breezy weather
Getting warmer soon
Arriving softly
Spring.
Gina Schroeder
Grade 4

i. Concrete poetry is poetry written in a design.

The City
Tall
Buildings
People
Climbing
Up the
Stairs.
Children
Peering
From the
Windows.
Tene-
ment.

PGC 9 Other card messages.

a. Repeat a greeting such as "Happy Birthday," "Merry Christmas," or "Thank You" in different languages.
Here are some translations of "Merry Christmas."

Spanish: *Feliz Navidad*
Italian: *Buon Natale*
French: *Joyeux Nöel*
German: *Frohliche Weinachten*
Greek: *Kala Christougenna*

b. Try cutting slogans from newspapers or magazines.
Slogans can be clipped and inspire messages. Children may paste one

on the outside of a card, and then complete the message inside. (For example, cut out "I Love New York," then add "but I love having you as a friend more.")

c. Consider similes and metaphors.
Birthdays are . . . Mothers Are . . . Fathers Are . . . Christmas is like . . . Having you as a friend is like . . . .

ACTIVITY PGC 10: Prepare envelopes for greeting cards.

PGC 10 Envelope instructions.

Envelopes may be of the same color paper as the card or of another.
To prepare:

Place the card with the longest dimension resting horizontally, on a piece of paper that is about 2 inches wider and one-and-a-half times longer than the card.
Fold the sides of the paper over the card.
Fold up the bottom of paper to the top of the card.
Fold the top of paper down to about one-half of the card.
Cut side folds on the bottom and top of the card (areas marked *x* in diagram).
Paste envelope together.
Top flap may be curved.
Outside of envelope may be decorated.

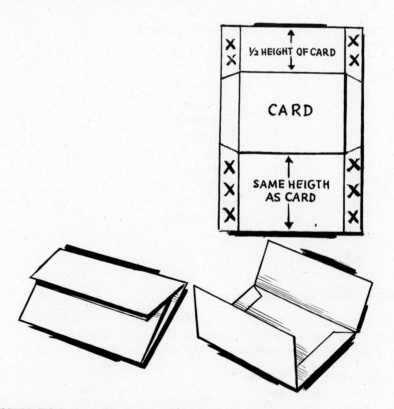

ACTIVITY PGC 10: Selling greeting cards.

PGC 10 Sell your cards.

Consider selling to people in the school or community in order to cover the expenses of making the cards.

First establish a "quality control" committee to approve items for sale and help set a price.

Sales may be made once a week at a specific time of day.

Cards may be displayed at PTA committee or general membership meetings. Orders may be taken for cards.

Receipts should be prepared in duplicate for each purchase, one to the customer and one for class records.

The class should decide on a worthwhile purpose for any profits.

RESOURCES FOR PART 5

Cummings, Richard, *Make Your Own Comics,* New York: Henry Z. Walck, 1976.

Bennett, Charles, Gerald Taylor, and Peggy Yatabe, *Make Your Own Greeting Card Book.* Los Angeles, Cal: J. P. Tarcher, 1977.

FOR CULTURAL JOURNALISM

Wigginton, Eliot, (ed.), *The Foxfire Books.* New York: Doubleday.

Wigginton, Eliot, *Moments: The Foxfire Experience.* Nederland, Col: IDEAS.

Wood, Pamela, *You and Aunt Arie.* Nederland, Col.: IDEAS, 1975.

Write to:

National Genealogy Society
1921 Sunderland Place, N.W.
Washington, D.C. 20036
     Request brochure: "Suggestions for Beginners in Genealogy."

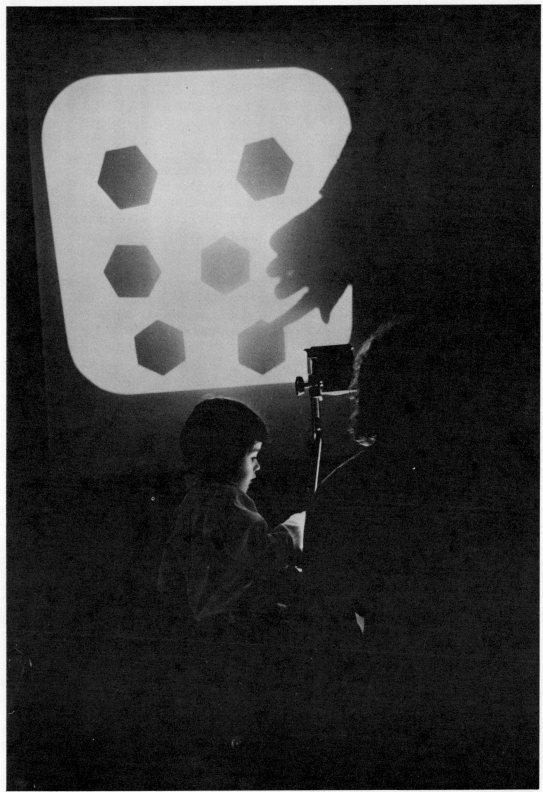

THE
CLASSROOM
AS A
MEDIA
CENTER

"Room 16 is on the air." This announcement was made over the school loud-speaker every Friday morning heralding a 5-minute weekly news broadcast by the fifth-graders in Room 16. The program was in its sixth week and had spurred an interest in current events throughout the school as children from other classes discussed and frequently "second-guessed" the selection of news stories.

The author was in the principal's office when the news program was announced. She had come to visit the school because she had heard it had a "strong media program." A tour of the school had confirmed this. Children were working on numerous media projects. In one classroom, a group was completing an animated movie; in another, they were creating a filmstrip from plain white paper to illustrate their report on the digestive system; and in still another, children were plotting a *storyboard* for a slide presentation of a spoof of *Superman*.

The principal explained the emphasis on media: "I was dissatisfied with the children's achievement on reading comprehension tests. Although our reading scores were generally improving, comprehension scores remained on a plateau. Children did not seem to be interacting with the written word. In analyzing this problem, I reasoned there was a dichotomy between the way children learned in school and outside of it. In school the emphasis was heavily on print, yet outside children absorbed information from television, radio, movies—nonprint media. There was a further concern. Teacher evaluation relied too exclusively on pen and pencil tests that at best only measured low-level cognitive skills.

"I decided to encourage nonprint media activities in the school. We could not afford to hire a media teacher, but working with a few interested classroom teachers, we set up an old broom-and-mop closet as a darkroom and purchased film and inexpensive instamatic cameras and some good media instruction books. Some faculty meetings were devoted to beginning techniques—making slides and filmstrips. Gradually, the approach has spread. We like to think of the classrooms as *media centers* where children have a choice of media, print and nonprint, to express their comprehension of a book, to report on a science or social studies topic, or to produce a creative work. I think the most heartening factor," the principal concluded, "has been the positive effect the program has had on our low-achieving students."

The salutary effect of media activities on students with reading problems has been noted by many teachers. For example, in Uniondale, New York, students who were reading at least two years below grade level participated in a special program *(Graphics Expression Reading System)*, which combined language instruction with television production. Children were taught to read and write by writing and staging their own television shows. The district reported "highly significant improvement [in reading] at the grade 4–6 level. The majority of students achieved at nearly twice the rate they had under previous traditional programs in word meaning and paragraph meaning."

Television is utilized to teach reading in other ways. Teachers are obtaining scripts of interesting programs in advance of their airing. (Most of the major television networks now have material available for schools.) Students read the scripts in class, analyze them, and then watch the programs when they are shown, frequently following along with the scripts to note any changes. The day after the airing the class reviews the scripts once again. Not only do the students become more discerning television viewers as a result of the program, but also more critical and motivated readers, often turning to books related to the subjects aired.

OBJECTIVES OF A MEDIA PROGRAM

Students will:

- Be introduced to a variety of nonprint media.
- Learn specific media production techniques.
- Be able to express themselves in nonprint forms.
- Sharpen their sensory perceptions of their environment and view it from different perspectives.
- Acquire interests and skills that can be a basis for future hobbies.
- Gain self-awareness and self-confidence through participation in media activities.
- Enlarge their vocabulary.
- Practice writing for a purpose.
- Become more discriminating television viewers.
- Acquire critical reading skills.
- Reinforce basic math and language skills.
- Learn to work cooperatively on projects.

CURRICULUM INTEGRATION

The media activities presented offer a substitute means of collecting and reporting information in every area of the curriculum. They are, therefore, particularly beneficial to students who are experiencing reading and writing difficulties. Suggestions for utilizing specific kinds of media in each subject follow.

Science

Demonstrate a procedure; combine with an oral report to culminate a unit (filmstrips, slides, videotape).

Demonstrate the sequence involved in a natural process, such as digestion or plant growth (filmstrips).

Record an experiment (videotape).

Social Studies

Community studies (slides).

Documentary (slides, videotape).

Record an historical event or biography of person studied (filmstrips).

Culminate a unit of study by noting key facts (filmstrips).

Mathematics

Pose mathematical problems or computations on filmstrips.

Mathematics is also involved in measuring films, filmstrips, and slides and in timing presentations.

Reading

Alternate means of reporting on a book or article (slides, filmstrips).

Present main ideas of a selection (filmstrips).

Read scripts (all media).

Writing

Write original materials for all media production.

Language Arts

Practice speaking, listening (all media).
Produce filmstrips illustrating parts of speech or synonyms, antonyms, and hononyms or vocabulary words, or to practice "spelling demons."

Art

Art is involved in all media production.

Miscellaneous

Provide information about topics such as consumerism, energy, environment, and careers (all media).

UNIT EXTENSIONS

1. Educators are becoming increasingly concerned about the impact of television on students, and urging that "critical viewing" be included in the curriculum. "Anything which equips students to deal with the barrage of information beamed at them by TV is a valid part of the curriculum," according to Dr. Calvert Schlick, superintendent of instructional services in Mamaroneck, N.Y. "We should define understanding media as a basic skill, identify component parts of the skill and then discover how to teach them."[1] Teachers should consider discussing television shows in the classroom, analyzing their content, plot, and characters, in the same manner as would be done with a book or play. As has been noted, scripts can frequently be obtained in advance of their airing from the major networks.
2. Suggestions for "Extensions" at the beginning of Chapter 6. "Advertising," contain ways children can survey their viewing habits and analyze shows. These can be adopted in conjunction with this part.
3. In Merrick, New York, a student "photo-journalism" squad was organized by the public information director, Marcia Handler. The district publishes regular newsletters to parents and faculty and a variety of other publications. Students were recruited and trained to cover events in their schools by writing stories and taking photographs. Since the formation of the squad numerous student articles and photographs have appeared in the school publications and the local press as well.[2]

[1]Quoted in *The New York Times*, December 18, 1979, p. C 1.
[2]For more details see Marcia E. Handler, "Elementary Students as Reporters and Photographers," *Journal of Educational Communication*, January 1978, vol 3, no. 1, p. 12.

12
PRODUCING NONPRINT MEDIA

Nonprint media have become pervasive in our environment. Their production in the classroom can add a new dimension to the curriculum and a deeper perception of the environment or a school topic. Many teachers are understandably apprehensive at the prospect of introducing nonprint media. Their concern may result from a lack of experience with the equipment, or from memories of an embarrassing moment when a movie projector jammed and a classroom of children waited impatiently for the teacher to unravel the film. Prior experience with media is not essential for this unit. A range of activities is presented; some do not require the use of any equipment.

This chapter is organized differently from the others. Teacher background notes continue to precede each topic, but **implementation** and **evaluation** have not been specified. It is assumed that students will receive necessary instruction in the use of equipment and the processes involved. Teachers will assess finished work in accordance with ability, maturity, and prior experience of students. The materials required by all the activities in this chapter are summarized below.

ACTIVITIES IN THIS CHAPTER REQUIRING SPECIAL MATERIALS

M 1: Carton, cloth, string, bulb and holder
M 2: Cardboard for puppets, thin sticks or plastic straws, paper fasteners
M 5: Overhead projector
M 6: Salad oil, magic markers or pens
M 7: Thermofax copier
M 8: Acetate
M 9: Old filmstrips, bleach
M 11: Acetate, slide mounts, markers, pens, common substances, glue
M 12: Old slides, bleach, or black leader film
M 13: Magazines, clear contact, slide mounts
M 14: Construction paper, natural objects
M 15: Blueprint paper, clorox or peroxide
M 16: Light-sensitive paper, fixing solution
M 18: 30: Camera, film
M 31: Pinhole camera (see details of activity)
M 32: Small pad
M 33–37: See details of activities
M 38–39: Camera, film, tape recorder
M 40–47: Video equipment and film
M 48–55: Tape recorder

SHADOW THEATER

Children have long enjoyed casting shadows with their hands or other parts of their bodies to imitate animals or strange creatures. In Shadow Theater this practice becomes an art form. Shadow plays can be produced in pantomime or with dialogue, with children or puppets as characters. If puppets are used, they can be one-dimensional cutouts or more elaborate ones in black or color.

TEACHER NOTES

Shadow Theater was a popular form of entertainment in ancient China over a thousand years ago. From there it spread to India, Java, the Middle East, and later to Europe. In Shadow Theater, puppets or people perform behind a screen with light focused behind them. Their figures are silhouetted on the screen, creating a dramatic effect.

Cochrane[1] relates that a Chinese emperor was unhappy because he had had his favorite jester killed. To please the emperor, a shadow was made from the jester's picture and a man manipulated the shadow and repeated some of the jester's jokes. This may have been one of the earliest examples of Shadow Theater. It was later adopted in some Far Eastern cultures, in which the shadow was said to represent the soul of a person.

The technique requires a minimum of materials. A permanent Shadow Theater in the classroom can inspire creative writing and dramatic expression and can serve as a means of reporting on books. It is particularly helpful to shy children who have difficulty performing in front of a class.

ACTIVITIES M 1–5: Be a theater impresario! Organize a Shadow Theater.

In Shadow Theater, plays are staged in *shadow* behind a screen. The audience sits in front of the screen watching the action and listening to a script read offstage. It is an art form that started over a thousand years ago. In this activity you will learn to make a Shadow Theater and puppets, operate your theater, and produce a play.

M 1   Build a theater.

You can make two kinds:

a.   A smaller puppet theater
You will need:

A carton about the size of a large television set.
White cloth (as from an old sheet).
150–200 watt bulb and holder such as a gooseneck lamp.
Scissors.

To proceed:
Leave the back of the box open, and cut a large *screen* in the front of the box.

Hang the white cloth across the front opening by stapling or pasting it tightly around the sides. The cloth must be taut.

Stand your theater on a table.

[1]Louise Cochrane, *Shadow Puppets in Color* (Boston, Mass: Plays, Inc., 1973), p. 5.

b. A larger Shadow Theater
You will need:

String or wire to reach across a corner of the room.
White cloth and bulb as in **a**.

To proceed:
Run the string from one corner of the room to another.
Hang the cloth across the wire anchoring the corners so the cloth is taut.
The theater should now be large enough to accommodate people as well as puppet characters.

M 2 Construct the puppets:

Cut the figures from light-weight cardboard. Start with simple one-dimensional figures. Attach them to light sticks so that they can be maneuvered in front of the screen.
Experiment with more complicated figures.
Give your puppets movable joints by attaching the limbs with paper fasteners. A thin stick or plastic straw taped on the limbs can be manipulated to make them move.
Dress the figures with tissue paper.
To add color to the puppets, cut them from different shades of construction paper. You will need to experiment to see which colors project best.

M 3 Prepare to operate your Shadow Theater.

Remember the following rules:

1. The audience sits in front of the screen.
2. Hold the puppets on sticks from behind the theater as close to the screen as possible.
3. Shine light from behind the theater onto the screen.
4. Scenery is generally unnecessary, but it may be hung around the edges of the theater. Be careful that it does not interfere with the action of the characters.
5. People as well as puppets can take parts in the larger Shadow Theater. If people participate, they should face sideways so their images are projected in profile.
6. Some plays will be only in pantomime; others will require a script. Scripts should be read offstage, out-of-sight if possible.

(*Note:* Interesting effects can be created with everyday objects. Cast shadows from scissors, paper clips, folded paper, or your fingers. The class can imagine what the shadows represent and write poems or stories involving them.)

M 4   Produce a shadow play.

It is best to write a script in advance. It may be taped or read as the play unfolds.

Arrange your puppets in order of appearance so that there is a minimum of distraction as the play proceeds.

Background music can be taped in advance. It may be used to set a mood or for sound effects.

Most plays will require a *stage director* to assure that the script flows smoothly.

M 5   Experiment with a different Shadow Theater.

Try an overhead projector theater. To project your figures, place them on a transparency, and move them around with a thin stick or drinking straw.

PHOTOGRAPHY WITHOUT A CAMERA

Filmstrips, slides, and photograms can be produced in a classroom without a camera. Each furthers an understanding of photography, offers creative experiences, and supplements and extends the curriculum.

TEACHER NOTES

FILMSTRIPS

Four methods of producing filmstrips in the classroom are described. There are also commercial kits available for this purpose. The ones presented below entail no cost for materials and permit children to produce filmstrips on numerous occasions.

ACTIVITIES M 6–10: Produce your own filmstrips. Here are four different methods and suggestions for presenting the finished strips.

M 6   Filmstrips from paper.

You will need:

Blank white paper
Any salad oil
Magic markers or nonsmear grease pens

To proceed:

1. Cut strips of paper 1⅜ inches wide.
2. Mark off ¾-inch frames for your pictures. (See diagram.) Leave two frames blank as a leader.

3. Draw pictures within each frame, and color with markers or pens.
4. Coat paper lightly with salad oil, and dry thoroughly.

To view:

Pull the strip gently through the projector. After a few times, slots will appear on the paper, and it will be easier to project. You may need to wrap a small strip of acetate around your leader, at first, for the projector to accept it.

M 7 Filmstrips from a Thermofax copier.

If your school has a Thermofax machine, more substantial strips can easily be made. The process is similar to that in the preceding activity.

Cut the strips of paper, mark off ¾-inch frames, and draw your pictures. Attach four or five strips to a sheet of 8½-inch-by-11-inch paper with Scotch tape. Only the top needs to be taped.

Run the paper through the Thermofax machine, taped end first. You will now have a transparency.

Cut the individual filmstrips apart. Color can be added and strips touched up. Longer strips can be made by splicing two together with Scotch tape.

To view:

Feed manually through the projector.

M 8 Filmstrips on acetate.

Follow the first three steps in Activity M 6, then place a piece of clear transparent acetate over the paper, and trace the drawings on to it.

Color the pictures to complete.

M 9 Filmstrips from previously used ones.

Old filmstrips (your school may have some that are obsolete) can be soaked in a solution of bleach and water to remove the images. When the film has dried, new pictures can be drawn on it.

M 10 Combine your filmstrips with oral or written notes.

Most filmstrips will require an explanation when viewed by others. Any of the following are acceptable:

1. Provide an oral presentation to accompany the strip when it is shown to the class or small group.
2. When strips are to be shown without the presence of the *producer,* either prepare a tape to be played with it or a written explanation. In the latter instance, number each frame of the filmstrip and a written script explaining it with corresponding numbers. The viewer will read the script while watching the filmstrip.

SLIDES WITHOUT A CAMERA

Almost any material that will permit light to pass through can be used to make slides. Clear 35-mm. film leader, blank filmstrips, acetate, old slides or movie film from which the previous image has been removed (by soaking in bleach and water) are examples. Activities M 11 and M 12 focus on creative slide production. When slides are made part of a report, students may wish to add some made from pictures in magazines or books. This process is described in Activity M 13.

ACTIVITIES M 11–13: Create slides directly on film.

M 11 Psychedelic slides.

Design abstract slides.

You will need:

Strips of clear acetate, 2 inches by 11 inches. Acetate can be purchased in sheets, 8½ inches by 11 inches and cut to size.
Slide mounts (packages of 100 can be purchased in photo shops[2]).
Magic markers or felt-tip pens.
Small amounts of common substances, such as jello powder, tea, coffee grounds, nail polish, brown sugar, sand.
Glue.

To proceed:

1. Spread some glue on acetate in abstract design. Then sprinkle some of the substances on the glue, varying colors and texture. Add design with magic marker or pen.
2. Cut acetate to fit slide mounts and insert.
3. Project finished slides with background music. If you can secure more than one slide projector, show a few slides simultaneously. The result is a true "art happening."

M 12 And more creative slides.

a. Old slides can be recycled by removing from mount and bleaching out the image (soak in bleach and water). They can then be painted or colored, or bits of paper glued on them for interesting effects.
b. Black leader film can be made into slides. You will need leader that is made of clear celluloid and work on the dark emulsion side.

Scratch designs on the film with a pin, nail, or paper clip. You can color the designs with a felt pen.

M 13 Picture transfers.

Pictures in magazines or books can be made into slides to illustrate your reports.
You will need:

Pictures with a glossy surface
Clear contact paper
Bowl of water
Scissors
Slide mounts

To proceed:

1. Cut a picture and piece of contact paper; each 2 inches square.
2. Remove the backing from the contact paper, and place it sticky side down, on the picture.

[2]It is possible to make mounts by copying a commercial one and cutting it out of light cardboard or oaktag. Experiment with this.

3. Rub together with blunt part of scissors or ruler to assure an even fit.
4. Soak the two in water for a few minutes. Peel off wet paper, and gently rub off the chalky residue on the contact paper.
5. The picture should now be on the contact paper. To preserve it place another piece of contact paper over it when it dries.
6. Place slide into slide mount.

PHOTOGRAMS

Light-sensitive paper when exposed to light, reacts and changes color. A *photograph* or *photogram* can be made by placing objects on portions of the paper before exposing it. The covered parts will remain unchanged, creating interesting designs. The process is in a sense a means of taking pictures without a camera and can serve as a basic introduction to photography.

ACTIVITIES M 14–16: Produce photograms: take pictures without a camera.

Have you ever left a piece of construction paper in the sun with a part covered? You probably found that the exposed part of the paper had faded, leaving an outline of your object. This is the basic idea of photograms. If you arrange objects on light-sensitive paper and then expose the paper to the sun or other bright light, the uncovered portions of your paper will *print,* leaving silhouette photographs of your objects. These silhouettes can later be colored or decorated. Three different kinds of photograms are described below.

M 14   Start with construction paper.

The red and blue shades work best.
Arrange natural objects, such as leaves, feathers, and blades of grass, on the paper, leaving uncovered areas.
Place the paper in a sunny but protected spot for at least a day. You can tell if your photogram is ready if the exposed parts of the paper have noticeably faded.
Remove from the sun and display your *photograms.*
(*Note:* You can also try paper designs instead of natural objects.)

M 15   Blueprint photograms.

You will need:

Blueprint paper, such as that used by architects. It can be purchased in rolls. Store the roll in a dark closet.
Clorox or 3 percent hydrogen peroxide.
Pan.
Water.

To proceed:

1. Cut off a part of the roll for your photogram in an area of the room without much light, and immediately return the unused part to the closet. Since the paper comes in long rolls, you can make large photograms—even people pictures.
2. Place objects on the paper—blue side up.
3. Expose the paper to sunlight or photoflood light for about two minutes.
4. Remove the objects out of the light.

5. Fix picture as follows: Place the paper in a solution of ½ cup of Clorox or peroxide to about 2 quarts of water for about one minute. Rinse the paper in plain water for a few minutes. Hang to dry.

M 16   Light-sensitive photographic paper photograms.

You will need:

Light-sensitive paper, such as Kodak Studio-Proof F, which can be purchased in sheets in a photography shop.
Fixing solution (Rapidfix or sodium thiosulphate crystals).
Pan.
Water.

To proceed:

1. The process is similar to the one described in blueprint pictures. Be certain to keep the light-sensitive paper in a dark closet, and do not expose unused sheets as others are removed.
2. Place objects on a sheet of the paper, shiny side up. Work in a dark area of the room.
3. Expose the paper to sunlight or photoflood light for about 5 minutes or until exposed portion of paper becomes dark purple.
4. Quickly remove the objects out of the light.
5. Fix the picture as follows: Immerse the paper in a fixing bath of Rapidfix solution or 5 tablespoons of sodium thiosulphate crystals dissolved in 2 quarts of cool water, for about 10 minutes. (The bath should be prepared before the pictures are printed.)
Shake off excess *fix,* and place the print in plain water for about an hour. Hang to dry.

(*Note:* Experiment with photograms. Vary arrangements and kinds of objects to achieve striking patterns. Research the effects of different intensities of light—sunlight, stronger and weaker bulbs, changing time exposures. Try, too, objects with different opacities. [Opacity is the degree to which an object prevents light from passing through.])

Mount your results for a photogram exhibit.

PHOTOGRAPHY (WITH A CAMERA)

TEACHER NOTES

Seeing the environment through the eye of a camera is a special sensory experience, a way of interpreting a scene by capturing only one aspect of it. Few young children have an opportunity to experiment with this art form, and yet photography can be a classroom activity and need not be too expensive. A few instamatic cameras may be within the school's budget; sometimes children can bring inexpensive cameras from home. Film can be purchased in bulk; outdated film that is still serviceable may be available. Establish a relationship with a local photo shop. It can be a source of professional help as well as budget film.

In the activities below, children first learn about photography and cameras and then are directed to specific subjects.

ACTIVITIES M 17–19: Learn basic facts about photography.

M 17   Introduction to photography.

The basic elements of photography are light, subject, camera, and film.
In learning about photography, each of these must be considered.

1.   Light: To photograph an image one must expose it to the proper amount of light. Too little will leave your pictures dark, too much will give them a washed-out appearance.

2.   Subject: Search for interesting subjects. "Good pictures are often initiated by minds that see the common in an uncommon way."[3]

3.   Camera: All cameras have the same basic parts.

4.   Film: Light-sensitive material that records an image. Different cameras use different-sized film.

(Note: See Figure 12.1, "Photography: How It Works," pp. 222–224.)

M 18   Get to know your camera.

Practice using it before you insert film. Are you holding it steady? Squeeze, do not push the trigger. Did the camera move? Look through the viewfinder. If your camera has an adjustable focus, practice using this.

If you will be using flash, remember this extends only 6 to 10 feet from your subject.

Note how to load your film.

M 19   Tips for better pictures.

1.   Keep your camera steady. Hold elbows close to your body, and stand still while you shoot.
2.   Vary your shots. Take closeups when possible. Check your camera manual to see how close you may get.
3.   Select different angles—shoot from below, above, side.
4.   Have one center of interest. Avoid cluttered backgrounds.
5.   If you are photographing people, have them doing something natural instead of just staring at the camera.
6.   Check your light source. It should be from behind you shining on the subject.

You should now be ready to proceed. Your first shots may be rough, but you will be learning from your errors. Try some of the activities described below. Different students may try similar themes. Note how each interprets them.

ACTIVITIES M 20–30: Be a photographer!

Here are picture suggestions.

M 20   Pictures tell a story.

Photograph four pictures that, when arranged in sequence, tell a story. (For example, a broken doll, someone finding it, repairing it, presenting it to a child.) Try this with a mystery, a surprise party, and so on.

Or create comics. Photograph "actors" in frozen positions as in comic strips. When pictures are developed, add dialogue to tell a story in balloons over the characters' heads.

[3]"Picture-taking in 5 minutes." Kodak Pamphlet AC-13, p. 1. Note: Basic elements of photography and tips for better pictures have been adapted from this pamphlet.

HOW IT WORKS

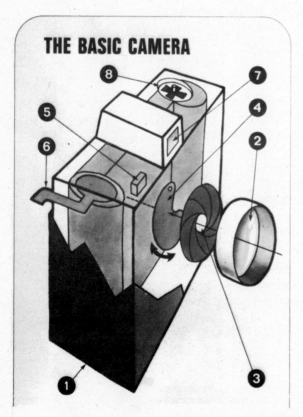

THE BASIC CAMERA

All cameras have these basic parts:

1 Lighttight box to keep light out and serve as a frame to hold other parts.

2 Lens to collect light reflected from a subject to form an image on the film.

3 Lens opening to control the amount of light reaching the film.

4 Shutter to control the time during which light reaches the film.

5 Shutter release to trigger the shutter.

6 Film-advance lever or knob.

7 Viewfinder to frame the picture area.

8 Most cameras have a socket for a flipflash, a magicube, a flashcube, a flashbulb, or a flashbulb holder.

Figure 12.1 Photography: How It Works. (Reproduced by permission of Eastman Kodak Compamy, Rochester, N. Y.)

WHEN YOU MAKE A POSITIVE PRINT FROM A NEGATIVE

You place the negative . . .

in contact with light-sensitive paper in a printing frame . . .

or to make an enlargement, you put the negative in an enlarger.

Then you shine light through the negative to form an image on the light-sensitive paper.

WHEN YOU PROCESS THE PAPER

The developer makes the positive image on the paper visible.

The acid stop bath stops the action of the developer.

The fixer preserves the positive image on the paper.

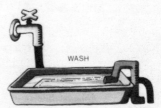

Washing the print in water removes the fixer and undeveloped silver. Then you dry the print.

WHEN YOU TAKE A PHOTOGRAPH

Light reflected from the subject
        passes through the lens and forms
an image on the light-sensitive film.

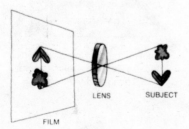

FILM   LENS   SUBJECT

WHEN YOU PROCESS THE FILM

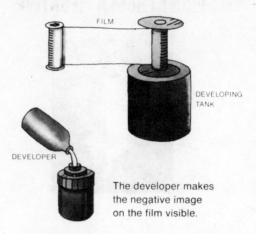

FILM

DEVELOPING
TANK

DEVELOPER

The developer makes
the negative image
on the film visible.

STOP

The acid stop bath
stops the action of
the developer.

FIXER

The fixer preserves
the negative image
on the film.

Washing the film
in water removes
the fixer and
undeveloped silver.

Then you hang the
film up to dry.

M 21   Pictures with a geometrical theme.

Photograph square things, round things, rectangular objects, circles.
Display these on a board cut in the same shape.

M 22   Everyday themes.

Shoot things that move, old things, young things, fun things, scary things.
Accompany your photos with cinquains (see Chapter 11, Greeting Card
Activity PGC 8).

M 23   Weather themes.

Take pictures that show scenes in the rain, snow, sun and some that suggest the weather, for example, a shadow, a puddle.

M 24   Neighborhood themes.

Try pictures that depict parts of your neighborhood or a special area, such
as the beach. What are the aspects of the beach that create the feeling of
beach? Without actually showing the entire area, create the mood of a beach
or park or playground through pictures.

M 25   Sensory themes.

Find scenes that represent special smells, tastes, feels.

M 26   People themes.

Photograph scenes that represent a special person: friend, parent, brother,
sister.

M 27   Mood themes.

Shoot pictures that represent a person's mood (a frown, tears, the back of
a dejected person).

M 28   Focus on one subject.

Photograph a tree or a plant regularly over a long period of time. Or a street
at different times of the day.

M 29   Interpret a scene.

Select a busy spot. Have each member of a group photograph the most
interesting aspect.

M 30   And for fun.

Add concrete objects to photographs, such as leaves to a tree, hair to a
face.

PINHOLE CAMERAS

Photography is basically the process of recording an image on film. Reduced to essentials, all that is required to accomplish this is a lightproof container, film, a tiny hole to permit a beam of light to reach the film, and a shutter to control the light. Photographers use complicated cameras for each step of this process, but simple cameras can be made in the classroom that will actually take pictures—some quite artistic.

ACTIVITY M 31: Construct and use a pinhole camera.

M 31   All about pinhole cameras.

You will need:

A container that has a tight-fitting lid, such as a coffee can, vegetable shortening can, cocoa tin, cylindrical oatmeal box.

A small piece of heavy aluminum foil about 2 inches (or 5 centimeters) square.

A #10 needle.

A small piece of black opaque paper or light cardboard same size as foil.

Flat black paint (spray or regular). If you use regular paint, you will need a small paint brush.

Masking tape.

Scissors.

To proceed:

1. Cut out a hole about 1 inch or (2½ centimeters) square in the center of the front of the box or, if possible, opposite the removable end.
2. Make a pinhole in the center of the aluminum foil with your needle. To do this, use only the point of the needle, and hold the foil on a piece of wood or cardboard to assure a smooth hole. Avoid jagged edges.
3. Paint or spray the inside of the container black. Be sure to paint the inside of the lid and around the edges so that no light can seep in.
4. Tape the aluminum foil with the pinhole over the 1-inch hole you made in the box.
5. Make a shutter over your pinhole by taping the piece of opaque paper or cardboard over the foil. The bottom should be tightly taped; the top, secured lightly with a small strip of tape so that the shutter can be dropped when you take pictures.

To load your camera:

1. You can use photographic paper to take pictures. (Some recommended papers are Kodak Royal Pan Sheet film 4141 or Kodabromide Paper F (glossy) No. 2, single weight. Consult a local photography shop for equivalent papers.) It is also possible to use Tri-X film and cut it into squares to fit your camera. However, this can only be handled in a darkroom or other completely dark area.
2. When handling the paper, you must work in a dark area under a *safelight*—a special lamp that is fitted with a filter to screen out light rays to which film and paper are sensitive. A safelight can be made by covering a flashlight with a few thicknesses of red cellophane.
3. Remove a sheet of paper. Cut it into pieces about 4 inches by 5 inches (or 10 x 12 centimeters). (Be sure to keep the box closed and store unused sheets of paper in a dark closet.)

4. Tape the paper lightly but securely into the camera on the inside across from the pinhole opening. The emulsion (shiny) side should face the opening.
5. Be certain the shutter is closed when you load the camera.

To take pictures:

1. You must keep your camera very still when taking pictures. Steady it on a table or other flat surface, and put a book over it or some modeling clay underneath to assure that it does not move.
2. Point the camera at the subject.
3. Drop the shutter to expose the pinhole and permit light to enter. Exposure time will vary. Royal Pan Film only requires about 1 to 2 seconds in bright sun; 4 to 8 seconds on a less bright day. Kodabromide paper needs about 2 minutes in bright sun and 8 minutes on a less bright day.
4. Cover the pinhole with the shutter.

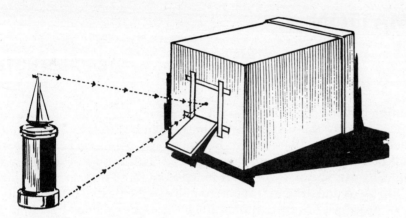

To develop the negative:

Remove the exposed paper in a dark area with only your safelight on.

You will also need:

Three plastic or glass trays and a pan or pail for washing the pictures
Paper towels
Developer (Dektol)
Vinegar, water
Fixer (such as Rapid Fix)
Watch with second hand

To proceed:

1. Prepare three trays in advance as follows:
   a. Developer (follow directions on container).
   b. Stop bath (1 tablespoon vinegar to 1 gallon of water.
   c. Fixer (follow directions on container).
2. Place your exposed paper in the developer for about 2 minutes, in the stop bath for about 30 seconds, and then in the fixer for about 8 minutes. As you move the picture from one tray to another, shake off the excess chemical in each tray.
3. Now wash in running water or soak your picture in water, stirring occasionally for about 10 minutes. Blot dry with paper towels, and hang to dry (a piece of string hung across a corner of the room makes a good line upon which to hang pictures with clothespins). You now should have a developed negative.

To print the negative:

1. Work under your safelight during this procedure.
2. Place your negative on a piece of unexposed photographic paper (shiny side on top of shiny side). If the negative is still wet, wet the unexposed paper.
3. Cover with a piece of glass.
4. Shine a 100-watt bulb on the picture about a foot away for about 5 seconds.
5. Now develop the print in the same manner you developed your negative, developer, stop bath, fixer as above and finally washing it and hanging it to dry. If the picture curls, complete drying it between paper towels under a book.

ANIMATION

TEACHER NOTES

Animation is defined as the process of "bestowing life," making something come alive. In film animation fantastic images can be produced: toy cannons can shoot out dinosaurs, lines become buildings, extra limbs grown on people, shoes walk off by themselves, and objects can be made to appear suddenly and then magically disappear. Techniques range from those that do not require a camera: flip cards and drawing on film to more sophisticated film animation. In each, the process is basically similar. It can best be explained by examining a piece of movie film. In 16-mm. film, each second on the screen embodies 24 different picture frames. (You can observe this by running a movie for a few seconds and noting how many frames have passed.) In animation, the camera is slowed so that only one or at most a few frames are shot at a time, permitting split-second control of the image.

As a classroom activity, animation has much to recommend it. The results are always visually exciting; it provides children with an understanding of *movies,* and involves reading and math. Animated movies can be abstract or short vignettes. They must be timed and frames per second computed. The vignettes require tight plotting, sequencing, and planning. They are unique creative experiences.

The activities below describe animation with and without a camera.

ACTIVITIES M 32–33: Try animation without a camera.

M 32   Make an animated flip book.

You will need a 3-inch-by-5-inch pad of thin, blank paper.

Place the pad on your desk with the binding on the right. Open the pad so that the bottom piece of cardboard is on the left, the paper on the right.

Turn over one page onto the cardboard, and draw a figure with hands at its side in the lower-left corner. Now turn over another page. The paper should be thin enough so that you can see the first figure underneath. Alter the position of the hands slightly. Now keep turning sheets one at a time, and on each alter the hands until the figure's hands are high in the air. Draw at least twelve frames.

When you have finished, flip the pages quickly, and you will see your figure move.

Try the same procedure with more complicated drawings or in color. Each picture should change only slightly.

(*Note:* Try other ways of making objects move. Draw a sequence of pictures around the edge of a cardboard circle. Insert a large nail through the center, and spin the circle around rapidly. Or experiment with drawing designs on pinwheels. As the wind blows them, the pictures will become *animated.*)

M 33 Animation by drawing on film.

Examine a piece of movie film, and note that each image varies only slightly. The process is similar to the one used in the preceding activity, making flip books. You can produce a *movie* without a camera by carefully drawing images directly on film. The illusion of movement results from the repetition of a drawing with only a slight change on each succeeding frame.

Here are some interesting math facts. On most movie film, it takes 24 frames of film to produce 1 second of a movie. Can you figure out how many frames you will need to produce 1 minute of a movie?

To draw a movie you will need:

1. 16-millimeter clear leader film. This can be purchased, or old 16-mm. film can be obtained from film libraries or suppliers and the original image removed. To do this, immerse the film in a solution of bleach diluted with water. As the image fades, rinse and wipe the film dry.
2. You will also need material to draw with—magic markers, felt pens, or india ink.

To proceed:

1. If you do not cut your film apart, you will be able to project it without splicing. Try, therefore, to leave the film in a long roll. Spread it out on a long table or the floor (corridor floors work well).
2. Measure off about 3 to 4 feet of film and leave it blank. This will be used for threading the projector.
3. Now measure and mark off about 2 feet of film for each child. You can place a piece of masking tape after each 2 feet to hold the film in place and separate the units.
4. The sprocket holes on the film outline each frame. The image must be placed within the sprocket perforations. Make an outline of the frame on a piece of cardboard, and move this as you work to assure that you stay within the sprockets.
5. Draw your pictures on the coated side of the film. The colors will be clearer. If the film is too smooth to absorb the ink, sand paper it very lightly.
6. Start with simple figures or abstract designs—dots growing and receding, circles advancing toward each other and merging, or a butterfly flying off. If the film has been cut apart, you will have to splice it with splicing tape, lining up the sprocket holes.
7. Preview your film. Note which designs work best, which colors are most effective, how many frames needed to set an image. If you are not satisfied with your first attempt, the images can be washed or bleached off.
8. The next time you may wish to plan a short scene. The class should decide on a theme, outline the plot, and sketch the frames in advance. Remember each frame will be only slightly different from the succeeding one. For

example, if you wish to draw a title for your movie, it will take about six frames for a letter to be seen.

After the frames are sketched, divide responsibility for drawing the finished pictures on the film.

Add sound:

Almost any movie is enhanced by the addition of sound. Preview the film, and decide where you wish to place the music. You may tape the sound to be shown with your movie. To do this, start the film, and start to record when the first image appears on the screen.

ACTIVITIES M 34–37: Producing animated movies.

M 34   Collect the necessary equipment.

You will need the following to film animated movies:

1. A super 8-mm. movie camera with a single-frame capacity and shutter release to enable you to shoot one picture at a time. *(This is desirable but not absolutely necessary. If your camera does not have a single-frame release, turn it to the least number of frames per second that it will take; and when you shoot pictures, just touch the trigger lightly to take the least number of frames.)*
2. Optional equipment on your camera: reflex viewing and focusing to show you just what the camera will film, zoom lens for close shots, light meter, film footage counter.
3. Cartridge of super 8-mm. film.
4. Tripod.
5. Two grip lights or standing lamps with 150- to 200-watt bulbs unless you can shoot in bright light.
6. Projector to show film.
7. Optional: Film editor and splicer.

For film mathematicians: Super 8-mm. film projects at 18 frames per second, ¼ of a foot of film each second. How many feet of film will be projected each minute?

There are 72 frames of film in each foot. How many per inch?

M 35   Experiment with different kinds of animation.

a.   Cutout.
Flat objects or figures are cut from magazines and mounted on cardboard, or original ones drawn, decorated, and then cut out.
Figures can be made to move by hinging the limbs with paper fasteners or thread.
People can appear to talk (sound can be added later) by preparing different shape mouths: closed, partially open, completely open. These are alternated in the filming.
Animation possibilities from cutout figures are endless: figures can appear from a circle that grows into a face; then suddenly features appear and disappear, a beard sprouts, and hair grows; chairs can take off and fly away; airplanes stand on their nose and walk off the page.

b.   Small object or figure.
Any object can be the focus of an animated movie: pebbles, miniature toys, flowers, pieces of string, or figures made of clay or wire. The figures will need to be solid enough so that they will withstand manipulation.
In animation, the objects will come alive—rocks grow from pebbles and develop features, then disappear. Boats can fly, plants eat people, and substances change shape—pieces of string take the shape of a bird and fly off.

c.   Pixillation.
Pixillation is the animation of larger objects or real people. When people are used, they create the effect of animated movies by moving very slowly from frame to frame.

d.   Time-lapse.
Time-lapse refers to a method of animating movies so that a long period of time is condensed. For example, a volcano can be built and explode; crystals grown; seeds planted and immediately shown in bloom—all in a few minutes.
It is accomplished by shooting a few frames at a time over an extended period.

M 36   Plan your animated movie.

Decide first what kind of animation it will be. Then plan carefully with attention to each of the following:

1.   Objective.
What is the purpose of your film? Is it to tell a story? Show an action? Establish a mood?
2.   Script.
A rough sketch showing what each character will do should be prepared in advance. If there is to be dialogue added, it should be written at this time so that the characters can be shown in proper positions.
3.   Prepare your characters or objects for the film (natural objects, figures, toys, puppets).
4.   Complete the set. Backgrounds should be bright but not white. Be certain they don't clash with the colors of the subjects.
5.   Complete your title, credit, and end cards. They can be printed on individual cards or animated, too. For example, the title may appear on the screen slowly one letter at a time:

J
JA
JAW
JAWS

A three-word title should run about 3 seconds or 54 frames.

6. Review how the camera works.
Collect your tripod and lights, load the camera, and screw in the cable release to enable you to shoot single frames.

M 37 Film your movie.

The procedure will differ depending on the kind of animation and figures used.

a. For cutout movies with flat figures, shoot the movie from above. Your set can be a table or the floor. Place your figures on a background sheet of paper.
Attach the camera to the tripod, making certain that it is steady and aim it down on your set.
Mark the boundaries as you see them through the viewfinder. This will encompass the action.
Position your lights on either side of the camera. Arrange your set and start shooting. You will need to film the title first unless you have a splicer. In that case, leave about 50 frames for the title to be added later.
Press the cable release twice (for two frames).
Move your figures about ¼ inch; press again twice. Continue shooting two frames for each ¼ inch of movement until your scene is completed.

b. To shoot dimensional objects.
Set up the stage on a table or desk enclosed on three sides with a learning carrel or three sides of a cardboard. Place the scenery and figures on the table, and the camera directly in front of the table on a tripod. The basic procedure is the same as in the above—objects are moved slowly for each succeeding shot.

c. To shoot pixillated movies.
These can be shot out-of-doors with natural light. Characters move slowly from frame to frame. There is a potential for magic. For example, a magician can produce a person or make her disappear from one scene to the next.

(*Note:* A roll of Super 8 film runs about 3 minutes and 20 seconds, or a total of 200 seconds. Each child in the class can make a short animated film. Divide 200 by the number of children in the class, and this will tell you how many seconds of film each may use. Twenty-five children could use 8 seconds of film or, at the rate of 18 frames per second, 144 frames of film. Even if reduced to permit a pause between each film, there is ample film for each child to experiment with animation.)

SLIDE SHOWS

TEACHER NOTES

Most schools have slide projectors and tape recorders. These plus any 35-millimeter camera, either belonging to the school or some of the children, are all the tools necessary to produce a slide show. The results can be a unique and worthwhile experience. Slide shows are an excellent medium for explaining the work of the class to parents and members of the community; they can be historical records of a class project from inception to completion; they can be used as teaching tools to communicate ideas or synthesize information at the end of a unit of study, a method of studying and recording aspects of the neighboring community or a field trip; an expression of an original story or theme, or creative media projects for *art's sake* alone.

ACTIVITIES M 38–39: Plan and film a slide show with sound.

M 38   Planning and filming the show.

You can make your own slides, add a narration, and produce a slide show in the classroom. Since film can become expensive, the whole class will probably want to collaborate on this. Some members will take pictures; others, write the narration; others, edit slides and script; and still others, add the sound.

You will need:

35-millimeter camera (instamatic will do) with flash attachment
Film
Slide projector and tape recorder

Before filming:

Plan your show in advance, using a checklist such as the one shown in Figure 12.2. Your show should be carefully plotted so that the result is not a haphazard collection of slides. The script should be written or sufficiently sketched so that you will take the right pictures to illustrate your story.

Possible subjects for a slide show include:

1.   A theme show: friendship, happiness, fear, and so on. Explore the theme through slides.
2.   An illustration of a popular song.
3.   A report: research a topic through slides, and report to the class. Explore the neighborhood, an industry, a science or social studies topic. One class investigated places of interest in their community; another, the local supermarket, showing how food arrived, was packaged and sold, how long it remained on the shelf, what happened to perishable food if it was not sold promptly, and the origin of different products.
4.   A story: illustrate a book or write an original story to be expressed in slides.
5.   A teaching tool: teach a craft or skill through slides.
6.   A career investigation: demonstrate through slides the work of different people—"a day in the life of a . . . "
7.   Whichever topic you choose, be specific. Slide shows are more effective when they contain a single concept.

Plan your visuals:

1.   Will you sketch the *title, credits,* and *end* directly onto a blank slide or photograph these? (Someone holding a card with the title might open the show.)
2.   Do you wish to include charts or statistics?
3.   Slides can be made from magazines, pictures, books with a Visual Maker Kit.[4] Will you include some?

4Sold at camera stores.

To proceed:

1. When taking pictures, bear in mind:
   The flash only extends about 6 to 10 feet.
   Vary your shots for interest (some closeup, some medium or long).
   If you have enough slides, take an extra shot of an important scene so that you can select the best.
2. After the pictures are printed, review the slides. (An inexpensive slide box with a light makes it possible to view all the slides at once.) Place them in proper sequence.
3. Review the script to see if changes should be made based on the actual slides. The script should enhance the pictures, not merely repeat what is obvious to the viewer.
4. You may wish to add slides previously shot or insert some made from magazine or book pictures.[5]

M 39   Sound in your slide show.

You will want different sounds for your show. Separate tapes can be prepared for background music, sound effects, dialogue, and commentary. (Your entire slide show should not run more than 10 minutes, so keep these short.)

SLIDE SHOW CHECKLIST

Objective of Show
_____Indicate the purpose: to teach something, illustrate a process, extend a unit, and so on.

Initial Planning
Do you have:
_____A complete list of all pictures you want to take
_____Complete list of all sounds (music, sound effects, dialogue, and so on.)
_____All narration written out

Production
_____Have you prepared title, credit, and "The End" slides?
_____Is your soundtrack ready?
_____Are all pictures shot (or selected from previous slides)?

After Pictures Are Printed
_____Have you previewed, eliminated unnecessary slides, and arranged balance in order?
_____Timed the show.
_____Synchronized the soundtrack and slides.
_____Completed the show and practiced presenting it.

Check each line as you complete it.

Figure 12.2   Checklist. (This checklist is based on one developed by Bob Kaplan, Shoreham-Wading River Middle School, Shoreham, New York. Mr. Kaplan was a consultant in the preparation of this entire chapter.)

[5]Do not discard old or extra slides. They can be recycled or be made part of a slide library and inserted in other slide shows.

To prepare your soundtrack, record the individual tapes on one master tape. Some recorders have a jack that permits a direct connection from the player to the recorder to eliminate outside sounds.

There is an advantage to preparing your soundtrack before shooting the pictures. You will know in advance exactly how many and what kinds of slides are needed to illustrate your show. It may eliminate filming unnecessary slides.

VIDEOTAPE

TEACHER NOTES

Modern videotape equipment is surprisingly easy to operate. With some basic instruction, teachers can quickly learn to use it and, in turn, teach students to do so. It is a particularly satisfying medium. Unlike other forms of film, it has instant feedback; no need to wait for film to be processed. Tapes can be erased and reused so that operating expenses are minimum. Finally, the result includes sound—no need for a separate audio track.

There is a special excitement in viewing oneself on television that can be ego-building as the children's performances improve. Even shy children blossom into outgoing actors and actresses when facing the camera. The use of videotape has been shown to significantly improve reading scores particularly at Grades 4–6.[6] Used selectively, videotape can enrich the curriculum at any grade level.

Teachers can utilize videotape themselves as a teaching tool, to demonstrate a procedure, to tape a lesson, or to record special events: a class play, the hatching of eggs in the classroom, an experiment that cannot easily be repeated, for example, the dissection of part of an animal. Students can be permitted to make short video tapes on topics of interest. In one school[7] where this is done, each student must first produce a written script and adhere to a set procedure:

1. Select a topic.
2. Research and make notes about it.
3. Find or create graphics to illustrate it.
4. Mount graphics for presentation.
5. Write the script.
6. Present it for editing of grammar, spelling, and style and then rewrite it.
7. Practice reading and delivering the script.
8. Videotape it.

The videotape activities that follow assume that equipment is available in the classroom or in the school building. They range from some that require just a few minutes to full productions.

ACTIVITIES M 40–47: Utilizing video in the classroom.

M 40   Each child a performer.

Videotape individual children in a performance of choice: dramatic reading, pantomime, song, dance.

[6]See introduction to Part 6.
[7]Oldfield Junior High School, Greenlawn, New York.

M 41 Stage a hobby show.

Individual children prepare a short segment on their hobbies with procedures demonstrated.

M 42 Produce a news show.

Divide into teams: news, weather, sports, features. Put it all together into a 15-minute news broadcast.

M 43 Conduct interviews.

First interview classmates and teacher; then invite others to the room—principal, school employees, parents, guest.
Questions should be prepared in advance and interview techniques carefully studied.

M 44 Produce a television commercial.

Base this on a real or fictitious product.
Time your commercial so that it is no longer than a minute. (See Activities CAD 9 and 10.)

M 45 Organize a game show.

Stage your own version of a television game show.

M 46 Present a variety show.

Have groups plan skits, dances, music.
Show off class talent.

M 47 Plan a television movie.

This will require detailed organization.
Write a script in advance. Create a *storyboard* showing: each scene, setting, characters, dialogue.
Rehearse before actual taping.

AUDIO

TEACHER NOTES

We are living in an electronic age, surrounded by sound. Audio activities aid children to become aware of these sounds and experiment with a popular means of communication. It requires only a tape recorder to transform a classroom into a *radio studio*. In the process, students practice language skills as they write scripts, listen to and record sounds in their environment, and speak on tape.

The following activities may be integrated with a science study unit on sound or a study of noise pollution as part of environmental studies.

ACTIVITIES M 48–55: Become radio journalists.

M 48 "Sounds of My City."

There is a record by a well-known tape recordist, Tony Schwartz, titled "Sounds of My City."[8] In it he has captured sounds of New York City: street sounds—a fire engine, construction, children playing and singing, people talking.

Here's an interesting assignment. Pick a street, listen to the sounds, and record different ones for about 5 seconds (10 at most). Put together a 3-minute tape. You can edit it, and if an additional recorder is available, make a montage—combining different sounds.

Try the preceding procedure with "Sounds of My School." Record sounds around the school—in the office, classroom, cafeteria, playground, bus, auditorium. Consider, too, "Sounds of My Home."

Or a more structured activity: Tell a story through sound. Without any narration, depict coming to school and going to class, getting ready for gym, going home, and so on.

M 49 Organize the classroom into a radio station.

Choose your call letters (such as TALK).
In a typical radio station, there are the following jobs.

Station manager
Program director
News director
News editors
Copy editors
Newswriters
Reporters
Technical director
Newscasters

You may wish to contact your local radio station to research the responsibilities of each and then select students for the roles.

M 50 Produce a news show.

Include a review of news, events to come, weather, sports, and possibly a short interview.

You may tape your show or broadcast it live. Can you secure permission to broadcast it to the school?

In one school, a class produced a brief radio show every Friday. In addition to a summary of the week's news, they researched a different topic for each broadcast. These included: community places of interest, school problems, energy facts, unique hobbies of school population, surveys of attitudes toward current issues, care of pets, and so on.

Points to bear in mind: When broadcasting, avoid outside noises caused by changing positions, shuffling papers, and so on. Also keep the microphone no more than one foot away from the speaker.

[8]Tony Schwartz. "Sounds of My City," Folkways Records Album # FC 7341 (New York: Folkways Records and Service Corp., 1956, 1962).

M 51   Still more radio shows.

Here are some more possibilities for radio shows:

1. A variety show featuring the members of your class.
2. Book reviews.
3. A "You Were There" show featuring interviews with historical figures: George Washington, Christopher Columbus, Susan B. Anthony, Harriet Tubman. Select an incident in their lives and then pretend you were a radio reporter interviewing them soon after.

M 52   Become a news correspondent.

Choose a news beat. Your assignment might be the school board or parent association. Try to cover the news of their meetings. Interview the board or parent association president regularly. Ask to be informed of key decisions or plans.

Tape a short report on your beat.

M 53   Radio interviews.

Tape an interview with an interesting person in the school or community. Keep it short—about 10 minutes. Plan your questions in advance.

Practice first by role-playing an interview with your teacher or member of the class.

Or plan an "Inquiring Reporter" radio segment. Interview students and teachers on topics of interest: "Should the sale of junk foods be banned in the cafeteria?"

M 54   Produce an original radio play.

a. Write an original play for radio. Since the characters cannot be seen in a radio show, the script must tell the complete story.
   Start with a short skit. See if you can enlarge this into a longer play.
b. Or invent characters for a radio play modeled after television soap operas. Write scripts of their adventures. Once a week, broadcast a 10-to-15-minute segment.
   You will need to pay attention to a number of details. Each script should end on a note of suspense so that people will want to *tune in* to see how it is resolved. Don't have too many characters, or it will be difficult to remember them.
   Each segment should be timed to last exactly 10 to 15 minutes and should start with a review of where the previous story ended.
c. Try this approach too with mysteries, science fiction.

   (*Note:* The key to sustaining interest is to include well-developed characters.)

M 55   More radio plays—*The Shadow.*

Some time ago, a popular radio show was called "The Shadow Knows . . . " It was about the adventures of a mystery figure called *The Shadow,* who solved crimes.

There is a collection of Shadow Plays that can be read and dramatized, then tape-recorded as radio plays.[9]

Read and record some of these.

[9]Deana Cohen and Irene Burns Hoeflinger eds., *The Shadow Knows.* (Glenview, Ill.: Scott, Foresman, 1977).

RESOURCES FOR PART 6

The following books include specific instructions for children in the use of media:

Andersen, Yvonne, *Make Your Own Animated Movies*. Boston, Mass: Little Brown and Co., 1970.

Andersen, Yvonne, *Teaching Film Animation to Children*. New York: Van Nostrand Reinhold Co., 1971.

Forbes, Robin, *A First Camera Book*. New York: Macmillan Publishing, 1979.

Holland, Viki, *How to Photograph Your World*. New York: Charles Scribner's Sons, 1974.

Holter, Patra, *Photography Without A Camera*. New York: Van Nostrand Reinhold, 1972.

Laybourne, Kit, and Pauline Cianciolo (eds.), *Doing the Media*. New York: McGraw Hill, 1978.

Lidstone, John, and Don McIntosh, *Children as Film Makers*. New York: Van Nostrand Reinhold, 1970.

Morrow, James and Murray Suid, *Media and Kids*. Rochelle Park, N. J.: Hayden Book Co., 1977.

The following are also recommended:

Workshop for Learning Things
5 Bridge Street
Watertown, Mass. 02172
     Publishes materials for teachers:
     Recommended: *The Camera Cookbook*
                 It's So Simple: Click and Print
                 Most of the Pictures Came out Real Well

Eastman Kodak Co.
Rochester, New York 14650
     Publishes more than 800 books, guides, and pamphlets on photography. Some recommended titles include:

     The Here's How Book of Photography, 1977.
     Classroom Projects Using Photography, Part I, 1975.
     Movies with a Purpose: A Teacher's Guide to Planning and Producing Super 8 Movies for Classroom Use

and the following pamphlets:

     How to Make and Use a Pinhole Camera
     Pocket Guide to Good Pictures
     Photo Reports: Make it Happen
     Easy Ways to Make Still and Movie Titles
     Loading and Handling 35mm Cameras
     Making a Movie
     Picture Taking in Five Minutes

     Write to the Eastman Kodak Co. for a more complete list of publications and single copies for the classroom.

APPENDIX
Activities Skill Charts

- List of all the activities in the book by chapter and page numbers.
- Skills stressed by each activity.
- Grade level of activities (where appropriate).

ENERGY AWARENESS

Chapter 1, pp. 17–20

Category	Skill	EA 1. What is energy?	2. Energy from the sun	3. More about photosynthesis	4. Plants are phototropic	EA 5. Two states of energy	6. Demonstrate examples of potential and kinetic energy	EA 7. More ways to think about energy	EA 8. Design an energy collage	9. Can you do without energy?	EA 10. Create a past and present energy mural	11. Life in the future
PROCESS	APPLYING SYNTHESIZING				×	×			×			
	COMPARING ANALYZING	×	×								×	
	PREDICTING INFERRING	×	×							×	×	×
	EXPERIMENTING		×	×	×							
	CLASSIFYING	×				×	×	×				
	OBSERVING		×	×								
ART	VISUALS					×		×	×	×	×	×
MATH	REPRESENTATION											
	COMPUTATION											
	MEASUREMENT											
LANGUAGE	RESEARCH		×					×	×		×	
	READING		×					×				
	WRITING			×						×	×	
	INTERVIEWING											
LEVEL: WHERE APPROPRIATE (I—INTERMEDIATE, U—UPPER)			U		U	U	U	U				

ACTIVITIES

NO.   TITLE

LEARN SOME BASIC FACTS ABOUT ENERGY
EA 1. What is energy?
2. Energy from the sun
3. More about photosynthesis
4. Plants are phototropic

DISTINGUISH BETWEEN POTENTIAL AND KINETIC ENERGY
EA 5. Two states of energy
6. Demonstrate examples of potential and kinetic energy

IDENTIFY OTHERS KINDS OF ENERGY
EA 7. More ways to think about energy

ENERGY IN OUR EVERYDAY LIVES
EA 8. Design an energy collage
9. Can you do without energy?

COMPARE THE USE OF ENERGY IN THE PAST AND THE PRESENT, AND THEN PROJECT INTO THE FUTURE
EA 10 Create a past and present energy mural
11. Life in the future

ENERGY: The Fossil Fuels

Chapter 2, pp. 24–29

Category	Skill	1	2	3	4	5	6	7	8	9	10	11	12	13	14	15	16	17
PROCESS	APPLYING SYNTHESIZING	×	×			×		×	×	×	×						×	×
	COMPARING ANALYZING				×	×		×		×	×							
	PREDICTING INFERRING	×	×		×	×		×			×						×	×
	EXPERIMENTING																	
	CLASSIFYING							×			×						×	×
	OBSERVING				×						×					×		
ART	VISUALS	×	×			×		×	×		×					×	×	×
MATH	REPRESENTATION																	
	COMPUTATION											×	×					
	MEASUREMENT																	
LANGUAGE	RESEARCH	×	×	×	×	×	×	×	×	×		×				×	×	×
	READING	×	×					×	×							×	×	×
	WRITING				×	×			×									×
	INTERVIEWING												×					
	LEVEL: WHERE APPROPRIATE I—INTERMEDIATE, U—UPPER			U	U	U	U			U		U					U	U

ACTIVITIES

NO. / **TITLE**

EXPLORE FOSSILS AND FOSSIL FUELS
EFF 1. What is a fossil?
2. What are the fossil fuels?

FOCUS ON PETROLEUM (OR CRUDE OIL)
EFF 3. In what kind of rock is petroleum found?
4. Draw a model of an oil well
5. Drilling for offshore oil
6. Danger of oil spills
7. Products from petroleum
8. Refining crude oil
9. Locate oil reserves
10. Study the oil-rich countries

CONCENTRATE ON GASOLINE: A KEY PRODUCT OF PETROLEUM
EFF 11. A shortage of gasoline
12. Construct a gasoline pump
13. What price gasoline?

STUDY COAL: OUR MOST ABUNDANT FOSSIL FUEL
EFF 14. Illustrate how coal forms
15. Extracting the coal
16. Research the different kinds of coal
17. Locate coal reserves in the U.S.

The Fossil Fuels—2

Chapter 2, pp. 29–32

NO.	TITLE	Applying/Synthesizing	Comparing/Analyzing	Predicting/Inferring	Experimenting	Classifying	Observing	ART: Visuals	MATH: Representation	Computation	Measurement	LANGUAGE: Research	Reading	Writing	Interviewing	Level (I—Intermediate, U—Upper)
EFF 18.	Products from coal					×		×				×				
19.	Debate the use of coal	×						×								
	INVESTIGATE NATURAL GAS: THE THIRD FOSSIL FUEL															
EFF 20.	Research natural gas											×	×	×		U
21.	The discovery of natural gas											×	×	×		U
22.	The uses of natural gas											×	×	×		U
23.	Manufactured gas											×	×	×		U
24.	Learn to read a gas meter							×		×						U

ENERGY: Solar Energy

Chapter 2, pp. 34–39

NO. / TITLE	PROCESS — Applying Synthesizing	Comparing Analyzing	Predicting Inferring	Experimenting	Classifying	Observing	ART — Visuals	MATH — Representation	Computation	Measurement	LANGUAGE — Research	Reading	Writing	Interviewing	LEVEL (I—Intermediate, U—Upper)
SURVEY ASPECTS OF THE SUN'S HEAT															
ESE 1. Heat from the sun		×	×	×		×	×		×	×					
2. Can the sun heat water?	×		×	×		×		×		×					
3. More heat from the sun	×	×	×	×		×		×	×	×					
4. Which materials store the sun's heat best?	×	×	×	×	×	×		×	×	×					
5. Which colors retain heat best?	×	×	×	×	×			×	×	×					
6. How can you concentrate solar energy?				×							×	×	×		
7. How hot is the sun?															IU
INVESTIGATE USES OF SOLAR ENERGY															
ESE 8. Solar energy for heating	×						×								U
9. Build a rooftop solar collector	×			×		×	×								
10. Demonstrate a problem with solar collectors			×												
11. Build a sun dial							×	×		×	×			×	
12. Can solar energy purify water?	×		×	×		×						×			IU
13. Can solar energy produce salt from seawater?	×			×		×				×	×				
14. Solar energy for cooking	×			×		×									
CONSIDER MORE FACTS ABOUT THE SUN AND BE INSPIRED BY IT															
ESE 15. Can the sun's rays be harmful?															
16. How would the sun's absence affect us?													×		IU
17. The sun in literature and myth			×								×		×		
18. Be inspired by the sun							×					×	×		

ENERGY: Wind Power

Chapter 3, pp. 42–44

ACTIVITIES — NO. / TITLE	PROCESS: Applying/Synthesizing	Comparing/Analyzing	Predicting/Inferring	Experimenting	Classifying	Observing	ART: Visuals	MATH: Representation	Computation	Measurement	LANGUAGE: Research	Reading	Writing	Interviewing	LEVEL (I—Intermediate, U—Upper)
THINK ABOUT THE WIND EWIP 1. Wind power	×		×	×		×	×								IU
2. Observe the power of the wind	×			×		×	×								
3. Construct a weather vane						×	×								
4. Make pinwheels						×	×								
5. All about windmills	×										×	×			
6. Build an anemometer	×			×		×	×			×					

ENERGY: Water Power

Chapter 3, pp. 45–46

NO. / TITLE — ACTIVITIES	Applying / Synthesizing	Comparing / Analyzing	Predicting / Inferring	Experimenting	Classifying	Observing	Visuals	Representation	Computation	Measurement	Research	Reading	Writing	Interviewing	Level: Where Appropriate (I—Intermediate, U—Upper)
	PROCESS						**ART**	**MATH**			**LANGUAGE**				
FOCUS ON WATER POWER															
EWAP 1. Can water move things?				×							×	×	×		I, U
2. Can water cut rock?			×	×			×								
3. Construct a water wheel			×			×	×								
4. What are hydroelectric plants?	×										×	×			I, U
5. Where are hydroelectric plants located?	×	×	×								×	×			I, U

ENERGY: Nuclear Power

Chapter 3, pp. 48–49

ENP 1. BECOME INFORMED ABOUT NUCLEAR POWER AND SOME OF THE PROBLEMS ASSOCIATED WITH ITS USE

Category	Skill	1. What is an atom?	2. Nuclear energy through fission or fusion	3. Nuclear energy produces electricity	4. Problems associated with nuclear power	5. Should nuclear plants be built?	6. Take a survey
PROCESS	APPLYING SYNTHESIZING				×	×	×
	COMPARING ANALYZING		×		×		
	PREDICTING INFERRING		×	×			
	EXPERIMENTING						
	CLASSIFYING						
	OBSERVING						
ART	VISUALS	×	×	×			
MATH	REPRESENTATION					×	
	COMPUTATION						
	MEASUREMENT						
LANGUAGE	RESEARCH	×			×	×	×
	READING						
	WRITING				×		
	INTERVIEWING				×	×	×
LEVEL: WHERE APPROPRIATE (I—INTERMEDIATE, U—UPPER)		U	U	U	U	U	

SOURCES OF ENERGY: An Overview

Chapter 3, pp. 53–55

NO. / ACTIVITIES TITLE	PROCESS: Applying / Synthesizing	Comparing / Analyzing	Predicting / Inferring	Experimenting	Classifying	Observing	ART: Visuals	MATH: Representation	Computation	Measurement	LANGUAGE: Research	Reading	Writing	Interviewing	Level (I—Intermediate, U—Upper)
NOTE HOW ENERGY SOURCES HAVE CHANGED															
ESEN 1. Prepare an energy time line	×	×	×				×								
RESEARCH SOME OF THE SOURCES OF ENERGY AND WHERE THEY ARE FOUND															
ESEN 2. Devise a "Sources of Energy" chart			×				×				×	×			
3. Locate the sources of energy					×						×	×			
FOCUS ON SPECIFIC SOURCES															
ESEN 4. Research a specific source of energy	×										×				
5. "Sell" a particular source of energy	×	×									×				
6. Prosecute a polluter	×	×					×				×		×		
7. Pantomime a source and an application	×						×						×		
CULMINATING ACTIVITIES															
ESEN 8. Energy in your home		×	×					×			×			×	
9. Energy in the school	×	×	×				×				×			×	
10. Daydream about energy in the future											×				
11. Write a poem													×		
12. Consider a special bulletin board							×				×				
13. Plan an open house or energy fair	×						×				×				

ENERGY CONSERVATION

Chapter 4, pp. 59–63

No. / Activity Title	PROCESS: Applying/Synthesizing	Comparing/Analyzing	Predicting/Inferring	Experimenting	Classifying	Observing	ART: Visuals	MATH: Representation	Computation	Measurement	LANG: Research	Reading	Writing	Interviewing	Level (I/U)
STUDY THE WORD CONSERVATION															
EC 1. What does conservation mean?													×		U
2. Why do we need to conserve energy?	×						×				×		×		U
LEARN ABOUT KILOWATTS, METERS AND THE COST OF ELECTRICITY															
EC 3. What is a kilowatt?									×						U
4. You can read an electric meter							×		×						U
5. Construct meters									×						U
6. How much does a kilowatt hour cost?									×		×				
7. Check your electric meter at home						×			×		×				
8. How much does your family pay for electricity?									×		×	×			U
9. What is the cost of electricity to the school?									×		×				
10. Electricity uses fuel															
ANALYZE THE USE OF ENERGY BY APPLIANCES															
EC 11. How much electricity does that appliance use?	×	×					×		×		×		×		U
12. Which appliances are most commonly used?	×	×			×			×						×	U
13. Cost of operating an appliance		×						×	×		×			×	U
14. Are all appliances necessary?		×			×										
CONSIDER CAR-POOLING TO SAVE GASOLINE															
EC 15. Collect information on car pooling					×				×		×		×		U
16. Complete a transportation survey					×	×		×	×		×				U

LEVEL: WHERE APPROPRIATE — I—INTERMEDIATE, U—UPPER

ENERGY CONSERVATION—2

Chapter 4, pp. 63–67

No.	Activities / Title	PROCESS — Applying / Synthesizing	Comparing / Analyzing	Predicting / Inferring	Experimenting	Classifying	Observing	ART — Visuals	MATH — Representation	Computation	Measurement	LANGUAGE — Research	Reading	Writing	Interviewing
	INVESTIGATE INSULATION														
EC 17.	What is insulation? Which materials insulate best?	×	×	×	×		×								
18.	Test for cold retention	×	×	×	×		×								
	EXAMINE MORE ENERGY-SAVING TIPS														
EC 19.	Lower thermostats	×			×		×			×					
20.	Save energy when cooking	×			×		×		×	×					
21.	Shower or bath?	×			×		×								
22.	Avoid waste of energy through drafts	×			×										
23.	Does this door need weather stripping?	×													
	HELP THE SCHOOL AND COMMUNITY BECOME ENERGY-SAVERS, TOO.														
EC 24.	Organize the class as a team of energy savers	×						×						×	
25.	Conduct a contest	×						×						×	
26.	Plan a poster campaign	×						×						×	
27.	Make energy filmstrips	×						×						×	
28.	Create a comic character or puppet	×						×						×	
29.	Be an energy "private eye"	×					×								
30.	Schedule an energy-saver day	×	×												
31.	Issue an energy-savers fact sheet	×													
32.	Prepare an energy news program	×										×		×	
33.	Complete an energy report card	×										×		×	

LEVEL: WHERE APPROPRIATE

I—INTERMEDIATE, U—UPPER

CONSUMERISM: Shopping

Chapter 5, pp. 77–80

LEVEL: WHERE APPROPRIATE — I—INTERMEDIATE, U—UPPER

Category	Skill	1	2	3	4	5	6	7	8	9	10	11	12	13	14	15	16	17	18
PROCESS	Applying / Synthesizing				X	X	X	X						X				X	X
	Comparing / Analyzing	X	X	X	X	X	X	X	X	X	X			X	X			X	X
	Predicting / Inferring			X	X	X					X		X	X	X			X	X
	Experimenting				X														
	Classifying	X	X	X			X	X					X					X	
	Observing				X	X													
ART	Visuals	X										X							
MATH	Representation	X																	
	Computation			X			X			X	X	X		X	X	X	X	X	X
	Measurement	X		X															
LANGUAGE	Research			X			X		X		X	X	X	X			X		X
	Reading						X	X											
	Writing			X	X		X	X											
	Interviewing					X						X					X		
LEVEL	Where appropriate (I/U)			U	U	U	U	U		U		U						U	U

ACTIVITIES — TITLE

EXAMINE PACKAGES
CS 1. Units of measurement
2. Classify packages
3. Compare packages
4. How does packaging influence purchasing?
5. Does packaging add to price?

LEARN ABOUT PRICES
CS 6. What is unit price?
7. Record unit prices
8. Unit prices as a guide to shopping
9. Price per serving
10. Which size is cheaper?
11. Does advertising affect prices?
12. Play "The Price is Right"
13. What is the cost of a lunch for four?
14. What can you buy for $5.00?
15. Practice consumer math

BE A COMPARISON SHOPPER: More tips
CS 16. Buy what you need
17. What price beans?
18. How expensive are frozen products?

Shopping—2

Chapter 5, pp. 81–88

LEVEL: WHERE APPROPRIATE — I—INTERMEDIATE, U—UPPER

Category	Skill	19	20	21	22	23	24	25	26	27	28	29	30	31	32	33	34	35	36	37
PROCESS	APPLYING SYNTHESIZING	×	×	×		×				×	×	×		×						
	COMPARING ANALYZING	×			×	×				×	×	×	×	×				×	×	×
	PREDICTING INFERRING				×	×							×	×				×		
	EXPERIMENTING				×					×	×	×	×	×						
	CLASSIFYING			×						×	×								×	×
	OBSERVING	×								×	×			×						
ART	VISUALS					×	×			×	×						×			
MATH	REPRESENTATION																			
	COMPUTATION	×	×		×					×	×			×				×		
	MEASUREMENT					×														
LANGUAGE	RESEARCH	×	×	×	×									×		×	×	×	×	×
	READING	×												×	×	×	×	×	×	×
	WRITING				×				×					×		×	×			×
	INTERVIEWING									×				×						×

ACTIVITIES

TITLE — NO.

- CS 19. Was that premium worth its price?
- 20. Learn to read food advertisements
- 21. How much are food coupons worth?
- 22. How can you determine quality?
- 23. Comparing prices of different-sized eggs
- 24. Juices vs. juice drinks
- 25. Juices vs. cola drinks
- 26. Do all stores charge the same?
- **ORGANIZE A PRODUCT-TESTING LABORATORY**
- CS 27. Test paper products
- 28. Try taste tests
- 29. Test cleaning powders
- 30. Test other products
- **SURVEY THE SUPERMARKET**
- CS 31. A trip to the supermarket
- **LABELS: DISCOVER WHY THEY ARE IMPORTANT AND HOW TO READ THEM**
- CS 32. How reading labels can save you money
- 33. Rules about labels
- 34. Understanding label vocabulary
- 35. How much sugar?
- 36. Read ingredients
- 37. Look for dates

Shopping—3
Chapter 5, pp. 88–92

Category groupings: **PROCESS** (Applying/Synthesizing, Comparing/Analyzing, Predicting/Inferring, Experimenting, Classifying, Observing) · **ART** (Visuals) · **MATH** (Representation, Computation, Measurement) · **LANGUAGE** (Research, Reading, Writing, Interviewing)

LEVEL: WHERE APPROPRIATE — I—INTERMEDIATE, U—UPPER

No.	Title	Applying/Synth.	Comparing/Anal.	Predicting/Inf.	Experimenting	Classifying	Observing	Visuals	Representation	Computation	Measurement	Research	Reading	Writing	Interviewing
	HELP OTHERS TO BE SMART FOOD SHOPPERS														
CS 38.	Issue a consumer report	×										×	×	×	
	BE A WISE TOY BUYER: Toy safety														
CS 39.	How safe is that toy?	×	×				×								
40.	Can broken toys be hazardous?	×	×	×			×								
41.	Read labels on toys and games	×	×									×	×		
42.	Promote toy safety	×	×												
43.	Stage a toy safety exhibit							×							
	SELECT TOYS CAREFULLY: Additional criteria for purchasing toys														
CS 44.	Do you still play with that toy?	×	×			×	×							×	
45.	Which toys break easily?	×	×	×		×	×	×		×				×	
46.	What do toys cost?		×			×									
47.	How well-packaged are toys	×	×					×						×	
48.	Criteria for a good toy		×												
49.	Can you write directions?					×	×			×			×	×	
50.	Organize a toy repair and exchange shop	×													
51.	Issue a toy bulletin													×	
	CHOOSE CLOTHES CAREFULLY														
CS 52.	If you had $100								×	×					
53.	Selecting clothes					×		×	×						
54.	Learn about fabrics											×			
55.	Which fabrics absorb water more easily?	×	×	×	×		×				×				
56.	Will that fabric shrink?	×	×	×	×		×				×				
57.	Read clothing labels		×									×	×		

CONSUMERISM: Advertising

Chapter 6, pp. 95–99

NO.	TITLE	PROCESS — Applying/Synthesizing	Comparing/Analyzing	Predicting/Inferring	Experimenting	Classifying	Observing	ART — Visuals	MATH — Representation	Computation	Measurement	LANGUAGE — Research	Reading	Writing	Interviewing	LEVEL: WHERE APPROPRIATE (I—Intermediate, U—Upper)
	START WITH TELEVISION: BE A CRITICAL VIEWER															
CAD 1.	Time those commercials		×			×	×		×	×	×					
2.	Study techniques used in television advertising		×	×		×	×							×		U
3.	Monitor commercials	×	×	×			×							×		U
4.	Are television commercials sexist?		×	×		×	×									
5.	Ask a professional		×									×		×	×	U
6.	Be a product tester	×	×		×		×							×		U
7.	Evaluate products	×	×													U
8.	Can politicians be "sold" to the public?	×		×		×	×							×		
9.	Produce commercials													×		U
10.	Produce timed commercials									×	×			×		
	FOCUS ON PRINT ADVERTISING															
CAD11.	Collect and analyze printed advertisements	×	×			×	×					×	×			U
12.	Study techniques used in printed ads	×	×				×					×	×	×		U
13.	Write advertising copy	×	×					×				×	×	×		U
14.	Write recruitment ads	×												×		U
	CONSIDER A DIFFERENT VIEWPOINT															
CAD15.	Can advertising help the consumer?	×		×										×		U

CONSUMERISM: Basic Economic Concepts

Chapter 7, pp. 101–104

ACTIVITIES (NO. / TITLE)	LEVEL: WHERE APPROPRIATE (I—INTERMEDIATE, U—UPPER)	LANGUAGE: RESEARCH	READING	WRITING	INTERVIEWING	MATH: REPRESENTATION	COMPUTATION	MEASUREMENT	ART: VISUALS	PROCESS: OBSERVING	CLASSIFYING	EXPERIMENTING	PREDICTING/INFERRING	COMPARING/ANALYZING	APPLYING/SYNTHESIZING
ANALYZE NEEDS AND WANTS															
CEC 1. Food, clothing, and shelter as basic needs						×			×		×			×	×
2. What determines your wants?											×			×	×
3. Distinguish further between needs and wants		×									×			×	
STUDY MORE ECONOMICS: PRICES, INFLATION, AND GOODS AND SERVICES															
CEC 4. What is meant by the law of supply and demand?	I					×			×		×		×	×	×
5. What other factors influence price?	U										×		×	×	×
6. Still other price determinants	U						×		×		×			×	
7. What is meant by inflation?	U	×					×							×	
8. Distinguish between goods and services		×							×		×				

CONSUMERISM: Rights and Responsibilities

Chapter 7, pp. 105–108

		CRR 1. Is the product guaranteed?	2. Classifying guarantees and warranties	3. Is this bike free of structural defects?	4. Consumers keep records	5. Consumers need records	CRR 6. Shopping by mail—1	7. Shopping by mail—2	8. Unordered merchandise	CRR 9. What price vandalism?	10. What price shoplifting?
PROCESS	APPLYING SYNTHESIZING	×	×	×				×		×	×
	COMPARING ANALYZING	×	×		×		×	×		×	×
	PREDICTING INFERRING	×									
	EXPERIMENTING										
	CLASSIFYING	×		×			×				
	OBSERVING						×				
ART	VISUALS	×		×			×			×	
MATH	REPRESENTATION										
	COMPUTATION									×	×
	MEASUREMENT										
LANGUAGE	RESEARCH		×								
	READING		×				×				
	WRITING			×			×			×	
	INTERVIEWING									×	×
LEVEL: WHERE APPROPRIATE I—INTERMEDIATE, U—UPPER		U	U	U	U	U		U	U	U	

ACTIVITIES TITLE

CRR 1. Is the product guaranteed?
2. Classifying guarantees and warranties
3. Is this bike free of structural defects?
4. Consumers keep records
5. Consumers need records

BE AWARE OF YOUR RIGHTS WHEN ORDERING MERCHANDISE IN THE MAIL

CRR 6. Shopping by mail—1
7. Shopping by mail—2
8. Unordered merchandise

CONSUMERS ARE RESPONSIBLE! THEY OPPOSE VANDALISM AND SHOPLIFTING

CRR 9. What price vandalism?
10. What price shoplifting?

(Row heading: **LEARN ABOUT GUARANTEES AND HOW TO PROCEED IF MERCHANDISE PURCHASED IS FAULTY**)

Chapter 7, pp. 109–114

CONSUMERISM: Money Management

Category	Skill	1	2	3	4	5	6	7	8	9	10	11	12	13	14	15	16	17	18	19	20	21	22
PROCESS	APPLYING / SYNTHESIZING						×	×		×	×	×	×				×	×			×	×	×
	COMPARING / ANALYZING	×	×		×						×		×					×	×				
	PREDICTING / INFERRING					×																	
	EXPERIMENTING																						
	CLASSIFYING		×		×													×					×
	OBSERVING			×																			
ART	VISUALS	×															×	×					×
MATH	REPRESENTATION				×																		
	COMPUTATION	×	×	×		×	×	×	×						×	×	×	×	×	×	×	×	×
	MEASUREMENT																	×					
LANGUAGE	RESEARCH	×	×	×				×		×	×	×		×			×		×				
	READING													×					×				
	WRITING																						
	INTERVIEWING			×																			
LEVEL: WHERE APPROPRIATE (I—INTERMEDIATE, U—UPPER)		U	U	U		U	U	U	U	U					U	U	U						

ACTIVITIES TITLE

NO.

UNDERSTAND MONEY VALUES
CMM 1. What does it cost
2. Investigate foreign currency
3. Visit a bank
4. Practice computations with money

ALL ABOUT BUDGETS
CMM 5. Do you receive an allowance?
6. Learn to budget
7. Budgeting for a party
8. Can you help the family budget?

EXAMINE SOME MONEY MANAGEMENT TECHNIQUES
CMM 9. Buying with credit cards
10. Credit card penalties
11. Borrowing money
12. Decisions on borrowing
13. Learn to read contracts

ENGAGE IN MONEY TRANSACTIONS
CMM14. Design a class scrip
15. Open classroom stores
16. Receive pay for classroom jobs
17. Help pay for your education
18. Organize an auction
19. Satisfy fantasies
20. Open a bank
21. Start a checking account
22. Organize a credit card company

CONSUMERISM: Culminating Activities

Chapter 7, p. 115

PROCESS						ART	MATH			LANGUAGE				LEVEL
APPLYING SYNTHESIZING	COMPARING ANALYZING	PREDICTING INFERRING	EXPERIMENTING	CLASSIFYING	OBSERVING	VISUALS	REPRESENTATION	COMPUTATION	MEASUREMENT	RESEARCH	READING	WRITING	INTERVIEWING	LEVEL: WHERE APPROPRIATE, I—INTERMEDIATE, U—UPPER

ACTIVITIES

TITLE: SUMMARIZE AND APPLY YOUR CONSUMER KNOWLEDGE

NO.	Activity	APPLYING SYNTHESIZING	VISUALS	READING	WRITING	LEVEL
CC 1.	Build your vocabulary	×			×	U
2.	Write a series of "How-To" Books	×			×	U
3.	Publish a newsletter in your community	×	×		×	U
4.	Other means of publicizing information	×	×		×	
5.	Organize a consumer fair	×		×		
6.	Consumers are environmentalists	×				

ENVIRONMENT: Air Pollution

Chapter 8, pp. 125–128

ACTIVITIES — TITLE	PROCESS — APPLYING SYNTHESIZING	PROCESS — COMPARING ANALYZING	PROCESS — PREDICTING INFERRING	PROCESS — EXPERIMENTING	PROCESS — CLASSIFYING	PROCESS — OBSERVING	ART — VISUALS	MATH — REPRESENTATION	MATH — COMPUTATION	MATH — MEASUREMENT	LANGUAGE — RESEARCH	LANGUAGE — READING	LANGUAGE — WRITING	LANGUAGE — INTERVIEWING	LEVEL: WHERE APPROPRIATE (I—INTERMEDIATE, U—UPPER)
INVESTIGATE POLLUTANTS IN THE AIR															
NAP 1. Can we see gases that pollute the air?			×	×		×									
2. Is the air dirty?			×	×		×									
3. Examine particles in the air		×	×	×	×	×									
4. Test a hypothesis about particles	×	×	×	×	×	×									
5. Do cars pollute?	×	×	×	×		×									
6. Cigarettes also pollute				×			×				×	×	×	×	U
DETERMINE SOME OF THE EFFECTS OF POLLUTION															
NAP 7. How does pollution affect plants?	×	×	×	×		×	×								
8. Does air pollution affect clothing?		×	×	×		×							×		
9. What is an inversion?			×	×		×									U
10. Why is an inversion dangerous?											×	×			U
WHAT CAN YOU DO ABOUT POLLUTION?															
NAP11. Become aware of air pollution in your community						×	×								
12. Fight air pollution	×						×				×		×		

ENVIRONMENT: Water Pollution

Chapter 8, pp. 130–134

LEVEL: WHERE APPROPRIATE — I—INTERMEDIATE, U—UPPER

Category	Skill	1	2	3	4	5	6	7	8	9	10	11	12	13	14	15	16	17
PROCESS	APPLYING / SYNTHESIZING	×					×						×	×				×
	COMPARING / ANALYZING		×	×	×	×			×	×	×	×	×	×				
	PREDICTING / INFERRING		×		×	×		×										
	EXPERIMENTING		×	×	×	×			×	×	×	×	×				×	
	CLASSIFYING	×			×	×			×									
	OBSERVING		×	×	×	×			×	×	×	×	×					
ART	VISUALS	×					×											×
MATH	REPRESENTATION																	
	COMPUTATION									×							×	×
	MEASUREMENT									×								
LANGUAGE	RESEARCH	×					×						×					
	READING																	
	WRITING	×		×			×		×	×	×	×	×	×	×			
	INTERVIEWING																	

ACTIVITIES / TITLE

BECOME AWARE OF WATER POLLUTION

NWP 1. Signs of water pollution
2. Are you a polluter?
3. Impurities in water
4. Oil spills on water
5. How can fertilizers pollute?
6. How do detergents pollute the water?
7. Suffocated fish—a sign of pollution

EXPERIMENT WITH METHODS OF PURIFYING WATER

NWP 8. Purifying water by sedimentation
9. Purifying water by coagulation
10. Purifying water by filtration
11. Purifying water to remove dyes and odors
12. Purifying water by evaporation
13. Purifying water by disinfection
14. Water for human consumption

WATER IS A FINITE RESOURCE. CONSERVE IT!

NWP15. Billions and billions of gallons of water
16. From drips to gallons
17. Conserve water

ENVIRONMENT: Waste Disposal

Chapter 9, pp. 138–143

NO. / ACTIVITIES TITLE	APPLYING SYNTHESIZING	COMPARING ANALYZING	PREDICTING INFERRING	EXPERIMENTING	CLASSIFYING	OBSERVING	VISUALS	REPRESENTATION	COMPUTATION	MEASUREMENT	RESEARCH	READING	WRITING	INTERVIEWING	LEVEL (I/U)
WHAT IS THROWN AWAY?															
NWD 1. Many words describe it	x	x			x	x			x		x	x	x		U
2. Take an inventory of solid waste	x	x			x	x							x		U
3. What is thrown away in class?	x	x			x	x							x		U
4. What is thrown away in the cafeteria?	x	x			x	x			x				x		U
5. What is thrown away in the school?	x	x			x	x			x				x		
6. What is thrown away on or near the school grounds?	x	x			x	x			x				x		
7. What is thrown away at home?															
WHAT HAPPENS TO THE WASTE?															
NWD 8. Methods of disposing of waste	x	x									x		x		U
9. Which methods are used in your community?	x				x						x	x	x	x	U
IT'S SMART TO RECYCLE AND CONSERVE															
NWD 10. Review your Solid Waste Inventory Forms	x					x									U
11. New uses for junk	x	x				x									U
12. Organize a "junk fair"	x		x			x	x		x						U
13. Let's save a tree	x	x		x		x									U
14. Recycle paper				x											U
15. Nature is a recycler				x											
16. Is it biodegradable?	x	x			x	x									
17. Plant a waste garden															
18. Is that packaging essential?	x	x			x	x							x		
19. How you can help	x						x				x		x		

ENVIRONMENT: Environmental Math

Chapter 9, pp. 147–150

NO. / ACTIVITIES TITLE	Applying / Synthesizing	Comparing / Analyzing	Predicting / Inferring	Experimenting	Classifying	Observing	Visuals	Representation	Computation	Measurement	Research	Reading	Writing	Interviewing	Level (I—Intermediate, U—Upper)
INVESTIGATE YOUR ENVIRONMENT TO FIND SETS, COUNT AND CLASSIFY															
NME 1. Sets in the environment		×				×		×	×		×				
2. Classify objects in the environment		×			×	×	×	×	×	×					
3. Go on a scavenger hunt		×				×			×	×					
4. Investigate a leaf		×	×		×	×			×						
5. How many different ways can you classify leaves?		×													U
PRACTICE MEASUREMENTS AND COMPUTATIONS, AND CONSTRUCT A TRUNDLE WHEEL															
NME 6. Measure by pacing			×												
7. How long is your pace?									×	×					
8. Unusual measurements									×	×					
9. Practice computations on the playground			×			×	×		×	×					
10. Construct a trundle wheel									×	×					
PRACTICE MORE ADVANCED MEASUREMENTS															
NME 11. Become acquainted with your shadow						×	×		×	×			×		U
12. Find the height of a tree by measuring your shadow	×	×				×			×	×					U
13. Other measurements with shadows	×					×			×	×					U
14. Investigate a small plot	×	×	×		×	×				×					U

CAREERS: Self-Awareness

Chapter 10, pp. 158–161

PROCESS	APPLYING SYNTHESIZING	× ×
	COMPARING ANALYZING	× × × × × × × × × × × × × × × × × × ×
	PREDICTING INFERRING	
	EXPERIMENTING	
	CLASSIFYING	
	OBSERVING	×
ART	VISUALS	
MATH	REPRESENTATION	× × × × × × × × × ×
	COMPUTATION	
	MEASUREMENT	
LANGUAGE	RESEARCH	
	READING	
	WRITING	× × × × × × × × × × × × × × ×
	INTERVIEWING	×
	LEVEL: WHERE APPROPRIATE I—INTERMEDIATE, U—UPPER	U U U

ACTIVITIES

TITLE

NO.

EXPLORE YOUR LIKES, DISLIKES, INTERESTS, CHARACTERISTICS

RSA 1. What is your favorite . . .?
2. Which is your favorite television program?
3. Which is your favorite kind of book?
4. Whom do you admire?
5. What would you change?
6. What are you proud of?
7. What would you buy?
8. What are your likes and dislikes?
9. What do you enjoy?
10. How would you like to spend your time?
11. Do you have a hobby?
12. Think about a friend
13. What is your best characteristic?
14. Do you have responsibilities?
15. How do you work with others?—1
16. Working with others—2
17. What will you expect from a job?

Self Awareness—2 Chapter 10, pp. 161–164

NO. ACTIVITIES TITLE	APPLYING SYNTHESIZING	COMPARING ANALYZING	PREDICTING INFERRING	EXPERIMENTING	CLASSIFYING	OBSERVING	VISUALS	REPRESENTATION	COMPUTATION	MEASUREMENT	RESEARCH	READING	WRITING	INTERVIEWING	LEVEL: WHERE APPROPRIATE I—INTERMEDIATE, U—UPPER
	PROCESS						ART	MATH			LANGUAGE				
THINK ABOUT YOUR FEELINGS															
RSA 18. Feelings affect us physically		×											×		
19. Analyze your feelings		×											×		
20. How do you react to feelings?		×													
21. More about your reactions	×	×	×			×									
22. How do you manage conflicts?		×													
23. Do you like to take chances?		×											×		
24. Do you wish you had the courage to . . .?		×													
HOW DO YOU MAKE DECISIONS?															
RSA 25. Are you a decision maker?	×	×	×												
26. How would you resolve these?	×	×	×										×		
27. Do you consider the consequences of your behavior?		×													
SUMMARY ACTIVITIES															
RSA 28. Make a booklet titled "A Very Special Person"	×												×		
29. Create a collage	×						×								
30. Consider a mobile	×						×								
31. Prepare a media presentation	×						×								
32. Try an acrostic	×												×		

CAREERS: Career Awareness

Chapter 10, pp. 165–169

	Skill	1	2	3	4	5	6	7	8	9	10	11	12	13	14	15	16	17
PROCESS	APPLYING SYNTHESIZING				×	×	×	×									×	×
	COMPARING ANALYZING				×	×	×	×		×	×	×	×	×	×	×		×
	PREDICTING INFERRING											×	×	×	×	×		×
	EXPERIMENTING																×	
	CLASSIFYING	×	×	×	×	×	×				×	×	×	×	×	×		
	OBSERVING																×	
ART	VISUALS		×									×	×	×				
MATH	REPRESENTATION			×		×	×											
	COMPUTATION																	
	MEASUREMENT																	
LANGUAGE	RESEARCH	×	×		×	×	×			×	×	×	×	×	×	×	×	
	READING																	
	WRITING				×		×											
	INTERVIEWING			×		×	×											
LEVEL: WHERE APPROPRIATE (I—INTERMEDIATE, U—UPPER)				U	U	U	U	U			U	U	U		U	U	U	U

ACTIVITIES

TITLE

COLLECT INFORMATION ABOUT DIFFERENT OCCUPATIONS

RCA 1. Maintain a class career file
2. What work do people do in your community?
3. Parents work
4. Still more jobs: The Yellow Pages
5. Identifying jobs by products
6. Interview people about their work
7. Job satisfaction
8. Play "What's My Line?"

ANALYZE AND CLASSIFY JOBS

RCA 9. Classifying jobs: goods and services
10. Analyzing occupations
11. Occupations and the five senses
12. Occupations and clothes
13. Hats tell the story
14. What do they need to know?
15. Many occupations require special tools
16. Invent a new tool
17. Working on an assembly line

Career Awareness—2

Chapter 10, pp. 169–174

NO. / TITLE	PROCESS — APPLYING SYNTHESIZING	COMPARING ANALYZING	PREDICTING INFERRING	EXPERIMENTING	CLASSIFYING	OBSERVING	ART — VISUALS	MATH — REPRESENTATION	COMPUTATION	MEASUREMENT	LANGUAGE — RESEARCH	READING	WRITING	INTERVIEWING	LEVEL: WHERE APPROPRIATE (I—INTERMEDIATE, U—UPPER)
INVESTIGATE HOW PEOPLE FIND OUT ABOUT AVAILABLE POSITIONS?															
RCA 18. How did you find out about your job?					×			×					×	×	U
19. "Help-Wanted"		×	×		×						×	×			U
20. What is an employment agency?		×	×								×	×			U
PRACTICE APPLYING FOR A JOB															
RCA 21. Complete a job application	×												×		U
22. Learn to write a résumé	×	×										×	×		U
23. Answer a newspaper "Help-Wanted" Ad	×	×										×	×		U
24. Write a "Situation-Wanted" Ad	×												×		U
25. Role-play a job interview	×													×	U
SUMMARIZE YOUR CAREER INFORMATION															
RCA 26. Acrobat to zoologist	×				×						×	×			U
27. Start a career library	×				×						×				U
28. Dramatize your career library							×						×	×	U
29. Add a media section													×		U
30. The vocabulary of careers											×	×			U
31. What do people earn?									×				×		U

CAREERS: Future Studies

Chapter 10, pp. 176–178

		RFS 1. Predicting the future	2. More predictions	3. Probability and chance	4. More probability exercises	RFS 5. How will I look?	6. What will I be doing?	7. Styles change	8. Neighborhoods change	9. Future changes	RFS 10. Careers—1	11. Careers—2	12. Careers—3	13. Careers—4
PROCESS	APPLYING SYNTHESIZING													
	COMPARING ANALYZING	×	×	×	×	×	×	×						
	PREDICTING INFERRING	×	×	×	×	×	×	×	×	×			×	×
	EXPERIMENTING													
	CLASSIFYING			×	×									
	OBSERVING						×	×						
ART	VISUALS						×		×					×
MATH	REPRESENTATION		×		×									
	COMPUTATION			×	×									
	MEASUREMENT													
LANGUAGE	RESEARCH										×	×		
	READING													
	WRITING							×	×		×	×		
	INTERVIEWING				×						×	×		
LEVEL: WHERE APPROPRIATE I—INTERMEDIATE, U—UPPER					U	U	U	U	U	U	U	U	U	U

ACTIVITIES TITLE

NO.

IS IT PROBABLE?
RFS 1. Predicting the future
2. More predictions
3. Probability and chance
4. More probability exercises

PEOPLE CHANGE, STYLES CHANGE, NEIGHBORHOODS AND CITIES CHANGE
RFS 5. How will I look?
6. What will I be doing?
7. Styles change
8. Neighborhoods change
9. Future changes

CAREERS IN THE FUTURE
RFS 10. The changing world of careers—1
11. The changing world of careers—2
12. The changing world of careers—3
13. The changing world of careers—4

PUBLISHING: Writing Books

Chapter 11, pp. 187–192

Skill categories: **PROCESS** (Applying/Synthesizing, Comparing/Analyzing, Predicting/Inferring, Experimenting, Classifying, Observing) · **ART** (Visuals) · **MATH** (Representation, Computation, Measurement) · **LANGUAGE** (Research, Reading, Writing, Interviewing) · **LEVEL: WHERE APPROPRIATE — I—INTERMEDIATE, U—UPPER**

No.	Title	Applying/Synthesizing	Comparing/Analyzing	Predicting/Inferring	Experimenting	Classifying	Observing	Visuals	Representation	Computation	Measurement	Research	Reading	Writing	Interviewing	Level
WRITING BOOKS																
PWB 1.	Write mystery stories	×											×	×		IU
2.	Invent superhuman characters	×				×							×	×		
3.	Write fables													×	×	
4.	Be biographers, autobiographers			×		×								×		
5.	Compile sensory books		×			×		×				×	×	×	×	IU
6.	Publish a book of hobbies					×						×		×		IU
7.	Publish a calendar with novel information											×		×	×	
8.	Publish a book of names											×		×		
9.	Publish an art book													×		
10.	Publish a comic book											×		×		
11.	Publish a holiday book					×		×			×		×	×		IU
12.	Organize a children's literature workshop											×	×	×	×	
13.	Publish a community directory	×										×		×	×	U
14.	Research the history of the school	×										×		×		
BINDING BOOKS																
PWB15.	Instructions for bookbinding	×														

PUBLISHING: Cultural Journalism

Chapter 11, pp. 194–199

ACTIVITIES — TITLE	PROCESS — APPLYING SYNTHESIZING	COMPARING ANALYZING	PREDICTING INFERRING	EXPERIMENTING	CLASSIFYING	OBSERVING	ART — VISUALS	MATH — REPRESENTATION	COMPUTATION	MEASUREMENT	LANGUAGE — RESEARCH	READING	WRITING	INTERVIEWING	LEVEL: WHERE APPROPRIATE I—INTERMEDIATE, U—UPPER
PUBLISHING A CULTURAL HISTORY															
PCJ 1. Identify your topics											×				
2. Identify your sources											×				
3. Prepare for the interview		×			×						×				
4. At the interview—five rules	×					×								×	
5. Writing the information	×												×		
DIGGING INTO ROOTS															
PCJ 6. Who am I?											×				
7. Who lives in this community?	×										×			×	U

PUBLISHING: Greeting Cards — Chapter 11, pp. 201–207

Activity	PROCESS: Applying/Synthesizing	Comparing/Analyzing	Predicting/Inferring	Experimenting	Classifying	Observing	ART: Visuals	MATH: Representation	Computation	Measurement	LANGUAGE: Research	Reading	Writing	Interviewing	Level (I—Intermediate, U—Upper)
CARDS FOR ALL OCCASIONS															
PGC 1. Start with an interesting shape					×		×			×			×		
2. Pressed flower cards							×						×		
3. More unusual covers							×			×			×		
4. Silhouette faces							×						×		
5. Banner cards							×						×		
6. Roller movie cards							×						×		
7. Figures as cards							×						×		
WRITE MESSAGES IN POETRY AND PROSE															
PGC 8. Forms of poetry											×		×		
9. Other card messages													×		
PREPARE ENVELOPES FOR GREETING CARDS															
PGC 10. Envelope instructions							×			×			×		
SELLING GREETING CARDS															
PGC 11. Sell your cards	×								×						

MEDIA

Chapter 12, pp. 214–220

LEVEL: WHERE APPROPRIATE
I—INTERMEDIATE, U—UPPER

No.	Title	PROCESS — Applying / Synthesizing	Comparing / Analyzing	Predicting / Inferring	Experimenting	Classifying	Observing	ART — Visuals	MATH — Representation	Computation	Measurement	LANGUAGE — Research	Reading	Writing	Interviewing	Level
BE A THEATER IMPRESSARIO: ORGANIZE A SHADOW THEATER																
M1.	Build a theater															
2.	Construct the puppets							×								
3.	Prepare to operate your shadow theater							×								
4.	Produce a shadow play	×					×	×						×		
5.	Experiment with a different shadow theater	×					×	×								
PRODUCE YOUR OWN FILMSTRIPS																
M6.	Filmstrips from paper				×			×								
7.	Filmstrips from a Thermofax copier				×			×								
8.	Filmstrips on acetate				×			×								
9.	Filmstrips from previously used ones				×			×								
10.	Combine your filmstrips with oral or writen notes.	×						×						×		
CREATE SLIDES DIRECTLY ON FILM																
M11.	Psychedelic slides							×								
12.	And more creative slides							×								
13.	Picture transfers							×								
PRODUCE PHOTOGRAMS: TAKE PICTURES WITHOUT A CAMERA																
M14.	Start with construction paper						×	×								
15.	Blueprint photograms						×	×								I
16.	Light-sensitive photographic paper photograms						×	×								U

MEDIA—2
Chapter 12, pp. 221–230

NO. / TITLE	APPLYING SYNTHESIZING	COMPARING ANALYZING	PREDICTING INFERRING	EXPERIMENTING	CLASSIFYING	OBSERVING	VISUALS (ART)	REPRESENTATION	COMPUTATION	MEASUREMENT	RESEARCH	READING	WRITING	INTERVIEWING	LEVEL (I/U)
LEARN BASIC FACTS ABOUT PHOTOGRAPHY															
M17. Introduction to photography						×					×				U
18. Get to know your camera						×									U
19. Tips for better pictures						×									U
BE A PHOTOGRAPHER															
M20. Pictures tell a story					×	×	×								U
21. Pictures with a geometrical theme					×	×	×	×							U
22. Everyday themes					×	×	×								U
23. Weather themes					×	×	×								U
24. Neighborhood themes			×		×	×	×								U
25. Sensory themes					×	×	×								U
26. People themes					×	×	×								U
27. Mood themes			×		×	×	×								U
28. Focus on one subject					×	×	×								U
29. Interpret a scene					×	×	×								U
30. And for fun					×	×	×								U
CONSTRUCT AND USE A PINHOLE CAMERA															
M31. All about pinhole camers	×						×			×					U
TRY ANIMATION WITHOUT A CAMERA															
M32. Make an animated flip book						×	×								U
33. Animation by drawing on film	×			×		×	×			×					U

LEVEL: WHERE APPROPRIATE — I—INTERMEDIATE, U—UPPER

MEDIA—3

Chapter 12, pp. 230–236

ACTIVITIES NO. / TITLE	PROCESS — APPLYING SYNTHESIZING	PROCESS — COMPARING ANALYZING	PROCESS — PREDICTING INFERRING	PROCESS — EXPERIMENTING	PROCESS — CLASSIFYING	PROCESS — OBSERVING	ART — VISUALS	MATH — REPRESENTATION	MATH — COMPUTATION	MATH — MEASUREMENT	LANGUAGE — RESEARCH	LANGUAGE — READING	LANGUAGE — WRITING	LANGUAGE — INTERVIEWING	LEVEL: WHERE APPROPRIATE (I—INTERMEDIATE, U—UPPER)
PRODUCING ANIMATED MOVIES															
M34. Collect the necessary equipment					×	×	×			×					U
35. Experiment with different kinds of animation				×	×	×	×						×		U
36. Plan your animated movie	×			×	×	×	×								U
37. Film your movie															U
PLAN AND FILM A SLIDE SHOW WITH SOUND															
M38. Planning and filming the show	×	×				×	×						×		U
39. Sound in your slide show	×	×				×	×						×		U
UTILIZING VIDEO IN THE CLASSROOM															
M40. Each child a performer						×	×							×	U
41. Stage a hobby show	×	×					×				×		×	×	U
42. Produce a news show							×						×		U
43. Conduct interviews							×						×		U
44. Produce a television commercial	×						×				×		×		U
45. Organize a game show	×						×				×		×		U
46. Present a variety show							×								U
47. Plan a television movie	×	×				×	×				×	×	×		U

MEDIA—4

Chapter 12, pp. 237–238

NO.	TITLE	PROCESS: APPLYING SYNTHESIZING	COMPARING ANALYZING	PREDICTING INFERRING	EXPERIMENTING	CLASSIFYING	OBSERVING	ART: VISUALS	MATH: REPRESENTATION	COMPUTATION	MEASUREMENT	LANGUAGE: RESEARCH	READING	WRITING	INTERVIEWING	LEVEL: WHERE APPROPRIATE I—INTERMEDIATE, U—UPPER
	BECOME RADIO JOURNALISTS															
M48.	"Sounds of My City"					×						×				U
49.	Organize the classroom into a radio station							×				×				U
50.	Produce a news show					×		×				×	×	×	×	U
51.	Still more radio shows	×	×					×								U
52.	Become a news correspondent	×	×					×							×	U
53.	Radio interviews	×						×				×	×	×	×	U
54.	Produce an original radio play	×						×					×	×		U
55.	More radio plays: "The Shadow"	×						×								U